GRUNDLAGE DEUTSCH 3

Fundamentals of German

Jessie G. McGuire

Walter G. O'Connell High School, Copiague, NY (retired)

Joseph Castine

Northport High School, Northport, NY (retired)

AMSCO SCHOOL PUBLICATIONS, INC.
315 Hudson Street / New York, NY 10013

Cover design by A Good Thing, Inc.

Please visit our Web site at:
www.amscopub.com

When ordering this please specify *either* **R 65 W** *or*
GRUNDLAGE DEUTSCH 3: FUNDAMENTALS OF GERMAN

ISBN   978-1-56765-409-7

NYC Item   56765-409-6

Printed in the United States of America

1 2 3 4 5 6 7 8 9 10   12 11 10 09 08 07 06

Preface

Grundlage Deutsch 3 is designed as a review of the material covered in a typical third-level German course. It offers learners a chance to review, practice and strengthen their understanding of the German language within communicative contexts. Vocabulary has been introduced contextually into each chapter, so that *Grundlage Deutsch 3* may be used independently or as a supplement to any basal text.

ORGANIZATION

Grundlage Deutsch 3 consists of 19 chapters, each organized around a single major grammar concept. As in previous levels, the base concept is explained succinctly and clearly, illustrated with usage examples, followed by relevant practice exercises for the learner, and then expanded upon. Each expansion explanation follows the same pattern of explanation, examples, and practice exercises. Chapters start with clear introductions to the new concept and expand in small increments until the required functions of third-level German related to this concept have been introduced, illustrated and practiced.

VOCABULARY AND GRAMMAR

Grundlage Deutsch 3 highlights culture within the German-speaking countries. Each chapter focuses upon a specific item of cultural interest: an event, a location, a famous person, a typical, leisure-time activity, or a notable work of literature. Vocabulary for each unit is introduced contextually within the examples and followed up in extensive in-chapter and appended word lists.

EXERCISES

Each grammar explanation is followed by a series of exercises. Exercises are based on communicative situations and develop a cultural theme throughout the chapter. They begin with simple recognition activities and scaffold toward more complex tasks. They progress from easy to more difficult in small, manageable steps that student can easily handle.

FLEXIBILITY

Grundlage Deutsch 3 can be used successfully whether students are working independently, in small learning groups, or in a classroom situation. Each chapter focuses on a single, or a few, related grammar concepts. Vocabulary lists, the grammar reference charts, and the extensive table of contents allow learners to identify readily where explanations and exercises relevant to their needs can be found. The book can be used independently or with little or no extra preparation as a classroom supplement to any basal level-three German text.

Mastering communicative functions gives learners confidence and a firm basis on which to continue building their knowledge of German. *Grundlage Deutsch 3* cements the essential skills necessary for mastery of level three and increases students' communicative abilities and cultural knowledge of German-speaking countries. Its gradual progression from simple to complex, review of previously learned concepts, clear explanations, and transparent organization make it ideal whether used as a classroom tool, a remedial tool, or an enrichment tool. We wish all learners ***Viel Glück*** as they work through the exercises in *Grundlage Deutsch 3*.

Jessie MGuire and Joseph Castine

Contents

CHAPTER 1
Present Tense
Present Tense of Stem Vowel Change Verbs
Separable Prefixes

1. Formation of the Present Tense

The present tense of the verb is used to express action taking place at the same time as the narrative. It has three direct translations:

Ich verdiene *I earn, I do earn, I am earning*

It is formed by adding personal endings to the stem of the verb.

PRESENT TENSE CONJUGATION OF REGULAR VERBS	
SINGULAR	PLURAL
ich verdien – e *I earn, I do earn, I am earning*	**wir verdien – en** *we earn, we do earn, we are earning*
du verdien – st *you (informal) earn, do earn, are earning*	**ihr verdien – t** *you (informal) earn, do earn, are earning*
er, sie, es verdien – t *he, she, it earns, does earn, is earning*	**sie verdien – en** *they earn, do earn, are earning*
Sie verdien – en *You (formal) earn, do earn, are earning*	

NOTE: If the stem ends in *–t*, *–d*, or two consonants followed by an *–n*, add *–e* before the *–te* ending to facilitate pronunciation. If the *du*-form already ends in *–s* or *–ß*, only *–t* is added.

ÜBUNG A   **Taschengeld verdienen.** The class is discussing its favorite topic – how everyone gets pocket money. Match a proposed method of getting money to a student, and then ask them to see if you were correct.

EXAMPLE: Frederika, babysittest du an Wochenenden?

Konrad	Geld von der Großmutter bekommen
Antje und Andy	an Wochenenden babysitten.
Frederika	den Rasen mähen
Herr Huster	im Supermarkt jobben
Jans Rolf und ich	Eintrittskarten im Kino verkaufen
Petra	Im Schnellimbiss arbeiten

1. Konrad, _____

2. Antje und Andy, _____

3. Frederika, _____

4. Herr Huster, _____

5. Jans Rolf (und ich), _____

6. Petra, _____

2.   Strong Verbs with Stem Vowel Changes

Certain verbs change the vowel when used in the second (*du*) and third persons (*er, sie, es*) singular. When the vowel changes occur, they are either:

a changes to **ä**	**fahren, er fährt**	*ride or drive*
e changes to **i**	**helfen, er hilft**	*help*
e changes to **ei**	**sehen, er sieht**	*see*

PRESENT TENSE CONJUGATION OF STEM-VOWEL VERBS							
SINGULAR				PLURAL			
	a to ä **fahren**	**e to i** **helfen**	**e to ie** **sehen**		**a to ä** **fahren**	**e to i** **helfen**	**e to ie** **sehen**
ich	fahr – e	help – e	seh – e	**wir**	fahr – en	help – en	seh – en
du	f**ä**hr – st	h**i**lf – st	s**ie**h – st	**ihr**	fahr – en	help - en	seh – en
er, sie, es	f**ä**hr – t	h**i**lf – t	s**ie**h – t	**sie**	fahr – en	help – en	seh – en
Sie	fahr – en	help – en	seh – en	**Sie**	fahr – en	help – en	seh – en

NOTE: If the stem ends in *–t, –d*, or two consonants followed by an *–n*, add *–e* before the *–te* ending to facilitate pronunciation. If the *du*-form already ends in *–s* or *–ß*, only *–t* is added.

ÜBUNG B   **Taschengeld verdienen.** Several students in your class earn extra spending money by working part time or doing odd jobs at home. Oskar, Frieder, Michaela, Gitti, and Annette told you about their jobs. They are all excellent students. You'd like to work, but your mother is afraid that your grades might suffer. Try and convince her by telling her what your five friends do and still get good grades.

EXAMPLE: Paulo / im Winter / Schnee / schaufeln   Paulo schaufelt Schnee im Winter.

1. Oskar / nach der Schule / Nachhilfestunden / geben

   _____

2. Frieder / jeden Nachmittag / seine Nachbarin / zum Seniorenzentrum / fahren

   _____

3. Michaela / ihrer Mutter / nachmittags / zu Hause / helfen

   _____

4. Gitti / samstags / Autos / waschen

   _____

5. Annette / am Samstagabend / mit einer Rockband / singen

   _____

| ÜBUNG C | **Dein Taschengeld.** And you? Write a list of four things you do, or could do, to earn spending money. |

EXAMPLE: Ich mähe den Rasen für meine Familie.

1. _____
2. _____
3. _____
4. _____

3. Verbs with Separable Prefixes

In English an adverb often completes the meaning of a verb.

I'll pick you up.   He's driving away.   Would you like to take your jacket off?

In German, the completer is attached to the beginning of the verb. It starts the infinitive, yet is separated and goes to the end of its utterance (clause, phrase or sentence) once the verb is used in a sentence.

Derek trägt jeden Tag Zeitungen aus. (austragen)

Derek delivers newspapers every day.

Adding a prefix is an easy way to increase vocabulary and the ability to express oneself. The list below shows the many meanings one stem-verb can take just by adding separable prefixes.

anfahren _drive towards something, knock something over, go at someone (verbally)_

abfahren _depart, drive away_

auffahren _drive up to, start up_

ausfahren _exit, drive out, drive a car to its full potential_

beifahren _ride as front seat passenger, ride shotgun_

einfahren	*drive into, enter*	**wegfahren**	*drive away, go away on vacation*
fortfahren	*continue, drive on*		
mitfahren	*drive along with someone*	**zurückfahren**	*return, drive back, drive backwards*
nachfahren	*follow someone in a moving vehicle*		
vorfahren	*drive in front of someone, precede, drive forward*	**zusammenfahren**	*crash into another car, drive together with someone*

Following is a chart of verbs commonly used with separable prefixes. Understanding how separable prefixes work is helpful in deciphering a difficult text.

COMMON VERBS WITH SEPARABLE PREFIXES

ab- *down, away from*

abbiegen	*turn into*	**abholen**	*pick up*
abfahren	*depart*	**abnehmen**	*take off, lose weight*
abhängen	*depend upon, hang from*	**abschließen**	*lock up*

an - *at, on*

anfangen	*begin*	**annehmen**	*assume*
anhaben	*have on, be wearing*	**anprobieren**	*try on*
anhalten	*stop (a vehicle)*	**anrufen**	*call up*
ankommen	*to arrive*	**anschauen**	*look at*
anmachen	*turn on*	**ansehen**	*look at*
sich anmelden	*register*	**sich anziehen**	*get dressed*

auf- *up*

aufbauen	*build up*	**aufschließen**	*unlock*
auffallen	*stand out, be conspicuous*	**aufschreiben**	*write down*
aufgeben	*give up*	**aufstehen**	*stand up, get up from bed*
auflösen	*solve*	**aufwachen**	*wake up (naturally)*
aufpassen	*watch out (for), pay attention*	**aufwachsen**	*grow up*
		aufwecken	*wake (someone) up*

aus- *out, from*

ausdrucken	*print out*	**ausmachen**	*turn off*
ausfallen	*be canceled*	**auspacken**	*unpack*
ausgeben	*to spend (money)*	**ausreichen**	*be enough*
ausfüllen	*fill out*	**sich ausruhen**	*relax*
ausgehen	*go out*	**aussehen**	*look (appearance)*
aushelfen	*help out*	**aussteigen**	*get out, climb out*
auslassen	*let out*	**sich ausziehen**	*undress*

bei- *along, with*

beibringen	*teach (someone, something)*	**beitreten**	*join*
beifügen	*add (something)*	**beistehen**	*stand with someone* *support someone*

ein- *in*

einbrechen	*break in*	**einpacken**	*pack*
einfallen	*to occur to someone (with dative)*	**einschlafen**	*fall asleep*
einkaufen	*shop*	**einsteigen**	*get in, climb in*
einladen	*invite*	**eintragen**	*register, enter*
		eintreten	*step in, enter*

fern- *far, at a distance*

fernsehen	*watch tv*

fest- *firm*

festhalten	*hold onto tightly*	**feststellen**	*determine*
festlegen	*establish, set firm*		

fort- *forth*

fortfahren	*continue*	**fortgehen**	*go on*

her- *motion towards speaker*

herkommen	*come from*

hin- *motion away from speaker*

hingehen	*go away from the speaker*	**sich hinsetzen**	*sit down*
		hinwerfen	*throw down*

mit- *with, along*

mitarbeiten	*work with someone*	**mitmachen**	*participate*
mitkommen	*come along*	**mitsingen**	*sing along (with)*

nach- *after*

nachahmen	*copy, ape*	**nachmachen**	*imitate*
nachdenken	*ponder, think about*	**nachschlagen**	*look up (reference), check*
nachfragen	*ask about*		
nachlassen	*let up, slack off*	**nachsehen**	*look after*

vor- *in front of, before*

vorbereiten	*prepare*	**vorlesen**	*read aloud*
vorführen	*perform*	**vorschlagen**	*suggest*
vorgehen	*precede, go ahead of*	**vorschreiben**	*prescribe*
vorhaben	*have planned*		

weg- *away*

wegbleiben	*stay away*	**wegschmeißen**	*throw away*
weggehen	*go away*	**wegsehen**	*look away*
wegnehmen	*take away*		

zu- *to, toward*

zudecken	*cover up*	zunehmen	*increase, gain weight*
zulassen	*admit, agree to*	zuordnen	*assign to*
zumachen	*turn off, close*		

zurück- *back*

zurückbringen	*bring back*	zurückschreiben	*write back, reply*
zurückgeben	*give back*	zurücksetzen	*set back, reset*
zurückgehen	*go back, recede*	zurückzahlen	*pay back, repay*

zusammen- *together*

zusammenbinden	*tie together*	zusammenkleben	*glue together*
zusammenfallen	*coincide*	zusammenschlagen	*break apart*
zusammenhalten	*stick together (people)*		*by force*
zusammenhängen	*associate, hang around together*	zusammenstehen	*stand together*

ÜBUNG D **Deine Vorschläge.** Your mother is listening to your arguments. She's willing to discuss the idea of you working after school, but she'd rather see you do volunteer work, either within the family or the community. She tells you what some of her friends' children are doing. What suggestions did she make? The pictures will help you.

EXAMPLE: (aushelfen) Magdalena hilft ihrer Mutter zu Hause aus.

1. (vorlååesen) _____

2. (aufräumen) _____

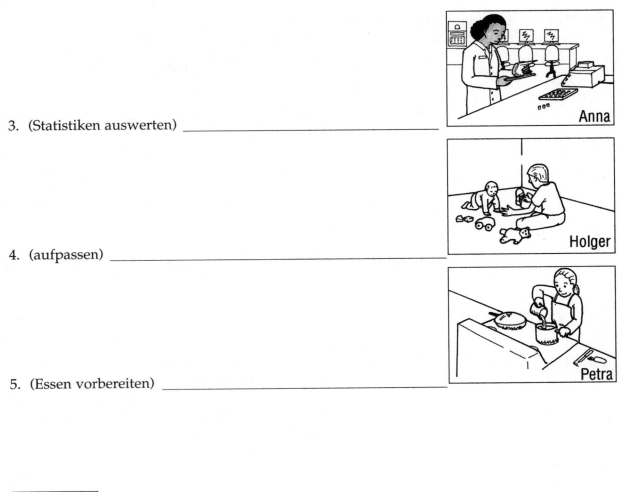

3. (Statistiken auswerten) _____

4. (aufpassen) _____

5. (Essen vorbereiten) _____

ÜBUNG E   **Hausarbeit.** You talk to your friends about their household chores. You're anxious to see what they do to help around the house.

EXAMPLE: Paula wäscht Geschirr ab.

1. Mustafa / seine Geschwister / vom Kindergarten / abholen.

   _____

2. Adelheid / das Wohnzimmer / aufräumen

   _____

3. Josef / den Hund / jeden Morgen / ausführen

   _____

4. Cassandra und Carsten / das Bad / saubermachen
   (**NOTE:** sometimes a word of more than one syllable can be used as a separable prefix.)

   _____

5. Aylin / ihrer Mutter / in der Küche / aushelfen

   _____

ÜBUNG F   **Das Interview mit meinen Freunden.** You start thinking about your friends and what they do in their *Freizeit* (leisure time). Some of them work and some don't. Some have volunteer jobs; others participate in clubs and sports. Interview several people and make a list of the seven after school activities you find most interesting.

EXAMPLE: Beatrix schwimmt Bahnen (laps), macht eine Online-Diät mit, und nimmt ab.

1. _____

2. _____

3. _____

4. _____

5. _____

6. _____

7. _____

ÜBUNG G   **Das Taschengeld.** You're writing a story for German class about the trials and tribulations of (not) having enough spending money when you're a teenager. It may be fictional or based on fact. Choose one separable prefix verb from each section of the chart above. That gives you 18 verbs. Use at least ten of them in your story titled „Das Taschengeld".

_____

_____

_____

_____

_____

_____

_____

_____

CHAPTER 2
Present Perfect Tense

The present perfect tense, often referred to as the conversational past or just the perfect tense, is used to express actions that occurred in the past. It is formed using the auxiliary verb *haben* or *sein* with the past participle of the verb.
It has three translations in English.

Er hat Theaterkarten für Samstagabend gekauft.

He bought, did buy, or has bought theater tickets for Saturday evening.

Jedes Wochenende im Oktober haben wir für meinen Vater gearbeitet.

We worked, did work, or have worked every weekend in October for my father.

1.   Formation of the Present Perfect Tense

Thinking of the present perfect tense in its third translation, i.e. "has bought," makes it easier to remember how it is formed. The correct form of the verb *haben* (see chart below) is used as the finite verb in the sentence. The past participle is added to the end of the sentence or clause.

Martina hat Herrn Marzipan seit fünf Jahren nicht gesehen.

Martina has not seen Herr Marzipan for five years.

Sie hat ihm ein altes Fotoalbum mitgebracht.

She brought him an old photo album.

HABEN	
SINGULAR	PLURAL
ich habe	wir haben
du hast	ihr habt
er, sie, es hat	sie haben
Sie haben	

+ past participle = present perfect tense

If the verb cannot take a direct object (for example, *ankommen*), or if it shows motion towards a goal (*laufen*), or expresses a state of being (*sein*) or a change of state (*sterben*), then the present perfect is formed using *sein* rather than *haben*.

Die alten Freunden sind zusammen nach Berlin gefahren.

The old friends traveled together to Berlin.

Michael Renza ist Pilot geworden.

Michael Renza has become a pilot.

SEIN	
SINGULAR	PLURAL
ich bin	wir sind
du bist	ihr seid
er, sie, es ist	sie sind
Sie sind	

+ past participle = present perfect tense

ÜBUNG A   **Sein oder haben?** Complete the following sentences with the correct form of *haben* or *sein*. Some verbs may take either depending upon their use in the sentence. Remember, if the verb has a direct object, then *haben* is used.

EXAMPLE: Michael __hat__ die Flugschule in Mühlheim besucht.

1. Er _____ seinen Flugschein dort bekommen.

2. Wir _____ jeden Samstag mit ihm nach Mühlheim gefahren.

3. Während er geflogen _____, _____ wir unsere Freunde besucht.

4. Dann _____ wir alle zusammen gegessen.

5. Die Routine _____ wir 18 Monate lang gemacht.

6. Am Ende von dem Flugprogramm _____ er Pilot geworden.

7. Wir _____ froh gewesen, und _____ ihm gratuliert.

2.   Formation of the Past Participle of Weak Verbs

The past participle of weak (regular) verbs is formed by removing the *-en* (or *-n* if there is no *-en*) from the infinitive, then adding a *ge-* before the stem and a *-t* after it.

> **ge + kauf + t = gekauft**   *bought*

If the verb stem ends in *-t*, *-d*, or two consonants followed by an *-n*, add *-e* before adding the *-t*. This exception occurs often in German. The *-e* simply makes the resulting verb form easier to pronounce.

> **ge + arbeit + e + t = gearbeitet**   *worked*
> **ge + send + e + t = gesendet**   *broadcast*
> **ge + öffn + e + t = geöffnet**   *opened*

If the verb ends in *-ieren*, no *ge-* is added before the stem. The *-en* is still replaced at the end of the verb by *-t*.

> **telefonier + t = telefoniert**   *telephoned*
> **synchonisier + t = synchronized**   *synchronized*
> **reduzier + t = reduziert**   *reduced*

If the verb starts with an inseparable prefix, there is also no *ge-*. Inseparable prefixes are: *be-, emp-, ent-, -er, ge-, miss-, ver-, voll-,* and *zer-*.

entdeck + t = entdeckt	*discovered*
verdien + t = verdient	*earned*
vollend + e + t = vollendet	*completed*

If the verb starts with a separable prefix, the *ge-* is added between the separable prefix and the stem. The stem then follows the same rules as above.

an + ge + schaut = angeschant	*watched, looked at*
auf + ge + räumt = aufgeräumt	*cleaned up*
ein + ge + kauft = eingekauft	*shopped*

ÜBUNG B   **Dein Tagesablauf.** You made a list of things you want to do today. As you complete the tasks mark them as having been done. What does your list look like at the end of the day?

EXAMPLE: mit Oma telefonieren.   mit Oma telefoniert.

1. Fernsehen schauen _____

2. neue Schuhe kaufen _____

3. neues Kuchenrezept ausprobieren _____

4. Pausebrot einpacken _____

5. Wecker auf 8 Uhr stellen _____

6. Internet surfen _____

7. den Hund ausführen _____

8. mit Herrn Marzipan reden _____

9. Michaela abholen _____

10. den Babysitter bezahlen _____

ÜBUNG C   **Gemacht ist gemacht.** You'd like to go to the library and study with your friends. Your father is home and confirms that you've done all your chores before you leave. Assure him that it's alright for you to leave.

EXAMPLE: Klavier / üben / und / die Mondlichtsonate von Beethoven / spielen
Ja, ich habe Klavier geübt und die Mondlichtsonate von Beethoven gespielt.

1. mit Tante Emma / telefonieren / und / ihr / für das Geburtstagsgeschenk / danken

_____

2. dein Zimmer / aufräumen / und / unter dem Bett / staubsaugen (sep. prefix)

_____

3. deine Hausaufgaben / machen / und / alle Matheaufgaben / lösen

   _____

4. etwas zum Abendessen / vorbereiten / und / Spaghetti / kochen

   _____

5. Kleider für morgen / auslegen / und / meine braune Hose und mein rotes Hemd / bügeln

   _____

ÜBUNG D | **Was hast du gestern nach der Schule gemacht?** Interview five classmates, either singly or in pairs. What did each of them do yesterday after school? Some of the things your friends might mention are *kochen, spielen, baden, verdienen, lernen, staubsaugen, plaudern* (chat)*, vorbereiten, fotografieren, kennen lernen, telefonieren.*

EXAMPLE: Jennifer, hast du Basketball geübt?   Nein, ich habe Mathe gelernt.

1. _____
2. _____
3. _____
4. _____
5. _____

3.   Formation of the Past Participle of Strong Verbs

Strong verbs do not follow the same, easy patterns of weak verbs. They indicate the tense via a change in the stem vowel. It's similar to English. A weak verb in English simply adds "–ed" to the verb stem to form the past and past participle. "I play, played, have played." Strong verbs change vowel forms and very often end in "–en" to form the past participle: "speak, has spoken." Or "forget, has forgotten."

The principle parts of strong verbs must be memorized. Like English, their past participle usually ends in –en rather than –t. A stem vowel change indicates tense. Learning the verbs in groups according to their stem change pattern makes memorization easier.

The most frequently-used strong verbs are the three auxiliary verbs. These should be learned first, since they are the building blocks for all six German verb tenses.

In this and all the charts below, the first column is the infinitive (*haben*). The second column is the third person singular present tense (*er, sie, es hat*). The third column is the first and third person singular past tense (*ich* and *er, sie, es hatte*). The fourth column is the third person singular present perfect tense (*er, sie, es hat gehabt*). The final column is the English translation for the verb.

The principle parts of the helping verbs are:

haben	hat	hatte	hat gehabt	*have*
sein	ist	war	ist gewesen	*be*
werden	wird	wurde	ist geworden	*become, will*

ÜBUNG E | **Erinnerungen an ehemalige Schüler.** Your teacher is remembering former students with whom he has not kept in touch. You catch him up to date using the present perfect tense.

EXAMPLE: Sebastian war immer gut im Deutschunterricht. (Autor / werden)
Er ist Autor geworden.

1. Jessica war immer gut mit Kindern. (5 Kinder / haben)

_____

2. Rainer spielte immer gern Flöte. (ein berühmter Konzertflötenspieler / werden)

_____

3. Die Zwillinge Gerd und Gerlinde waren immer so lustig. (Komikerteam des Jahres / sein)

_____

4. Paulo studierte immer so viel. (Physikprofessor / werden)

_____

5. Bart und Benno waren immer gute Athleten. (in der Sommerolympiade 2004 / sein)

_____

The following list of principal parts is divided into stem-vowel change pattern groups. Practice one pattern group until you have memorized it and then go on to the next. Many of the patterns will be familiar from English.

a. Principal Parts of Verbs with an **A** that Show a Stem-Vowel Change

a	ä	u	a	
backen	bäckt	backte (buk)	hat gebacken	*bake*
begraben	begräbt	begrub	hat begraben	*bury*
einladen	lädt ein	lud ein	hat eingeladen	*invite*
fahren	fährt	fuhr	ist/hat gefahren	*ride, drive*
graben	gräbt	grub	hat gegraben	*dig*
laden	lädt	lud	hat geladen	*load*
schlagen	schlägt	schlug	hat geschlagen	*hit, beat*
tragen	trägt	trug	hat getragen	*carry, wear*
wachsen	wächst	wuchs	ist/hat gewachsen	*grow*
waschen	wäscht	wusch	hat gewaschen	*wash*

a	ä	ie	a	
anhalten	hält an	hielt an	hat angehalten	*stop (motion)*
blasen	bläst	blies	hat geblasen	*blow*
braten	brät	briet	hat gebraten	*roast (food)*
fallen	fällt	fiel	ist gefallen	*fall*

halten	hält	hielt	hat gehalten	*hold, stop (motion)*
lassen	lässt	ließ	hat gelassen	*let, allow*
laufen	läuft	lief	ist gelaufen	*run, walk*
raten	rät	riet	hat geraten	*guess, advise*
schlafen	schläft	schlief	hat geschlafen	*sleep*
ä	ä	i	a	
hängen	hängt	hing	hat gehangen	*hang (clothes, pictures)*
a	a	u	a	
schaffen	schafft	schuf	hat geschaffen	*create*

ÜBUNG F	**Was aus uns geworden ist.** Herr Marzipan is on memory lane. He continues to ask you about former students with whom you've stayed in touch. You update him as best you can.

EXAMPLE: Elise? Tennisspielerin / werden // Steffi Graf / im Endspiel / schlagen
Elise ist Tennisspielerin geworden. Sie hat Steffi Graf im Endspiel geschlagen.

1. Katrina? Filmstar / werden // uns / zur Premiere von ihrem letzten Film / einladen

_____

_____

2. Petra? Backmeisterin / werden // den 2005 preisgekrönten Kuchen des Jahres / backen

_____

_____

3. Dieter? Archäologe / werden // eine alte Inka Stadt in Peru / ausgraben

_____

_____

4. Stefan? Filmregisseur / werden // den Film „Terror auf Ahornstraße" / schaffen

_____

_____

5. Renate? Fotomodel /werden // letztes Jahr / Karl Lagerfelds Sammlung / tragen

_____

_____

6. Elena? Rennfahrerin / werden // im Mai / auf dem bekannten Nürburg-Ring / fahren

_____

_____

| ÜBUNG G | **Mein Superfreund Henner.** Imagine you have a friend Henner with super powers. Using verbs from the list on pages 13–14, write a list of 5 amazing things he has done in the last week. Make his week as varied and interesting as you can. If the past participle lists the auxiliary verb _ist_, use that instead of _hat_.

EXAMPLE: Henner ist 2 Meter gewachsen und hat seinen Kopf an der Decke geschlagen.

1. _____

2. _____

3. _____

4. _____

5. _____

b. Principal Parts of Verbs with an **E** that Show a Stem-Vowel Change

e	i	o	o	
schmelzen	**schmilzt**	**schmolz**	**ist/ hat geschmolzen**	_melt_
e	e	i	a	
gehen	**geht**	**ging**	**ist gegangen**	_go, walk_
e	e	a	a	
stehen	**steht**	**stand**	**hat gestanden**	_stand_
e	i	a	e	
essen	**isst**	**aß**	**hat gegessen**	_eat (human)_
fressen	**frisst**	**fraß**	**hat gefressen**	_eat (animal), devour_
geben	**gibt**	**gab**	**hat gegeben**	_give_
messen	**misst**	**maß**	**hat gemessen**	_measure_
treten	**tritt**	**trat**	**ist/hat getreten**	_step, step on_
vertreten	**vertritt**	**vertrat**	**hat vertreten**	_represent_
e	i	a	o	
gelten	**gilt**	**galt**	**hat gegolten**	_be valid_
helfen	**hilft**	**half**	**hat geholfen**	_help_
nehmen	**nimut**	**nahm**	**hat genommen**	_take_
sterben	**stirbt**	**starb**	**ist gestorben**	_die_
werfen	**wirft**	**warf**	**hat geworfen**	_throw_

e	ie	a	e	
lesen	liest	las	hat gelesen	*read*
geschehen	geschieht	geschah	ist geschehen	*happen*
sehen	sieht	sah	hat gesehen	*see*

e	ie	a	o	
befehlen	befiehlt	befahl	hat befohlen	*command, order*
empfehlen	empfiehlt	empfahl	hat empfohlen	*recommend*
stehlen	stiehlt	stahl	hat gestohlen	*steal*

e	e	o	o	
heben	hebt	hob	hat gehoben	*raise, lift*

ÜBUNG H **Der nächste Spielberg?** Your former classmate Stefan is working on his latest movie and has asked you not only to read part of the screenplay but also to help draw some of the story boards. Create a series of pictures of the scenes he has created here.

(1) Frieder hat lange Stunden in der Bank gestanden. Er hat sich nicht bewegt, nur Nüsse gegessen und seine Zeitung gelesen. (2) Der Banksicherheitsdienst hat ihn fast hinausgeworfen. In dem Moment ist aber der Geldtransporter vor die Bank eingefahren. (3) Zwei Männer haben Geldsäcke in die Bank hereingetragen. Aber was ist dann geschehen? (4) Ein Sack ist heruntergefallen. (5) Frieder ist schnell hingegangen und hat den Sack aufgehoben. Hat er ihn stehlen wollen? Nein. (6) Unser Frieder ist ein so guter Mensch gewesen, dass er den gefallenen Sack mit zur Kasse getragen hat. Er hat den zwei Männern geholfen, nicht bestohlen.

c. Principal Parts of Verbs with an **EI** that Show a Stem-Vowel Change

ei	ei	i	i	
beißen	beißt	biss	hat gebissen	*bite*
gleichen	gleicht	glich	hat geglichen	*equal, equate*
gleiten	gleitet	glitt	ist geglitten	*glide*
greifen	greift	griff	hat gegriffen	*grasp, grap*
kneifen	kneift	kniff	hat gekniffen	*pinch*
leiden	leidet	litt	hat gelitten	*suffer*
pfeifen	pfeift	pfiff	hat gepfiffen	*whistle*
reißen	reißt	riss	hat gerissen	*rip*
reiten	reitet	ritt	ist/hat geritten	*ride (an animal)*
schleichen	schleicht	schlich	ist geschlichen	*sneak, creep*
schmeißen	schmeißt	schmiss	hat geschmissen	*throw*
schneiden	schneidet	schnitt	hat geschnitten	*cut*
streichen	streicht	strich	hat gestrichen	*strike; (expunge), stroke, paint*
streiten	streitet	stritt	hat gestritten	*quarrel*

vergleichen	vergleicht	verglich	hat verglichen	*to compare*
weichen	weicht	wich	hat gewichen	*yield*
ei	**ei**	**ie**	**ie**	
bleiben	bleibt	blieb	ist geblieben	*stay, remain*
gedeihen	gedeiht	gedieh	ist gediehen	*thrive, prosper*
leihen	leiht	lieh	hat geliehen	*borrow, lend*
meiden	meidet	mied	hat gemieden	*avoid, shun*
reiben	reibt	rieb	hat gerieben	*rub*
scheiden	scheidet	schied	had geschieden	*separate, part*
scheinen	scheint	schien	hat geschienen	*appear, seem, shine*
schreiben	schreibt	schrieb	hat geschrieben	*write*
schreien	schreit	schrie	hat geschrien	*scream, yell*
schweigen	schweigt	schwieg	hat geschwiegen	*remain silent*
steigen	steigt	stieg	ist gestiegen	*climb*
treiben	treibt	trieb	ist/hat getrieben	*drive, propel*
weisen	weist	wies	hat gewiesen	*point to*
ei	**ei**	**ie**	**ie**	
heißen	heißt	hieß	hat geheißen	*be called*

ÜBUNG I | **Eine Filmstory.** Now it's your turn. Stefan has sent you the above list of verbs and asks you to create another episode in Frieder's life. Choose at least seven of the above verbs and create the story using the present perfect tense. Your classmates may ask you to read it aloud, so make it as interesting as you can.

_____

_____

_____

_____

_____

_____

ÜBUNG J | **ABC-Geschichte.** You have been asked to write a story based on the alphabet. Choose any five verbs from the last two lists of verbs and use them in alphabetical order to tell a story. Try to make the story interesting by using the vocabulary you know.

_____

_____

_____

_____

_____

d. Principal Parts of Verbs with an **IE** that Show a Stem-Vowel Change

ie	ie	o	o	
biegen	biegt	bog	hat gebogen	*bend*
bieten	bietet	bot	hat geboten	*offer*
fliegen	fliegt	flog	ist/hat geflogen	*fly*
fliehen	flieht	flog	ist geflohen	*flee*
fließen	fließt	floss	ist geflossen	*flow*
frieren	friert	fror	hat gefroren	*freeze*
gießen	gießt	goss	hat gegossen	*pour*
genießen	genießt	genoss	hat genossen	*enjoy*
kriechen	kriecht	kroch	ist gekrochen	*crawl, creep*
riechen	riech	roch	hat gerochen	*smell*
schieben	schieb	schob	hat geschoben	*push, shove*
schießen	schießt	schoss	hat geschossen	*shoot*
schließen	schließt	schloss	hat geschlossen	*close, lock*
verlieren	verliert	verlor	hat verloren	*lose*
wiegen	wiegt	wog	hat gewogen	*weigh*
ziehen	zieht	zog	hat gezogen	*pull*
ie	**ie**	**a**	**e**	
liegen	liegt	lag	hat gelegen	*lie (position)*

| ÜBUNG K | **Eine Geschichte schreiben.** You are enjoying these creative writing assignments. This time your teacher has given you a list of nouns, adverbs and adjectives. You're to use at least two of her words plus any one of the verbs above in the present perfect tense to create 5 interesting sentences. You may not use any prompt word or verb twice.

Nouns –Tennisspieler, Kleinkind, Buch, Fotomodel, Dichter, Mörder, Polizeikommissar, Kusine, Koffer, Tag, Kaffee, Diamantenring, Katze, Apfelkuchen

Adjectives and Adverbs – schnell, heimlich, endlich, mysteriös, nervös, determiniert, ärgerlich, furchtbar, traurig, ekelhaft, krank, munter, freundlich, nett, gesund, klug

EXAMPLE: Das kluge Kleinkind hat den Apfelkuchen gerochen und ist determiniert in die Küche gekrochen.

1. _____

2. _____

3. _____

4. _____

5. _____

e. Principal Parts of Verbs with an **I** that Show a Stem-Vowel Change

i	i	a	u	
binden	bindet	band	hat gebunden	*tie, bind*
dringen	dringt	drang	hat gedrungen	*urge, put pressure on*
empfinden	empfindet	empfand	hat empfunden	*feel, sense*
findet	findet	fand	hat gefunden	*find*
gelingen	gelingt	gelang	ist gelungen	*be successful*
klingen	klingt	klang	hat geklungen	*peal (bell), ring*
misslingen	misslingt	misslang	ist misslungen	*be unsuccessful*
ringen	ringt	rang	hat gerungen	*wrestle, struggle*
schwingen	schwingt	schwang	hat geschwungen	*swing, sway*
singen	singt	sang	hat gesungen	*sing*
springen	springt	sprang	ist gesprungen	*jump*
stinken	stinkt	stank	hat gestunken	*smell badly*
trinken	trinkt	trank	hat getrunken	*drink*
verschwinden	verschwindet	verschwand	ist verschwunden	*disappear*
winden	windet	wand	hat gewunden	*wind*
zwingen	zwingt	zwang	hat gezwungen	*force*

i	i	a	o	
beginnen	beginnt	begann	hat begonnen	*begin, start*
schwimmen	schwimmt	schwamm	ist/hat geschwommen	*swim*
spinnen	spinnt	spann	hat gesponnen	*be crazy, spin tales*

i	i	a	e	
bitten	bittet	bat	hat gebeten	*request, ask (for)*
sitzen	sitzt	saß	hat gesessen	*sit*

NOTE: *Dass* (that) and *ob* (whether) are both subordinating conjunctions. When they introduce a clause, the finite verb (that part which shows endings) moves to the end of that clause.

Er ist weit gesprungen.   Weißt du, dass er weit gesprungen ist?

Use that knowledge and the above verbs to complete the exercise below.

ÜBUNG L	**Weißt du was?** You are asking your friend Udo about recent accomplishments of your fellow students.

EXAMPLE: Elli / ihn / schon / darum / bitten (ob)
          Weißt du, ob Elli ihn schon darum gebeten hat?

1. Melanie / ihre Brille / schon / finden (ob)

_____

2. Hans und Gerlinde / am Samstagabend / im Konzert / singen (ob)

_____

3. Mein Hund / letzte Woche / verschwinden (dass)

_____

4. Die Küche / nach Rauch / stinken (dass)

_____

5. Wir / auf der Party / nur Limo / trinken (dass)

_____

6. Der Film / um zwanzig Uhr / beginnen (dass)

_____

7. Ihr / drei Stunden / im Kino / sitzen (dass)

_____

8. er / spinnen (ob)

_____

NOTE: Question words often act like subordinate conjunctions when introducing a dependent clause, i.e. they also move the verb to the end of the sentence or clause.

Hat er gesagt? Wann hat der Film begonnen?

Did he say? When did the movie start?

Hat er gesagt, wann der Film begonnen hat?

Did he say when the movie started?

ÜBUNG M   **Partygeflüster.** You're at a party and having a hard time hearing over the loud music. Ask your friend for clarification using verbs from the list on page 19. Use the present perfect tense in both clauses.

EXAMPLE: fragen // was / wir / trinken   Hat er gefragt, was wir getrunken haben?

1. sagen warum / der Hund / ihn / beißen

_____

2. fragen // wann / Melissa / verschwinden

_____

3. sagen // wer / ihn / zwingen

_____

4. sagen // wie weit / Tarzan / in dem Film / schwimmen

_____

5. sagen // worum / die Kinder / bitten

_____

    e. Principal Parts of Verbs with an **O** or **U** that Show a Stem-Vowel Change

o	o	a	o	
bekommen	**bekommt**	**bekam**	**ist bekommen**	_receive_
kommen	**kommt**	**kam**	**ist gekommen**	_come_
u	**u**	**ie**	**u**	
anrufen	**ruft an**	**rief an**	**hat angerufen**	_call on telephone_
rufen	**ruft**	**rief**	**hat gerufen**	_call_
u	**u**	**a**	**a**	
tun	**tut**	**tat**	**hat getan**	_do, make_

ÜBUNG N	**Mir ist nicht klar!** You're still having a hard time hearing at the party. Ask for clarification using the above verbs in the present perfect tense, this time using a question word to introduce the clause.

EXAMPLE: sagen // was / er / zu Weihnachten / bekommen
Hat er gesagt, was er zu Weihnachten bekommen hat?

1. sagen // wo / das Eis / schon / schmelzen

_____

2. fragen // wann / wir / kommen

_____

3. sagen // wen / er / anrufen

_____

4. fragen // was / wir / tun

_____

5. sagen // wie / wir / ohne Studentenausweis / in dieses Lokal / einkommen

_____

4.   Mixed Strong Verbs in the Present Perfect Tense

There are a few verbs, including all the modal verbs (see following page), that exhibit a stem-vowel change to form their past, yet take a –t in the past participle like the weak verbs do. These are called irregular strong verbs, or often mixed strong verbs.

The principle parts of the irregular strong verbs are:

brennen	brennt	brannte	hat gebrannt	*burn, be on fire*
niederbrennen	brennt nieder	brannte nieder	ist niedergebrannt	*burned down*
bringen	bringt	brachte	hat gebracht	*bring*
denken	denkt	dachte	hat gedacht	*think*
kennen	kennt	kannte	hat gekannt	*know, be acquainted with*
nennen	nennt	nannte	hat genannt	*name*
rennen	rennt	rannte	ist gerannt	*run*
wissen	weiß	wusste	hat gewusst	*know (a fact)*

ÜBUNG O   **Hausbrand!** You're reporting for the school newspaper. Susanna Meier's house has burned. The fire department thinks that lightning hit the house. The Meiers knew that the storm was dangerous. They didn't know however how dangerous it was. The students have collected money for the family. This afternoon your German club brought them food and blankets. Write the article.

_____

_____

_____

_____

_____

_____

_____

5.   Modal Verbs in the Present Perfect Tense

The principle parts of the modal verbs are:

dürfen	darf	durfte	hat gedurft	*may, be allowed*
können	kann	konnte	hat gekonnt	*can, be able*
mögen	mag	mochte	hat gemocht	*like*
müssen	muss	musste	hat gemusst	*must, have to*
sollen	soll	sollte	hat gesollt	*should, supposed to*
wollen	will	wollte	hat gewollt	*want to*

The present perfect of modal verbs is unique. If there is no infinitive completer, you use the past participle just as you would a normal verb.

Das habe ich nie gekonnt.   *I was never able (to do) that.*
Ihre Kinder haben Eis nie gemocht.   *Her children have never liked ice cream.*

ÜBUNG P   **Das hat er immer schon gewusst.** You are talking to Herr Marzipan once again about former students. He is claiming that he always knew certain things about his students.

EXAMPLE: Josef ist jetzt Lehrer geworden. wollen   Das hat er immer gewollt.

1. Marika kann jetzt gut Schi laufen.

 können _____

2. Martin darf jetzt mit den besten Schachspielern spielen.

 dürfen _____

3. Danika ist Tierärztin geworden.

 wollen _____

4. Francesca hat jetzt ein Haus in Berlin.

 wollen _____

5. Frank darf jetzt so oft er will, nach New York fliegen.

 dürfen _____

Most often, however, the modal is used with an infinitive completer, even in the present perfect tense. In that case, the past participle is replaced by an infinitive. The order of the three verbs in the sentence becomes VIM (auxiliary verb-infinitive-modal).

Mein Vater hat nie schwimmen können.   *My father has never been able to swim.*
Habt ihr gestern mit ihm fahren können?   *Were you allowed to go with him yesterday?*

ÜBUNG Q   **Damals!** You are now going to tell Herr Marzipan what you remember about your friends. Use each of the modals and the sentence elements to write something about them. Make up the last three.

EXAMPLE: Niels hat damals immer vor 10 Uhr abends zu Hause sein sollen.

1. Klara / nie / alleine / in die Stadt / dürfen/ fahren

_____

2. Michael / Tennis / nie / können / spielen

_____

3. Lucia / immer / Eis / mögen / essen

_____

4. müssen _____

5. sollen _____

6. wollen _____

| ÜBUNG R | **Dann haben wir . . .** Now write about life *damals* (i.e. then, a while ago). What did you and your friends do, what could you do, etc. Write at least five sentences.

EXAMPLE: Wir haben damals nicht mit dem Auto fahren dürfen und (wir) sind immer mit dem Bus zur Schule gefahren.

_____

_____

_____

_____

_____

_____

_____

_____

CHAPTER 3
Simple Past Tense

1. Written vs. Spoken Text

The simple past tense, often called the imperfect or narrative past, is used more often in written texts than in spoken. It is used to tell a story or relate a series of events.

The creative stories in the previous chapter became wordy and awkward. Compare this narrative from chapter 2 (pg. 16) with the same story written in the past tense. The simple past tense makes the paragraph much easier to read.

<table>
<tr><td align="center">Conversational Past</td><td align="center">Narrative Past</td></tr>
<tr><td>

Frieder hat lange Stunden in der Bank gestanden. Er hat sich nicht bewegt, nur Nüsse gegessen und seine Zeitung gelesen. Der Banksicherheitsdienst hat ihn fast hinausgeworfen. In dem Moment ist aber der Geldtransporter vor die Bank gefahren. Zwei Männer haben Geldsäcke in die Bank hereingetragen. Aber was ist dann geschehen? Ein Sack ist heruntergefallen. Frieder ist schnell hingegangen und hat den Sack aufgehoben. Hat er ihn stehlen wollen? Nein. Unser Frieder ist ein so guter Mensch gewesen, dass er den gefallenen Sack mit zur Kasse getragen hat. Er hat den zwei Männern geholfen. Er hat sie nicht bestohlen.

</td><td>

Frieder stand lange Stunden in der Bank. Er bewegte sich nicht, aß nur Nüsse und las seine Zeitung. Der Banksicherheitsdienst warf ihn fast hinaus. In dem Moment fuhr aber der Geldtransporter vor die Bank. Zwei Männer trugen Geldsäcke in die Bank herein. Aber was geschah dann? Ein Sack fiel herunter. Frieder ging schnell hin und hob den Sack auf. Wollte er ihn stehlen? Nein. Unser Frieder war ein so guter Mensch, dass er den gefallenen Sack mit zur Kasse trug. Er half den zwei Männern. Er bestahl sie nicht.

</td></tr>
</table>

In discussing a single event in the past, the present perfect, or conversational past, is preferred.

Schiller hat das Drama „Wilhelm Tell" geschrieben.

Schiller wrote / did write / has written the drama "Wilhelm Tell".

When you are discussing a series of events in the past, which is the case when telling or writing a story, then the narrative, or simple past, is used.

Schiller lebte eine Weile in Kanton Uri in der Schweiz. Dort hörte er die Sage von Wilhelm Tell. Er fand sie so interessant, dass er ein Drama darüber schreib. Das Drama wurde schnell sehr populär. Es machte die Geschichte von Wilhelm Tell weltberühmt.

Schiller lived for a while in Canton Uri in Switzerland. There he heard the legend of Wilhelm Tell. He found it so interesting, that he wrote a drama about it. The drama quickly became very popular. It made the story of Wilhelm Tell world famous.

2. Formation of the Simple Past of Weak Verbs

The simple past tense of weak verbs is formed by adding *-te* (or *-ete*) to the verb stem, and then the personal verb endings.

SIMPLE PAST TENSE OF WEAK VERBS	
SINGULAR	PLURAL
ich spiel – te *I played, I did play, I was playing*	**wir spiel – ten** *we played, we did play, we were playing*
du spiel – test *you (informal) played, did play, were playing*	**ihr spiel – tet** *you (informal) played, did play, were playing*
er, sie, es spiel – te *he, she, or it played, did play, was playing*	**sie spiel – ten** *they played, they did play, they were playing*
Sie spiel – ten *You (formal) played, did play, were playing*	

NOTE: If the stem ends in *–t*, *–d*, or two consonants followed by an *–n*, add *–e* before the *–te* ending to facilitate pronunciation. If the *du*-form already ends in *–s* or *–ß*, only *–t* is added.

ÜBUNG A | **Die Geschichte von Wilhelm Tell.** Your class has plans to write and illustrate Wilhelm Tell for students in the class below yours. Before you actually create your book you want to understand the setting of the story. Your classmates have found a history article about his canton in Switzerland. Now you must answer questions about it. This article was written in the present tense. Because you will be telling a story, you want to make sure that your answers are in the simple past tense.

Wilhelm Tell lebt im 14. Jahrhundert. Er wohnt auf dem Land in Kanton Uri in der Schweiz. Er hat einen Sohn Walter. Er jagt oft im Wald mit seiner Armbrust (crossbow). Weit weg in Wien Österreich regiert die Habsburger Familie. Die habsburgischen Prinzen schicken einen Beamten (official) namens Hermann Gessler in die Schweiz. Er arbeitet in Altdorf (der Hauptstadt vom Kanton) und versucht den Handel (trade) zwischen Österreich und der Schweiz zu kontrollieren. Er versucht die Schweiz unter Kontrolle von Österreich zu bringen. Die Schweizer lieben ihre Freiheit und wollen Gessler nicht helfen. Das vereint sie gegen ihn.

EXAMPLE: Wann hat Wilhelm Tell gelebt? Wilhelm Tell lebte im 14. Jahrhundert.

1. Wo hat Wilhelm Tell gelebt?

   _____

2. Wen haben die Habsburger in die Schweiz geschickt?

   _____

3. Wo hat Hermann Gessler gearbeitet?

   _____

4. Wen hat er repräsentiert?

   _____

5. Was hat Gessler machen wollen?

   _____

6. Was hat die Schweizer gegen Gessler und die Habsburger vereint?

   _____

ÜBUNG B | **Die Atmosphäre in Kanton Uri.** The people in three nearby towns had sworn an oath to stand up to Gessler. Meanwhile Gessler had erected a pole in town and placed his hat on top of it. The Swiss who passed this pole were supposed to bow and honor it. Wilhelm Tell refused to do so. That started the events that made him a hero. Create the story using the prompts. Use the past tense, since the end result is a series of events.

EXAMPLE: Leute / in 3 Nachbarstädten / sich / gegen Gessler / vereinen (unite)
         Die Leute in drei Nachbarstädten vereinten sich gegen Gessler.

1. Sie / ein Eid gegen die Habsburger / leisten (take an oath)

   _____

2. Gessler / einen Pfosten / im Stadtzentrum / errichten

   _____

3. Er / seinen Hut / darauf / stellen

   _____

4. Die Schweizer / vor dem Hut / Respekt zeigen / sollen

_____

5. Wilhelm Tell / außerhalb der Stadt / wohnen

_____

6. Er / Gesslers Worte / nicht / hören / und / den Hut auf dem Pfosten / ignorieren

_____

3.   Formation of the Simple Past of Strong Verbs

The simple past of strong verbs usually differs from the present tense by a vowel change. It must be memorized as part of the principle parts of the verb. (See chapter 2 or table 4 in appendix.) Personal endings are added, as seen in chart below.

geben, gibt, *gab*, hat gegeben – *give*

schreiben, schreibt, *schrieb*, hat geschrieben – *write*

SIMPLE PAST TENSE OF STRONG VERBS	
SINGULAR	PLURAL
ich gab *I gave, I did give, I was giving*	**wir gab – en** *we gave, did give, were giving*
du gab – st *you (informal) gave, did give, were giving*	**ihr gab– t** *you (informal) gave, did give, were giving*
er, sie, es gab *he, she, or it gave, did give, was giving*	**sie gab – en** *they gave, did give, were giving*
Sie gab – en *You (formal) gave, did give, were giving*	

NOTE: If the *du*-form already ends in *–s* or *–ß*, you need only add a *–t*

ÜBUNG C   **Die Geschichte von Wilhelm Tell - der Anfang.** You can now create the first draft of your Wilhelm Tell book. You've found a children's book that tells the story in the present tense. You'd prefer to use the past. As your partner reads the present tense to you, change it to the past. Refer to the charts in chapter 2 if you cannot remember the appropriate vowel change for the strong verb.

EXAMPLE: Eines Tages kommt Wilhelm Tell in die Stadt.
Eines Tages kam Wilhelm Tell in die Stadt.

1. Er geht an dem Pfosten mit dem Hut vorbei und biegt sich nicht.

_____

2. Hermann Gessler ist empört und nimmt ihn fest.

   _____

3. Die Leute in der Nähe wissen, dass Tell sehr gut mit der Armbrust schießen kann.

   _____

4. Gessler befiehlt, dass Tell einen Apfel von dem Kopf seines Sohnes abschießt.

   _____

5. Tell bringt zwei Pfeiler (arrows) mit sich. Er stellt einen in die Armbrust (crossbow) und den anderen in seinem Köcher (quiver).

   _____

6. Gessler bindet die Hände von Tells Sohn und stellt einen Apfel auf seinen Kopf.

   _____

7. Dann schießt Tell. Sein Pfeil trifft den Apfel. Er rettet das Leben von seinem Sohn.

   _____

ÜBUNG D | **Gessler nimmt Tell in Haft.** Gessler was impressed with Tell's marksmanship, but also curious why he had brought two arrows. Tell told him the second arrow was meant for Gessler's heart, had he missed and killed his son. Continue the story using the word prompts.

EXAMPLE: Gessler / sich / über Tells Antwort / ärgern
Gessler ärgerte sich über Tells Antwort.

1. Er / ihn / sofort / in Haft / nehmen.

   _____

2. Gessler / sagen // dass / Tell / sein Leben / im Gefängnis / verbringen / müssen

   _____

3. Das Gefängnis / über dem See in der Stadt Küssnacht / sein

   _____

4. Unterwegs / ein Sturm auf dem See / ausbrechen

   _____

5. Tell / der Ruderstock / nehmen // und das Boot / sicher / ans Land / bringen

   _____

6. Er / vom Boot / abspringen / und / weglaufen

   _____

ÜBUNG E	**Das Ende der Geschichte.** Tell has jumped from the boat taking him to prison for life and escaped. He could avoid Gessler and spend the rest of his life with his family. Instead he chose to take revenge on Gessler. His actions made him a hero whom the Swiss still honor each year on *Wilhelm Tell Tag*. Write the end of the story.

EXAMPLE: Er / frei / sein // Er / in die Stadt / laufen / und / auf Gessler / warten
Er war frei. Er lief in die Stadt und wartete auf Gessler.

1. Gessler / später / durch die hohle Gasse / kommen

   _____

2. Tell / aus seinem Versteck / springen / und Gessler / erschießen

   _____

3. Die Schweizer / diesem bösen Menschen / nicht mehr / gehorchen / müssen

   _____

4. Wilhelm Tell / dem Schweizer Folk zum Helden (Hero) / werden

   _____

4.   *Als* Used with the Simple Past Tense

We often link two simultaneous actions in the past using the word "when" or "as." This construction uses the simple past in German coupled with the word *als*.

Als ich jung war, ging ich jeden Tag 2 Meilen zu Fuß zur Schule.
When I was young, I walked 2 miles to school every day.
Als ich ins Bett ging, kam sie endlich nach Hause.
As I was going to bed, she finally came home.

This construction is often used with the word *gerade* (just) for emphasis.

Gerade als ich weggehen wollte, kam er an.   *He arrived just as I wanted to leave.*
Ich las gerade etwas über Schiller im Internet, als das Telefon klingelte.
I was just reading something about Schiller in the Internet when the telephone rang.

In the sentences above, there are two clauses in each sentence. The finite verbs end up next to each other. *Als* introduces the first clause, which is the subordinate clause. The verb in that clause moves therefore to the end of its clause followed by a comma. That *als*-clause becomes the first element in the sentence; the verb therefore has to come next. The result is that the two finite verbs often occur next to each other.

Gerade als ich meine Emails las, kam meine Mutter ins Zimmer.
My mother came into the room just as I was reading my emails.

ÜBUNG F **Meine Autobiografie.** You're getting ready to write an autobiography. Choose 6 significant things that happened in your life and write them here.

EXAMPLE: Als ich fünf Jahre alt war, bekam ich meine erste Katze Maggie.

1. Als ich zwei Jahre alt war, _____

2. Als ich sechs Jahre alt war, _____

3. Als ich acht Jahre alt war, _____

4. Als ich zehn Jahre alt war, _____

5. Als ich dreizehn Jahre alt war, _____

ÜBUNG G **Berühmte Deutsche, Schweizer und Österreicher.** You've been researching famous people from German-speaking countries. Eventually you'll choose one for a class report. You have a problem, however. Your note cards have gotten out of order. Connect the facts and then combine them into one sentence so that this can't happen again.

EXAMPLE: Adi Dassler war 24 Jahre alt. Er schuf die ersten Sportschuhe besonders für Fußballer. Als Adi Dassler 24 Jahre alt war, schuf er die ersten Sportschuhe besonders für Fußballer.

Bonus Question:
   What is the name of the famous sport shoe company that Adi Dassler and his brother started?

1. Albert Einstein war 40 Jahre alt. Er wurde amerikanischer Staatsbürger.

    _____

2. Max Ernst und Jans Arp studierten Kunst in Köln. Sie gründeten die moderne Kunstform Dadaismus.

    _____

3. Wolfgang Amadeus Mozart war 4 Jahre alt. Er gab sein erstes Konzert.

    _____

4. Friedrich Schiller war 45 Jahre alt. Er schrieb „Wilhelm Tell".

    _____

5. Der berühmte Boxer Max Schmeling starb. Er war 100 Jahre alt.

    _____

6. Arnold Schwarzenegger war 44 Jahre alt. Er wurde Gouverneur von Kalifornien.

    _____

ÜBUNG H | **Ein Teil meines Lebens.** Now you are ready to write a story, real or imagined, from your life. Pick an age and write about your life, school, friends, family, etc.

EXAMPLE: Als ich zehn Jahre alt war, zogen wir von New York City nach Austin um.

_____

_____

_____

_____

_____

_____

_____

_____

CHAPTER 4
Future Tense

1. Expressing the Future with the Present Tense

The present tense is often paired with an adverb or adverbial phrase to express futurity.

Die nächsten Winterolympiaden finden in zwei Jahren statt.
The next Winter Olympics will take place in two years.

In the above sentence, the present tense is used, but it is obvious that the future is being discussed. Adding the adverbial phrase *in zwei Jahren* establishes this fact.

Some of the adverbs or adverbial expressions you may use to express futurity are:

sofort	*immediately*
gleich	*at once*
bald	*soon*
morgen	*tomorrow*
übermorgen	*the day after tomorrow*
später	*later*
am Donnerstag	*on Thursday*
in einer Stunde/Woche	*in an hour/week*
in drei Tagen/Wochen	*in three days/weeks*
in einem Monat/Jahr	*in a month/year*
im Mai	*in May*
nächsten Dienstag	*next Tuesday*
nächste Woche	*next week*
nächsten Monat	*next month*
nächstes Jahr	*next year*

ÜBUNG A   **Den Kinobesuch planen.** You and your sister Annemarie want to go to the movies together. Write the conversation. Use an adverbial time expression in each sentence.

EXAMPLE: ANNAMARIE: Wann spielt der neue Wilm Wender Film?
DU: Die erste Vorführung ist heute Nachmittag.

1. ANNAMARIE: Wollen wir dann den Film sehen? Wann können wir hingehen?

   Du: _____

2. ANNAMARIE: Sollen wir am Nachmittag oder zur Abendvorführung hingehen?

   Du: _____

3. ANNAMARIE: Bist du noch nicht fertig? Wir müssen jetzt gehen.

   Du: _____

4. ANNAMARIE: Wann dann? Mach schnell. Der Film beginnt in einer halben Stunde.

   Du: _____

5. ANNAMARIE: Und wann soll das sein?

   Du: _____

| ÜBUNG B | **Eine Email.** Compose an e-mail to your friend inviting him or her to a performance of the school play followed by an activity. Make sure you confirm all the details: where you want to go, when you will pick him or her up, what time the performance begins, when you will get the tickets, what you will do afterward, etc. |

_____

_____

_____

_____

_____

_____

_____

_____

2. The Future Tense

The use of the present tense is the preferred method of expressing futurity in German. However, a formal future tense also exists. The helping verb *werden* becomes the finite verb and the completer infinitive goes to the end of the sentence.

Wir werden Karten für die Olympischen Winterspiele bekommen.

We will get / are going to get tickets for the Winter Olympic Games.

Mein Bruder wird die Schweiz in Eiskunstlauf vertreten.

My brother will represent Switzerland in figure skating.

CONJUGATION OF **WERDEN**	
SINGULAR	PLURAL
ich werde	wir werden
du wirst	ihr werdet
er, sie, es wird	sie werden
Sie werden	

ÜBUNG C   **Was ich bei den Olympischen Winterspielen tun werde.** You are writing your pen pal a message telling him that sometime in the future you will attend the Olympics. Use the cues to help you write about what you will see and do. Add two more sentences of your own.

EXAMPLE: zu den Olympischen Winterspielen fahren
        Ich werde zu den Olympischen Winterspielen fahren.

1. das Rennrodeln bestimmt anschauen
    _____

2. nicht unbedingt zu den Biathlonwettkämpfen hingehen
    _____

3. meine erste olympische Schlussfeier dort erleben
    _____

4. _____

5. _____

3.   The Future Tense in a Subordinate Clause

If the clause with the future tense is introduced by a subordinate conjunction, then the finite form of the verb (which is *werden*), goes to the end of the clause.

Wissen Sie, wann die Olympiade beginnen wird?

Do you know when the Olympics will begin?

Ich hoffe, dass die Schweizer einige Medaillen im Eiskunstlauf gewinnen werden.

I hope that the Swiss will win a few medals in figure skating.

ÜBUNG D | **Die nächste Winterolympiade.** You want to know how much your friend knows about the next winter games. Write at least five questions using werden and the cues below. Begin each with *"Weißt du,..."*. You may add your own thoughts.

EXAMPLE: wann / beginnen
       Weißt du, wann die nächsten Winterolympiaden beginnen werden?

1. wo / stattfinden

   _____

2. wie / Karten bekommen

   _____

3. wie viele / in der Eishockeymannschaft mitspielen

   _____

4. warum / die Olympiaden / nicht / in Griechenland / stattfinden

   _____

5. wer / Österreich / vertreten

   _____

6. wie viel / Eiskunstlaufkarten / kosten

   _____

7. _____

8. _____

ÜBUNG E | **Was wird bei den Olympiaden passieren?** Many of your friends express their thoughts about the next Winter Olympics. Write down what they are saying. Connect the two clauses using *dass*.

EXAMPLE: Ralf / glauben // das US-Eishockyteam / nicht / siegen
       Ralf glaubt, dass das US-Eishockyteam nicht siegen wird.

1. Mario / hoffen // die Schweizer / einige Medaillen / gewinnen

   _____

2. Arno / denken // die Spiele / wunderbar / sein

   _____

3. Lisa / wissen // sie / irgendwann / auch / in den Olympiaden / mitspielen

   _____

4. Maria / hoffen // die Schlussfeier / interessant / sein

_____

5. Lena / hoffen // es / Frieden auf der Erde / geben

_____

4.   The Future Tense with a Modal Verb

The word order for the present perfect tense with a modal is VIM (verb-infinitive-modal).

Er hat lange für die Schweiz laufen wollen.
     verb   infinitive modal

He has wanted to skate for Switzerland for a long time.

The VIM (verb-infinitive-modal) rule also applies in the case of a modal verb used in the future tense.

Leider wird seine Freundin ihn nicht sehen   können.
       verb   infinitive modal

His girlfriend will unfortunately not be able to see him.

ÜBUNG F   **Was wirst du während der Olympiade tun?** You have an acquaintance who lives in an upcoming Olympic city. Ask what his plans are for the big event.

EXAMPLE: zu allen Wettbewerben / hingehen / können
         Wirst du zu allen Wettbewerben hingehen können?

1. von der Schule / wegbleiben / dürfen

_____

2. oder / jeden Tag / in die Schule / gehen / müssen

_____

3. Karten für die Eishockey-Spiele / bekommen / können

_____

4. die Spieler / persönlich / kennen lernen / können

_____

5. an der Schlussfeier / teilnehmen / können

_____

5.   Using the Future Tense to Express Probability

The future tense is paired often with the word _wohl_ to express probability. It translates into English as "probably."

Die Schweizer werden wohl die Bronzemedaille in Eiskunstlauf gewinnen.
The Swiss will probably win the bronze medal in figure skating.

ÜBUNG G | **Deine Vorhersagen für die Olympischen Winterspiele.** Make some predictions for the next Winter Games. Who do you think will win or lose? Make your predictions for individuals or countries.

EXAMPLE: Jamaika wird wohl keine Medaille in Rennrodeln gewinnen.

1. _____

2. _____

3. _____

4. _____

5. _____

6.   Future Perfect Tense

Used rarely, the future perfect tense exists to discuss something that will have been completed before a specific time point in the future.

Er wird viel geübt haben, bevor er nächste Woche aufs Eis auftritt.
He will have practiced a lot before he steps out onto the ice next week.

werden + past participle + **haben** or **sein** = future perfect

FUTURE PERFECT TENSE CONJUGATION	
SINGULAR	PLURAL
ich werde gespielt haben	wir werden gespielt haben
du wirst gespielt haben	ihr werdet gespielt haben
er, sie, es wird gespielt haben	sie werden gespielt haben
Sie werden gespielt haben	

ÜBUNG H | **Was wird bis zur Winter-Olympiade passiert sein?** What will have happened before the next Winter Olympics take place? Make predictions about your life, the world, and sports. Use the cues and then add four of your own sentences.

EXAMPLE: Mein Bruder wird bestimmt viele Stunden auf dem Eis geübt haben.
Die USA wird noch viele Eishockeyspiele gewonnen haben.

1. wir / die Gewinner von den letzten Olympiaden / noch nicht / vergessen

_____

2. Die US Eishockeymannschaft / wohl / ihr Spiel gegen die Russen / gewinnen

_____

3. die Olympiastadt / eine neue Eiskunstlaufhalle / bauen

_____

4. Meine Familie und ich / unsere Flugpläne / machen

_____

5. Der österreichische Schispringer Andreas Goldberger / mindestens /10 Schier / brechen

_____

| ÜBUNG I | **Ich und meine Freunde bei den Olympischen Spielen.** Imagine that you and some friends will be competing someday in the Olympic Games. Write about the things you will do. Use both the present tense with time adverbs and the formal future tense in your narrative. It should be at least 7 sentences long. |

_____

_____

_____

_____

_____

_____

_____

_____

CHAPTER 5
Conjunctions

1. Coordinating Conjunctions

Coordinating conjunctions combine equal words, phrases or independent clauses. An independent clause is one that can stand alone as a sentence.

Christian Breuer hat viele Jahre zur Olympiade hintrainiert und viel Geld darin investiert.

Christian Breuer trained several years for the Olympics and invested much money in it.

Georg Hackl nahm an den 2006er Spielen in Torino teil, aber er hat keine Medaille gewonnen.

Georg Hackl participated in the 2006 Games in Turin, but he didn't win a medal.

In the sentence above, the clauses are connected by the coordinating conjunctions *und* and *aber*. Both clauses are independent, i.e. if the word *und* were removed, both clauses still function as sentences on their own. Coordinating conjunctions connect independent clauses, words or phrases.

Coordinating conjunctions in German are:

aber	*but, however*
denn	*because*
oder	*or*
sondern	*but rather, but on the contrary*
und	*and*

When clauses are combined with one of these coordinating conjunctions, both clauses take regular word order. The finite verb, i.e. the part of the verb that takes endings, is the second element in each clause.

ÜBUNG A **Die deutsche Mannschaft.** Combine the facts you have read about members of a recent German Winter Olympics Team into single sentences using the suggested conjunction.

EXAMPLE: Langläufer / in Scheidegg / trainieren // aber // Skispringer / in Davos / sein
Die Langläufer trainieren in Scheidegg, **aber** die Skispringer **sind** in Davos.

1. Björn Kircheisen / nicht / an dem Biathlon / teilnehmen // sondern // er / die nordische Kombination / machen.

2. die Snowboarder / viele Hamburger und Käseburger / essen // aber // die Alpinskier / viel gesünder / essen. NOTE: Either spelling Ski or Schi is acceptable.

_____

3. Anna Lena Zuck / Bundesmeisterin in Snowboard / sein // aber // sie / immer noch / jeden Tag / trainieren / müssen

_____

4. sie / so intensiv / trainieren // denn // sie / in diesen Spielen / gewinnen / möchten

_____

5. Claudia Pechstein / nicht / Eiskunstlauf / machen // sondern // sie / an den Eisschnelllauf / teilnehmen

_____

ÜBUNG B | **Die Winter Olympiade im Fernsehen.** You and your friends are discussing your TV plans for today's Olympic coverage. Complete the sentences.

EXAMPLE: Wir sehen uns den Langlauf an, und _____
Wir sehen uns den Langlauf an, und dann gehen wir essen.

1. Wir können das Eishockeyspiel Italien gegen die Schweiz leider nicht sehen, denn

_____

2. Andreas Schlütter fährt ja nicht den Skislalom, sondern

_____

3. Das Bobrennen ist schnell, aber das Skeletonrennen

_____

4. Wollen wir den Biathlon anschauen, oder

_____

5. Christoph Gruber fährt Skialpin zum zweiten Mal in den Olympiaden, aber

_____

2. Subordinating Conjunctions

Subordinating conjunctions connect an independent with a dependent clause. The independent clause can stand alone as a complete sentence; the dependent clause usually cannot.

Bevor die Athleten zur Olympiastadt fliegen, müssen sie einen Fahnenträger
dependent clause - cannot stand alone   independent clause - can stand alone

auswählen.
Before the athletes fly to the Olympia, they must choose a flag bearer.

Common subordinating conjuntions are:

als	*when (single event in the past)*	**obwohl**	*although*
bevor	*before*	**seit(dem)**	*since (temporal, time)*
bis	*until*	**sobald**	*as soon as*
da	*since (causal, reason)*	**solange**	*as long as*
damit	*so that*	**sooft**	*as often as*
dass	*that*	**während**	*while*
indem	*in that*	**weil**	*because*
nachdem	*after*	***wenn**	*when, whenever*
ob	*if, whether*		

**wenn* can also mean "if", but usually only when used with the subjunctive form of the verb (see page 85).

In clauses introduced by subordinating conjunctions, the verb goes to the end of the clause. When the subordinating clause comes first, the two verbs in the sentence end up being next to each other in the middle of the sentence.

Nachdem sie gegessen hatten, gingen die Jungen zurück vor den Fernseher.
After they had eaten, the boys went back in front of the TV.

Sie hatten schnell gegessen, weil sie das Ende des Riesenslaloms sehen wollten.
They had eaten quickly, because they wanted to see the end of the giant slalom.

ÜBUNG C | **Fernseholympiaden.** The TV coverage continues. The ladies giant slalom is still underway and the boys find themselves rooting for their favorite, the Austrian Renate Götschl.

EXAMPLE: bevor // sie / weggehen // die Jungen / den Riesenslalom / ansehen
Bevor sie weggegangen waren, schauten die Jungen den Riesenslalom an.

1. der Riesenslalom / sehr interessant / sein // weil // der Favorit / Renate Götschl / dabei / sein

_____

2. da / Götschl / am vorigen Sonntag / auf der Schneepiste / fallen // die Jungen / an ihr Laufen / besonders / interessiert / sein

_____

3. seitdem / sie / fallen // sie / aus der Öffentlichkeit / bleiben

_____

4. sooft / Leute / Renate Götschl / sehen // es / nie genug / sein

_____

5. wenn / sie / den Riesenslalom / machen // alle / Skifans / begeistert / zuschauen

_____

6. Rainer sagt: „Bis // ich / wissen // ob / Renate / gewinnen // ich / nicht / nach Hause / gehen"

_____

ÜBUNG D   **Es klingelt.** Just as Götschl is ready for her second jump, your friend's cell phone rings. He tries to hurry the conversation so that he doesn't miss what you both hope will be the winning jump. Write his half of the conversation using a different subordinate conjunction in each sentence.

EXAMPLE: Ich kann nicht lange sprechen, weil _____

Ich kann nicht lange sprechen, weil Renate Götschl bald springt.

1. _____, rufe ich dich zurück.

2. Ich kann nicht kommen, _____

3. _____, komme ich dich besuchen.

4. Marco wird nicht mitkommen, _____

5. Also ich bin bei dir, _____

ÜBUNG E   **Email über die Olympiade.** The ski jumping competition is over. E-mail your friend in the US, whose coverage hasn't started yet, and tell her about your day, including the results of Renate Götschl's attempt for the Gold. Use at least six subordinating conjunctions.

Hallo, Christiane!

_____

_____

_____

_____

_____

_____

_____

Dein Marco

3.   Interrogatives as Subordinating Conjunctions

Question words act as subordinating conjunctions when they are used to combine two clauses.

Wissen Sie, wer gewonnen hat?   *Do you know who won?*

Habt ihr gesehen, wie weit sie gesprungen ist?   *Did you see how far she jumped?*

Kannst du mir bitte sagen, wann der Eisschnelllauf beginnt?

Can you please tell me when the speed skating will start?

ÜBUNG F   **Dein Interview mit einem Rennrodler.** You have a wonderful opportunity. You were permitted to interview Georg Hackl, one of the greatest Olympians of all times. He won the luge event in at least 5 consecutive Olympics. Now you are telling your friends about the interview. Using at least 5 of the interrogatives *wer, wie, was, wann,* and *warum,* supply the correct question words. If you use *wie,* you may combine it with an adverb (*wie oft, wie viel(e), wie früh,* etc.).

NOTE: *Wie* is often combined with an adverb, e.g. *wie oft* (how often), *wie schnell,* etc. When asking how much or how many, use *wie viele* if the quantity can be counted in units (*viele Münzen*), *wie viel* if it can't (*viel Geld*).

EXAMPLE: Ich habe ihn gefragt, <u>wann</u> er mit dem Sport angefangen hat.

1. Dann hat er erklärt, _____ man in einem Rennrodel einsteigt.

2. Er hat mir auch erzählt, _____ er trainiert. Jeden Morgen um halb neun.

3. Er hat mir gezeigt, _____ er seine Hände während der Fahrt hält.

4. Natürlich hat er auch gesagt, _____ er den Sport so toll findet.

5. Ja, ich habe ihn gefragt, _____ ihm seinen ersten Rennrodel gekauft hat.

6. Und zuletzt habe ich ihn gefragt, _____ Olympia-Medaillen er schon hat.

4.   *Was für ein,* as Interrogative

The expression *was für (ein/eine/ein)* is an interrogative meaning "what kind of." The adjective *ein* takes the GNC of the noun it modifies. **NOTE:** The question "what kind of" is *was für ein* in the singular; the plural form is *was für* without the word *ein*.

Auf was für einem Rennrodel fahren Sie, Herr Hackl.
       MSD

What kind of luge do you ride Herrr Hackl? (literally, on what for a luge do you ride?)

ÜBUNG G | **Was für ein Leben.** You have only your friend's notes from her Olympic interview with a mogul skier. Can you reconstruct the questions from the answers? Use the *was für ein* construction.

EXAMPLE: Answer: Ich wohne in einer sehr kleinen Stadt in den Bergen.
Question: In was für einer Stadt wohnen Sie?

1. Meine Schier? Ich fahre auf Rossignol Schiern.

   Auf _____

2. Mein Glücksbringer? Ich habe meinen Glücksknopf.

   Was _____

3. Mein Wagen? Ich fahre einen BMW.

   Mit _____

4. Meine Skibrille? Ich trage eine Carrera Tiger Skibrille®.

   Was _____

5. Medaille? Ich hoffe, ich werde eine Goldene gewinnen.

   Was _____

ÜBUNG H | **Dein Interview.** You now have the opportunity to interview a Winter Olympian from your country. Write five questions you would like to ask him or her. One of your questions must use the *was für ein* construction and two must contain a subordinate clause.

EXAMPLE: Können Sie mir sagen, wie viele Gold Medaillen Sie schon gewonnen haben?

1. _____
2. _____
3. _____
4. _____
5. _____

5.   Correlative Conjunctions

There are a series of conjunctions, called correlatives, which are always used in pairs. Often there are two things which one wishes to connect in a sentence. Using the paired correlative conjunctions rather than a simple conjunction is not only more interesting, but also more specific.

a. entweder . . . oder   *either . . . or*

Entweder er gewinnt die Gold Medaille am Sonntag oder (er gewinnt) die Silber Medaille.

Either he will win the gold medal on Sunday or (he will win) the silver medal.

ÜBUNG I   **Entweder/ oder.** The German ice hockey team coach gives his group some ultimata. Fill in the missing words in the first three, and then create two more that you think are appropriate.

EXAMPLE: Entweder wir trainieren härter, oder wir werden verlieren.

1. Entweder ihr passt gut auf ihr Diät auf, oder _____.

2. Entweder ihr kriegt genug Schlaf, oder _____.

3. Entweder ihr _____, oder ihr werdet krank.

4. _____.

5. _____.

---

b. je (mehr) . . . desto (weniger)   *the (more) . . . the (less)*

Je mehr er trainiert, desto besser wird er.   *The more he trains, the better he becomes.*

ÜBUNG J   **Je mehr!** You have designed a chain response game in which each sentence repeats the second part of the previous sentence and then continues to tell the story. Fill in the sentences to make sure that you can do the task.

EXAMPLE: Je mehr er trainiert, desto besser wird er.
Je besser er wird, desto mehr gewinnt er.

1. Je mehr er gewinnt, desto _____.

2. Je mehr er _____.

3. Je mehr _____.

4. Je _____.

5. _____.

---

c. nicht nur . . . sondern auch   *not only . . . but also*

Nicht nur er qualifizierte für die Skimannschaft, sondern auch sein Bruder (qualifizierte).

Not only he qualified for the ski team, but also his brother (qualified).

ÜBUNG K   **Bei den Olypiaden.** Imagine you are at the Olympic Games and looking around with amazement. You make statements like, "Not only is it exciting here, but also beautiful." "Not only are the athletes in good shape, but also very charming." You write an e-mail to your cousin to tell about this experience by completing the sentences, then add one of your own.

EXAMPLE: Nicht nur es ist sehr spannend hier, sondern auch sehr schön.

1. Wettbewerbe / interessant // Medaillezeremonien / beeindruckend

   _____

2. Chinesen gut im Eiskunstlauf // Amerikaner und Italiener

   _____

3. wir Karten für / Eiskunstlauf / Eishockeyendspiel

   _____

4. Snowboarder kämpfen // in Herren- und Frauen Halfpipe / in Cross und
   Parallelriesenslalom

   _____

5. Peking / Vancouver // auch Olympiastädte

   _____

    d. sowohl . . . als auch   _both . . . and, both . . . as well as_
   Sowohl er als auch sein Bruder gehen also zur Winterolympiade.
   Both he and (as well as) his brother are going therefore to the Winter Olympics.

| ÜBUNG L | **Die Beiden.** Think of the Winter Olympics of the past or the future and create statements about two things or people in each sentence. |

EXAMPLE: Sowohl Thomas Morgenstern als auch Andreas Kofler sind österreichische
Schiläufer. Sowohl die Amerikaner als auch die Russen haben Medaillen in
Bobsport gewonnen.

1. _____
2. _____
3. _____
4. _____
5. _____

    e. weder . . . noch   _neither . . . nor_
   Ich sehe weder meinen Bruder noch meine Schwester in dieser Menge.
   I see neither my brother nor my sister in this crowd.

| ÜBUNG M | **Weder . . . noch.** You are writing your pen pal a message and telling him about the things you dislike about the Olympics. Include all aspects of the games (location, teams, events, etc.) in your answers. In order to make the message interesting you use _weder . . . noch_ in every sentence. |

EXAMPLE: Ich mag weder den Riesenslalom noch den Langlauf.

1. _____

2. _____

3. _____

4. _____

5. _____

Experimenting with complex sentences and combining smaller sentences into longer ones are excellent stylistic devices. The resulting German sounds more natural and sophisticated. It becomes even more fluid and interesting with the use of compound verb forms and varying word order. The rules are the same regardless of the length or complexity of the sentence:

- ○ If the clause is introduced by a *coordinating conjunction*, the finite verb is the *second* element in its clause.
- ○ If the clause is introduced by a *subordinating conjunction*, the finite verb goes to the *end* of its clause.

| ÜBUNG N | **Mein Olympiatraum.** Have you ever dreamed of being in the Olympics or dreamed of attending? Write a story about your Olympic dream. Use at least six of the following words.

aber, als, oder, sondern, bevor, damit, dass, ob, obwohl, seitdem, solange, sooft, während, weil, wenn, entweder . . . oder, je . . . desto, sowohl . . . als auch

_____

_____

_____

_____

_____

_____

_____

_____

_____

CHAPTER 6
Reflexive Verbs

1. Reflexive Verbs

A reflexive verb is a verb used in combination with a reflexive pronoun to show that the subject and the direct (or indirect) object are the same. In English we use –self (himself, e.g.) to show that the pronoun is the same as the subject.

Ich wasche mich immer hinter den Ohren.   *I always wash (myself) behind the ears.*

Er hat sich neben mich hingesetzt.   *He sat (himself) down next to me.*

2. Reflexive Pronouns

The reflexive pronoun will either be in the dative (indirect object) or the accusative (direct object).

REFLEXIVE PRONOUNS		
ENGLISH	DATIVE	ACCUSATIVE
me, myself	mir	mich
you, yourself (singular, informal)	dir	dich
him, her, it, himself, herself, itself	sich	sich
us, ourselves	uns	uns
you, yourself (plural, informal)	euch	euch
them, themselves	sich	sich
you, yourself (singular & plural, formal)	sich	sich

3.   Reflexive Verbs with Parts of the Body

A reflexive verb is one that must be used with one of the above reflexive pronouns. Verbs used when discussing (parts of) the body are usually reflexive.

sich *(acc.)* **baden**	*bathe*	**sich** *(acc.)* **rasieren**	
sich *(acc.)* **waschen**	*wash (oneself)*	*shave (oneself)*	
sich *(acc.)* **duschen**	*shower (oneself)*	**sich** *(dat.)* **die Nase putzen**	
sich *(acc.)* **schminken**	*put on makeup*	*blow one's nose*	
sich *(acc.)* **kämmen**	*comb one's hair*	**sich** *(dat.)* **die Zähne putzen**	
sich *(dat.)* **die Haare kämmen**	*comb one's hair*	*brush one's teeth*	
sich *(dat.)* **die Haare waschen**	*wash one's hair*	**sich** *(dat.)* **etwas brechen**	
		break something (a leg, an arm, etc.)	

ÜBUNG A   **Oma's Morgenroutine.** Your great grandmother, who lives with you, has been asked to wear a cardiac monitor. She has to write down everything she does so that the doctor can coordinate her heartbeat with her activities. Since she has trouble with her eyesight you decide to help her. Write down exactly what she did with accurate times. You are using the past tense because you are writing a series of events.

EXAMPLE: aufstehen / sich das Gesicht waschen
    Um 7:34 stand sie auf und wusch sich das Gesicht.

1. sich duschen _____

2. sich die Beine rasieren _____

3. sich die Zähne putzen _____

4. sich die Haare kämmen _____

5. sich anziehen _____

6. sich schminken _____

ÜBUNG B   **Beim Arzt.** It's 10:30 and you're now with your great grandmother in the doctor's waiting room. You're listening to people discuss what's the matter with them. Tell us about their complaints. Use the present perfect tense since each is only relating a single event in the past.

EXAMPLE: junges Mädchen / sich erkälten   Ein junges Mädchen hat sich erkältet.

1. alter Mann / sich das Bein brechen

    _____

2. zwei / Kleinkinder / sich anstecken (to infect someone, give an illness to someone)

    _____

3. junge Dame / am Knie / sich verletzen (to injure)

_____

4. mein Schulfreund Egon / in den Finger / sich schneiden

_____

5. meine Urgroßmutter / nicht / sich wohl fühlen (pres. tense since this is ongoing)

_____

4. Reflexive Verbs that Require the Accusative Pronoun

When the reflexive is used as the direct object, it takes the accusative pronoun.

Ich habe mich erkältet.   _I caught a cold._

Sein Büro befindet sich im 16. Stock.   _His office is located on the 16th floor._

Reflexive verbs in German that require an accusative pronoun are:

NOTE: See appendix for additional verb examples.

sich ändern	_change_
sich anziehen	_dress_
sich ärgern	_get angry_
sich ausziehen	_undress_
sich bedanken (bei + dat.) (für + acc.)	_thank (someone) (for)_
sich beeilen	_hurry_
sich befinden	_be located_
sich benehmen	_behave_
sich beschäftigen (mit + dat.)	_occupy oneself (with)_
sich blamieren	_embarrass oneself_
sich umziehen	_change clothes_

ÜBUNG C   **Gedanken im Wartezimmer.** Your _Urgroßmutter_ is now in with the doctor and you are thinking about what you must do today. You were a bit annoyed yesterday because you're in the school play and had too many changes in one scene. Write down some of your thoughts using the word prompts. Use the appropriate tense, depending upon whether you are discussing yesterday's events or your situation right now.

EXAMPLE: ich / in der Schule / sein / sollen / aber / ich / noch / beim Arzt / sich befinden
Ich soll in der Schule sein, aber ich befinde mich noch beim Arzt.

1. ich / gestern / in der Schule / sich ärgern

   _____

2. ich / dreimal in einer Szene / sich umziehen

   _____

3. ich / wirklich / sich beeilen / müssen

   _____

4. das Kind / dort drüben in der Ecke / nicht so gut / sich benehmen

   _____

5. meine Urgroßmutter / jetzt / kommen / und / bei mir / für das Warten / sich bedanken

   _____

sich beschweren (über + _acc._)	_complain (about)_
sich bewegen	_move, stir_
sich bewerben (um + _acc._)	_apply (for)_
sich entscheiden	_decide_
sich erholen	_recuperate_
sich erkälten	_catch a cold_
sich erinnern (an + _acc._)	_remember_
sich entschuldigen (bei + _dat._) (für + _acc._)	_apologize (tor someone) (for something)_
sich freuen (auf + _acc._)	_look forward to_
sich freuen (über + _acc._)	_be happy about_

ÜBUNG D   **Die Heimfahrt.** In the taxi on the way home from the doctor's you and your grandmother discuss lots of things. Write your conversation. You may write as many sentences as you want, but you should use at least 6 verbs from the list above. Don't be afraid to vary the tense, just as you would in normal conversation.

GROßMUTTER: _____

DU: _____

GROßMUTTER: _____

DU: _____

GROßMUTTER: _____

DU: _____

GROßMUTTER: _____

DU: _____

GROßMUTTER: _____

DU: _____

sich fühlen	*feel (health)*
sich gewöhnen (an + *acc.***)**	*get used (to)*
sich interessieren (für + *acc.***)**	*be interested (in)*
sich irren	*err, make a mistake*
sich schämen	*be ashamed*
sich setzen	*sit down*
sich treffen (mit + *dat.***)**	*meet (with someone)*

ÜBUNG E   **In der Schule schreiben.** You've dropped your grandmother off and are back at school. The class is in the middle of a grammar-oriented creative writing exercise. The teacher has given them the above list of seven verbs and asked them to create one sentence for each.

EXAMPLE: sich interessieren (für + acc.)   Er interessiert sich für die Konzertkarten, weil die Rockgruppe so toll ist.

1. sich fühlen / weil / Erkältung haben

   _____

2. sich gewöhnen an (+ acc.) / die schwere Arbeit

   _____

3. sich irren // wenn / du / meinen // dass / es / nicht / regnen / werden

   _____

4. sich schämen // dass / er / gestern / in der Schlussprüfung / schummeln (cheat)

   _____

5. sich setzen (+ acc.) / neben / mein Bruder

   _____

6. sich treffen mit (+ dat.) / Schulrektor

   _____

sich unterhalten (mit + *dat.***)**	*converse (with)*
sich verabreden (mit + *dat.***) (für +** *acc.***)**	*make a date (with someone) (for time)*
sich verabschieden (von + *dat.***)**	*say good-bye (to)*

sich vorstellen	*introduce oneself*
sich umdrehen	*turn around*
sich verlieben (in + *acc.*)	*fall in love (with)*
sich verloben (mit + *dat.*)	*get engaged (to)*

ÜBUNG F | **Eine Liebesgeschichte.** Write a modern romantic fairy tale using five of the verbs in the list above. Use the simple past tense since this is a narration. Perhaps two people make a date, converse, fall in love, and then must say good-bye.

EXAMPLE: Lisa und Leon stellten sich vor.

1. _____

2. _____

3. _____

4. _____

5. _____

5. Reflexive Verbs that Require the Dative Pronoun

Reflexive verbs in German that require a dative reflexive pronoun are:

sich (etwas) einbilden	*imagine something (that's usually not correct)*
sich (etwas) kaufen	*buy something for yourself*
sich (etwas) überlegen	*consider something*
sich (etwas) vornehmen	*decide to do something*
sich (etwas) vorstellen	*imagine something*

NOTE: *sich (acc.) vorstellen* is to introduce yourself!
        Stell dich vor! *Introduce yourself!*
sich (dat.) etwas vorstellen is to imagine (something)
        Stell dir vor, du bist reich! *Imagine (that) you are rich!*

ÜBUNG G | **Der Egoist.** Your classmate Axel Ichbingut is quite an egotist, which you find annoying. Imagine a conversation you might have with him, trying to point out his flaws or offering him constructive advice.

EXAMPLE: Du bildest dir immer ein, dass du besser als deine Klassenkameraden bist.

1. sich (etwas) einbilden / besser als andere

   _____

2. sich (etwas) kaufen / zu viel

   _____

3. sich (etwas) überlegen / wie / aussehen

   _____

4. sich (etwas) vornehmen / nicht so arrogant zu sein

   _____

5. sich (etwas) vorstellen // du / keine Freunde mehr / haben

   _____

6. *Lassen* Plus the Reflexive Verb

The verb *lassen* to let or allow is often used with the dative reflexive. It then means to have something done for you rather then do it yourself. Compare what happens when you add *lassen* to the sentences below.

Ich schneide mir die Haare.	*I'm cutting (my own) hair.*
Ich lasse mir die Haare schneiden.	*I'm having my hair cut.*
Er kauft eine Zeitung.	*He's buying a newspaper.*
Er lässt sich eine Zeitung kaufen.	*He's having a newspaper bought for him.*

ÜBUNG H   **Ich lasse mir alles machen.** Your arrogant friend is at it again. Every time you tell her what you do, she tells you that she has the same thing done for her. She starts every sentence with *echt*? (Really?) What does the conversation sound like?

EXAMPLE: DU: Ich putze mein Zimmer jeden Tag.
DEINE FREUNDIN: Echt? Ich lasse mir jeden Tag mein Zimmer putzen.

1. DU: Ich bereite immer mein Pausebrot am Abend vorher vor.

   DEINE FREUNDIN: _____

2. DU: Ich wasche mir alle drei Tage meine Haare und föhne (blow dry) sie.

   DEINE FREUNDIN: _____

3. DU: Ich lackiere mich alle fünf Tage die Fingernägel.

   DEINE FREUNDIN: _____

4. DU: Ich färbe einmal im Monat meine Haare, normalerweise brünette.

   DEINE FREUNDIN: _____

5. DU: Wir bringen jeden Freitagabend eine Pizza ins Haus.

   DEINE FREUNDIN: Echt? Wir _____

ÜBUNG I   **Ich lasse mir . . .** Do you wash your own car? Do you cook your own meals? There are many things that you do yourself and many that you allow others to do for you. Make a list of at least five things you allow others to do for you. Do not repeat sentences from exercise H.

EXAMPLE: Ich lasse mir die Schuhe putzen.

1. _____

2. _____

3. _____

4. _____

5. _____

ÜBUNG J   **Deine Abendroutine.** You are now ready to write out your evening routine. Using reflexive verbs and *lassen* list at least six things you do or allow to be done each day.

EXAMPLE: Nach der Schule ziehe ich mich um.

1. _____

2. _____

3. _____

4. _____

5. _____

6. _____

CHAPTER 7
Present Perfect Tense
Past Perfect Tense
Doch

1.   Review of the Present Perfect Tense

The present perfect tense is formed by the present tense of *haben* or *sein* with the past participle. The translation of *hat gespielt*, for example, is "has played."

Wolfgang Amadeus Mozart hat „die Zauberflöte" komponiert.

Wolfgang Amadeus Mozart composed the "Magic Flute."

Most verbs use the auxiliary verb *haben*. If the verb cannot take a direct object (for example, *ankommen*), or if it shows motion towards a goal (*laufen*), or expresses a state of being (*sein*) or a change of state (*sterben*), then the present perfect is formed using *sein* rather than *haben*.

Mozart ist im Jahre 1756 geboren und im Jahre 1791 gestorben.

Mozart was born in 1756 and died in 1791.

NOTE: See appendix page 186 for a complete list of principal parts of the strong verb.

ÜBUNG A   **Das Leben Mozarts.** Below are notes you took for a report on the Austrian composer Mozart. Create sentences in the present perfect tense that summarize his life.

EXAMPLE: er / sein erstes / Konzert / mit 6 Jahren / geben
          Er hat sein erstes Konzert mit 6 Jahren gegeben.

1. er / 1769 / in Salzburg / leben

   _____

2. er / oft / nach / Italien / fahren

   _____

3. er / 1780 / in München / seine erste Oper *Idomeneo* / komponieren

   _____

4. er / 1781 / nach Wien / umziehen

   _____

5. in Wien / er / 1791 / *Die Zauberflöte* / inszenieren (produce theatrically)

   _____

2. Past Perfect Tense

The past perfect tense, often called the pluperfect or the *Plusquamperfekt* in German, is formed by the past tense of the auxiliary verbs *haben* or *sein* and the past participle. The translation of *hatte gespielt*, for example, is "had played."

Mozart hatte sein erstes Werk komponiert, bevor er 5 Jahre alt war.

Mozart had composed his first work before he was 5 years old.

3. Past Tense Forms of *haben* and *sein*

The past perfect tense is formed by the past tense of *haben* or *sein* and the past participle. The charts below show the two auxiliary verbs in the past tense.

CONJUGATION OF HABEN IN THE PAST TENSE			
SINGULAR		PLURAL	
ich hatte	I had	**wir hatt –en**	we had
du hatt – est	you (informal) had	**ihr hatt – et**	you (informal) had
er, sie, es hatt – e	he, she, or it had	**sie hatt –en**	they had
Sie hatt – en	You (formal) had		

CONJUGATION OF SEIN IN THE PAST TENSE			
SINGULAR		PLURAL	
ich war	I was	**wir war –en**	we were
du war – st	you (informal) were	**ihr war–t**	you (informal) were
er, sie, es war	he, she, or it was	**sie war –en**	they were
Sie war – en	You (formal) were		

4. Using the Past Perfect Tense

The past perfect tense is used to express an action in the past that was completed before another action in the past. It is most often used with the word *bevor* or *ehe*.

Mozart hatte nur Konzerte mit seiner Schwester gegeben, bis er seine Frau kennen lernte.
first completed action   second, more recent completed action

Mozart had given concerts only with his sister, until he met his wife.

There are two distinct actions and two distinct clauses in any sentence using the past perfect tense. The first action (in one clause) is completed before the second action (in the other clause) was completed. The first completed action is in the past perfect tense. The second completed action is usually in the simple past tense.

Mozart hatte den Vater von seiner Frau um ihre Hand gebeten, bevor er sie heiratete.
first completed action   second, more recent completed action

In the above sentence, Mozart had asked for his wife's hand before he married her. There are two distinct actions in the sentence. The first action was asking for her hand. The second action (marrying her) also occurred in the past, but it happened more recently than when he asked for her hand. The first action is always expressed using the past perfect tense. The second action is usually in the simple past.

Sie hatten ihn schon gekannt, bevor sie ihn heiratete.
first completed action   second, more recent completed action understood

She had known him before she married him.

ÜBUNG B   **Mozart in Prag.** Your workgroup is writing a report on Wolfgang Amadeus Mozart. You've all taken notes, and now have to put them into chronological order and transfer them into report-ready sentences. Combine each set of two facts into one sentence using the conjunction *bevor*. Remember that the first completed action is in the past perfect tense and the second, more recent completed action in the simple past.

EXAMPLE: er / 1787 / die Oper / *Die Hochzeit des Figaro* / komponieren
// bevor / Mozart / nach Prag / reisen
Er hatte die Oper *Die Hochzeit des Figaro* 1787 in Wien komponiert,
bevor er nach Prag reiste.

1. am 28. Mai / sein Vater / sterben
// bevor / Mozart / am 10. August / *Eine Kleine Nachtmusik* / fertig / komponieren

_____

2. er / schon wieder / in Prag / ankommen // bevor er *Don Giovanni* / fertig / schrieb

_____

3. er / schon wieder / nach Wien / gehen
// bevor / seine erste Tochter / zur Welt / kommen

_____

4. 51 Jahre / nach seinem tod vorbeigehen // bevor / die Leute in Salzburg / ein
Mozart-Denkmal / errichten

_____

5. bevor / die Stadt / das Denkmal / offiziell / widmen
// die Stadtväter / ein Mozartkonzert / veranstalten (hold an event)

_____

Past perfect clauses can also be introduced by *nachdem*. It depends on whether the emphasis is on the first or the second completed action.

Nachdem ich die Opernwerke von Mozart gehört hatte, fuhr ich nach Salzburg.

After I had heard the operatic works of Mozart, I traveled to Salzburg.

| ÜBUNG C | **Umgekehrt!** You've been told that your teacher would prefer you to write your report using the word *nachdem*. How would this change the sentences you wrote in exercise D? Remember that the finite verb in a compound sentence goes to the end of its clause. The first word of the following clause is then the verb. |

EXAMPLE: er / 1787 / die Oper / *Die Hochzeit des Figaro* / komponieren
// bevor / Mozart / nach Prag / reisen
Nachdem er 1787 die Oper *Die Hochzeit des Figaro* komponiert
hatte, reiste Mozart nach Prag.

1. _____

2. _____

3. _____

4. _____

5. _____

| ÜBUNG D | **Meine Leistungen.** What had you accomplished before you went on to the next grade? |

EXAMPLE: Bevor ich in die 5. Klasse kam, hatte ich schon viele Bücher von Cornelia Funke gelesen.

1. _____

2. _____

3. _____

4. _____

5. _____

5.   *Doch*

German has a form of negation that no longer exists in English, i.e. the word *doch*. It may be used alone or in a sentence and tells the previous speaker, who had made a statement assuming that the listener would agree with him, that he was mistaken. In English we usually repeat the speaker's words with the word "yes," which is exactly the opposite answer of what the first speaker expected.

You can't come with us.   *Yes, I can.*   *That's not correct.*   *Yes, it is.*
Du kannst nicht mitkommen.   **Doch.**   **Das stimmt nicht.**   **Doch.**

In both these sentences the speaker expected the listener to agree with the negative statement. "You're right," "I can't go with you." or "You're right," "it's not correct."

But the above negative statements were wrong and the listener could not agree. The listener needed only one word to say: "You're wrong." "I know you expected me to agree, but I cannot agree with you." *Doch* is a one-word expression used in these situations. It means "yes," when a negative answer is expected or "no" when a positive answer is expected. It tells the person he or she was mistaken.

| ÜBUNG E | **Mozart auf der Reise.** Mozart and his sister were young when their father took them on concert tours. The older sister often tried to control her younger brother's behavior. They had to be well dressed at all times, punctual, polite, practice several hours a day, etc. Imagine a conversation between the two. |

EXAMPLE: Wolfgang, du hast heute nicht geübt.   Doch, ich habe eine Stunde geübt.

1. NANNERL: _____

   MOZART: Doch. Ich habe heute früh gebadet.

2. NANNERL: Aber du hast dir die Zähne noch nicht geputzt.

   MOZART: _____. _____. Aber, sprich leise. Vater ist noch nicht wach.

3. NANNERL: _____. _____.

   MOZART: Unser Konzert war gestern Abend nicht sehr gut. Der Prinz hat unsere Violin-Sonate nicht gemocht.

4. NANNERL: _____

   MOZART: Wird er uns noch weiter bezahlen?

5. NANNERL: Doch. Aber du magst es hier nicht.

   MOZART: _____

| ÜBUNG F | **Ein Kinderstreit.** While you seldom worry about whether the prince will like your music well enough to continue employing you, you can sympathize with Mozart and his sister. You often had a spat with your older sister when you were younger. Try and remember some of the things you said to each other, using the word *doch* at least 5 times in the conversation. |

1. DU: _____

   DEINE SCHWESTER: _____

2. Du: _____

   Deine Schwester: _____

3. Du: _____

   Deine Schwester: _____

4. Du: _____

   Deine Schwester: _____

5. Du: _____

   Deine Schwester: _____

CHAPTER 8
Verb Tenses

1. Verb Tenses

German has six tenses, three simple and three perfect tenses. They are:

Simple Tenses

past	*he plays, did play, was playing*	**er spielte**
present	*he plays, does play, is playing*	**er spielt**
future	*he will play*	**er wird spielen**

Perfect Tenses

past perfect	*he had played*	**er hatte gespielt**
present perfect	*he played, did play, has played*	**er hat gespielt**
future perfect	*he will have played*	**er wird gespielt haben.**

NOTE: Which tense to use is determined by the answers to three questions:

a. When does the action take place?

b. If completed, when was the action completed?

c. When is the action being discussed? Is it before, during or after the action?

2. Action that Takes Place in the Present – The Present Tense

Actions that take place at the same time the event is being related are in the present tense.

Er komponiert seine eigenen Musikstücke.   *He composes his own musical pieces.*

ÜBUNG A   **Die Musikstunde.** What happens in your music classes every week? Choose at least six of the verb phrases from the list and write full sentences about your music classes. Be sure to add adverbs and adjectives.

EXAMPLE: Wir müssen jeden Tag singen.

Instrumente spielen	ruhig zuhören	im Chor singen
singen müssen	Musikstücke komponieren	in der Klasse vorsingen
Gedichte vorlesen	Musik lesen	tief ein- und ausatmen

1. _____

2. _____

3. _____

4. _____

5. _____

3. Action that Will Take Place in the Future – The Present and Future Tenses

Actions taking place in the future are in the present or the future tense. If there is an adverbial phrase expressing futurity, the verb is most often in the present tense, although either tense is acceptable. They are interchangeable.

Er spielt morgen mit dem Chor.   *He is going to play for the choir tomorrow.*
Er wird morgen mit dem Chor spielen. *He is will play for the choir tomorrow.*

ÜBUNG B   **Das Konzert.** Your choral group is going on a trip to perform in a neighboring city on Tuesday. Write a list of questions for your music teacher to find out what you will be doing. Use both adverbs expressing the future with the present tense and the future tense in your questions.

EXAMPLE: wir / mit dem Bus / fahren   Fahren wir am Dienstag mit dem Bus?
Werden wir mit dem Bus fahren?

1. Karl / Klavier / spielen

_____

2. das Konzert / in der prachtvollen Konzerthalle / stattfinden

_____

3. wie viel / die Konzertkarten / kosten

_____

4. wann / das Hauptkonzert / beginnen

_____

5. wir / im Jugendhotel / auf dem Marktplatz / übernachten

_____

4. Action That Took Place in the Past – The Past, Present Perfect, Past Perfect and Future Perfect Tenses

a. The Simple Past (Narrative Past)

The simple past is used to relate a series of events in the past, as in a story. It must be used if the English translation is "was" or "were" followed by an -ing verb, e.g. "was playing," "were eating."

Er spielte, als ich in das Zimmer kam.   *He was playing, when I came into the room.*

ÜBUNG C   **Email über das Konzert.** The concert you were discussing in *Übung B* has taken place. You are now writing a quick e-mail to your parents telling them about it. Because you are relating a series of events, you are writing it in the simple past. Rewrite the sentences from *Übung B* into the sample past, this time as statements, not questions.

EXAMPLE: Wir fuhren wir am Dienstag mit dem Bus.

1. _____

2. _____

3. _____

4. _____

5. _____

ÜBUNG D   **Ludwig van Beethoven.** This famous composer was born into a musical family. His father wanted him to be a child prodigy like his peer Mozart. You have been researching Beethoven and are now writing a report about his life.

EXAMPLE: als / er / noch / sehr jung / sein / / / sein Vater / ein Wunderkind / aus / er / wollen machen
Als er noch sehr jung war, wollte sein Vater ein Wunderkind aus ihm machen.

1. Beethoven / erst (just) / fünf Jahre alt / sein // als / sein Vater / er / Klavierunterricht / geben

   _____

2. er / noch tief / schlafen // als / sein Vater / er / um Mitternacht / wecken // damit / er / üben / können

   _____

3. manchmal / er / in der Schule / einschlafen // weil / er / so müde / sein

   _____

4. er / erst elf Jahre alt / sein // als / er / nicht mehr / in die Schule / gehen

   _____

5. als / er / 14 Jahre alt / werden // er / seine erste bezahlte Stelle / bekommen

_____

b. The Present Perfect (Conversational Past)

The present perfect is used to relate an isolated event in the past. It is also used often in conversation to relate past events, even if there is a series of events.

Er hat gestern mit dem Chor gespielt.   _He played with the choir yesterday._

Er hat immer gut gespielt.   _He has always played well._

| ÜBUNG E | **Gesprochenes!** You're now telling your friend about the concert. Since this is conversation and not at all formal, you're using the present perfect tense. Rewrite the sentences in _Übung C_ into the present perfect tense.

EXAMPLE: Wir sind am Dienstag mit dem Bus gefahren.

1. _____

2. _____

3. _____

4. _____

5. _____

| ÜBUNG F | **Die Musikstunde.** You are going to give an oral report in your German class about what you did in your music class last week. Mention at least 5 activities using the present perfect tense. You may refer to _Übung A_ for vocabulary.

EXAMPLE: Am Montag habe ich Musik gelesen.

1. _____

2. _____

3. _____

4. _____

5. _____

c. The Past Perfect Tense

The past perfect is used to relate an incident in the past that was completed before a more recent action in the past. (See chapter 7.)

Beethoven hatte seine Mondlichtsonate komponiert, bevor er taub wurde.

Beethoven had composed his Moonlight Sonata before he became deaf.

The sentence fragment "He became deaf" (action 2) discusses something that happened in the past. However, the completion of the Moonlight Sonata (action 1) happened even before that past episode. Action 1 must therefore be expressed using the past perfect tense.

ÜBUNG G | **Was passiert war.** You're explaining your concert trip to a friend. You preface each of your sentences with "before we knew it." Therefore your sentences are in the past perfect tense.

EXAMPLE: Bevor wir es wussten, waren wir am Dienstag mit dem Bus gefahren.
Bevor wir es wussten, . . .

1. _____

2. _____

3. _____

4. _____

5. _____

ÜBUNG H | **Beethovens Reisen.** You are writing a report on Beethoven's life. Your teacher has returned some of your notes to you and asked that you combine your simple sentences into complex ones using the past perfect tense and the suggested conjunctions. Remember, the first action is in the present perfect. The second action, the more recent of the two, is in the simple past.

EXAMPLE: (bevor) Beethoven reiste 1787 nach Wien. Er hatte schon eine bezahlte Stelle als Hoforganist.
Bevor Beethoven 1787 nach Wien reiste, hatte er schon eine bezahlte Stelle als Hoforganist gehabt.

1. Er blieb nur zwei Wochen in Wien. (bevor) Er musste nach Hause reisen.

_____

2. (nachdem) Beethoven kam in Bonn an. Seine Mutter starb.

_____

3. Mozart starb. (bevor) Beethoven mit 22 Jahren wieder nach Wien reiste.

_____

4. (nachdem) Er schon in Wien war. Joseph Haydn nahm er als Student an.

_____

5. Er führte sein erstes Konzert in Wien auf. (nachdem) Er wurde schon 25.

_____

5. The Future Perfect Tense

The future perfect tense follows the same pattern.

Actions in the future perfect tense start and end before an event in the future.

Er wird eine Stunde gespielt haben, bevor die Chorprobe um acht Uhr zu Ende ist.
He will have played an hour, before choir practice is over at eight o'clock.

In the above sentence, choir practice isn't over yet. It isn't eight o'clock yet. But, by the time it is eight o'clock (the event in the future), he will have played for one hour (the event that will be completed before that event in the future).

| ÜBUNG I | **Was wird passiert sein?** Before you leave for home from your last concert trip, several things will have happened. Describe them using the sentences from *Übung C*, this time using the future perfect tense. |

EXAMPLE: Wir werden am Dienstag mit dem Bus gefahren sein.

1. _____
2. _____
3. _____
4. _____
5. _____

| ÜBUNG J | **Was werden wir gemacht haben?** Your concert is in one week. What will you and your classmates have completed before the concert? Use the sentence elements to build sentences and add at least two of your own. |

EXAMPLE: in den Bus einsteigen // unsere Instrumente einpacken
Bevor wir in den Bus einsteigen, werden wir unsere Instrumente schon eingepackt haben.

1. bevor / wir / die Schule verlassen // viel üben

_____

2. aus dem Bus aussteigen // viel lachen

_____

3. das Konzert beginnen // eine Vorprobe machen

_____

4. zu singen beginnen // das Publikum klatschen

_____

5. _____
6. _____

ÜBUNG K | **Mein erstes Konzert.** Imagine that you are a musician getting ready to perform in your first solo-concert. What have you done to get there? What are you thinking now? What will you be doing in a few minutes when you start your performance? What will you have done before you start? Write a six to ten sentence story about this imaginary (or real) experience.

EXAMPLE: Ich habe jahrelang Klavier gespielt und jetzt ist es so weit. Ich gebe . . .
OR
Als ich 10 Jahre alt war, fing ich mit meiner Karriere an. Jetzt . . .

_____

_____

_____

_____

_____

_____

_____

_____

_____

_____

CHAPTER 9
Passive Voice

In most sentences the subject performs the action of the verb.

Meine Mutter bringt die Wäsche in den Keller.
   subject   verb   direct object

My mother is taking the laundry into the basement.
   subject   verb   direct object

In some sentences however the subject receives the action of the verb. For example, the sentence above can be reworded so that the direct object becomes the subject of the verb.

Die Wäsche wird von meiner Mutter in den Keller gebracht.
  subject   verb   agent   verb

The laundry is being taken into the basement by my mother.
  subject   verb   agent

When the subject is being acted upon, not performing the action, the verb is said to be in the passive voice.

1.   Formation of the Passive Voice

The passive voice is formed with the auxiliary verb *werden* followed by the past participle.

WERDEN	
SINGULAR	PLURAL
ich werde	wir werden
du wirst	ihr werdet
er, sie, es wird	sie werden
Sie werden	

+ past participle = passive voice
present tense

Die Wäsche wird in die Waschmaschine geladen.

The laundry is being loaded into the washing machine.

ÜBUNG A   **Die Wäsche waschen.** You are in a hurry to leave the house. You're also a little annoyed that your parents have asked you to fold and sort the laundry before you can go. Not willing to let things rest, you announce loudly each time you start a new step of the task.

EXAMPLE: Du machst den Trockner auf.   Der Trockner wird aufgemacht.

NOTE: Notice that the direct object in the active sentence becomes the subject of the passive voice sentence.

1. Du nimmst die Wäsche aus dem Trockner.

_____

2. Du faltest die Handtücher.

_____

3. Du sortierst die Socken.

_____

4. Du bringst die Wäsche vom Keller hoch.

_____

5. Du verteilst die Wäsche in die richtigen Zimmer.

_____

2.   The Agent with the Passive Voice

The subject in a passive sentence is being acted upon. The person or animal performing the action of the verb is called the agent. The agent is expressed using the dative preposition *von*. In the exercise above, the speaker might have emphasized that he or she was folding the laundry by saying: *Die Wäsche wird von mir gefaltet, von mir sortiert*, etc.

ÜBUNG B   **Endlich Geschafft!** You did it! The laundry is folded, sorted and distributed. Now all you have to do is tell your parents where you'll be and with whom and you're free to leave. Answer your mother's questions using the passive voice and turning the direct object of the mother's question into the subject of your sentence.

EXAMPLE: DEINE MUTTER: Wer holt dich ab?
          DU: Ich werde von meinem Freund Dieter abgeholt.

1. DEINE MUTTER: Wer wählt der Film aus?

    DU: _____

2. DEINE MUTTER: Wer packt eure Esspakete?

    DU: _____

3. DEINE MUTTER: Wer fährt euch ins Kino?

    DU: _____

4. DEINE MUTTER: Wer bringt dich nach Hause?

   DU: _____

5. DEINE MUTTER: Rufst du mich nach dem Film an?

   DU: _____

3. The Instrument with the Passive Voice

If the action of the verb is performed by a thing, rather than a person or animal, that instrument is expressed using the accusative preposition *durch*.

Der Film wird durch Spenden finanziert.

The film is being financed by contributions.

ÜBUNG C | *Twister.* You're home after seeing a movie and having dinner with your friends. You're anxious to tell your parents about the movie you saw, *Twister*.

EXAMPLE: Haus / großer Wirbelsturm / zerstören
         Ein Haus wird durch einen großen Wirbelsturm zerstört.

1. Mann / ein fallender Baum / verletzt

   _____

2. Auto / starker Wind / aufheben

   _____

3. Kind / Wind / aus den Armen seiner Eltern / wegreissen

   _____

4. Fenster von der Schule / Rückwind / einblasen

   _____

5. Familie / Autoblockade / retten

   _____

4. Changing from Active to Passive Voice

There are three steps in changing a sentence in the active voice to the present.

1. The direct object becomes the subject.
2. The subject becomes the agent (*von + dat.*) or the instrument (*durch + acc.*)

3. The verb becomes passive using a form of *werden* plus the past participle.

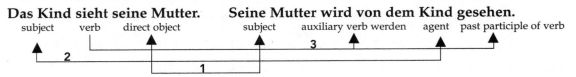

Das Kind sieht seine Mutter.   **Seine Mutter wird von dem Kind gesehen.**
subject   verb   direct object   subject   auxiliary verb werden   agent   past participle of verb

---

ÜBUNG D | **Mahlzeit.** Your brother is complaining about dinner time behavior at home. Rewrite his statements so that they are in the passive voice.

EXAMPLE: Unser Vater isst immer das letzte Stück Schnitzel.
Das letzte Stück Schnitzel wird immer von unserem Vater gegessen.

1. Unsere Mutter bereitet das Essen immer vor.

   _____

2. Dein Freund Thomas ruft dich immer vor der Mahlzeit an.

   _____

3. Das Telefon stört unsere Mahlzeit jeden Abend.

   _____

4. Du trinkst immer das größte Glas Apfelsaft.

   _____

5. Und unsere Schwester nimmt immer die letzte Portion Eis.

   _____

5.   Passive Voice with Dative Verbs

A few verbs require a dative rather than an accusative direct object.

antworten	*answer*	**gratulieren**	*congratulate*
befehlen, befiehlt	*command*	**helfen**	*help*
danken	*thank*	**passen**	*fit*
dienen	*serve*	**passieren**	*happen*
erlauben	*allow*	**schaden**	*harm*
folgen	*follow*	**verzeihen**	*pardon, forgive*
gehorchen	*obey*	**wehtun, tut weh**	*hurt*
glauben	*believe (someone)*	**zuhören (sep. prefix)**	*listen to*

Changing the active voice to the passive voice when the sentence contains a dative verb is different in step one (above) only. The last two steps are the same.

1. The dative object is unchanged. It does not become the subject of the sentence.
2. The introductory word *es* is added as the subject. (See note on following page.)

3. The subject becomes the agent (*von + dat.*) or the instrument (*durch + acc.*)
4. The verb becomes passive using a form of *werden* plus the past participle.

Das Kind hilft seiner Mutter.   Es wird seiner Mutter vom Kind geholfen.

NOTE: the dative object is the first element in the sentence, then the word **es** is not added.

Das Kind hilft seiner Mutter.   Seiner Mutter wird vom Kind geholfen.

ÜBUNG E   **Bei dir zu Hause.** Your brother is now complaining about his position in the family. You don't want to listen to it anymore and are contradicting him. In doing so, change his sentences to the passive voice. Remember that a dative verb keeps the dative direct object even in the passive voice.

EXAMPLE: BRUDER: Mutter dankt mir nie für meine Arbeit.
          DU: Das stimmt nicht. Dir wird von Mutter immer für deine Arbeit gedankt.
          OR   Das stimmt nicht. Es wird dir von Mutter immer für deine Arbeit gedankt.

1. BRUDER: Mutter glaubt mir nie etwas.

   DU: _____

2. BRUDER: Und das Telefon dient nur dir in diesem Haus.

   DU: _____

3. BRUDER: Und die Eltern erlauben mir bestimmt nicht so viel wie dir.

   DU: _____

4. BRUDER: Der Hund und die Katze gehorchen mir nicht immer.

   DU: _____

5. BRUDER: Unsere Eltern gratulieren mir nie zum Geburtstag.

   DU: _____

6. BRUDER: Du verziehst meinen Freunden nie, wenn sie dir weh tun.

   DU: _____

ÜBUNG F   **Gute Manieren.** Your grandmother believes that every child should behave properly. Use the cues to write out some sayings that your grandmother would use. Vary your answers between using the introductory *es* and starting the sentence with the dative direct object.

EXAMPLE: die Mutter / von / ihr Kind / gehorchen
Der Mutter wird von ihrem Kind gehorcht.
OR
Es wird der Mutter von ihrem Kind gehorcht.

1. die Mutter / von / ihre Kinder / immer / glauben

_____

2. das Kind / von / die Eltern / oft / befehlen

_____

3. der Vater / von / seine Kinder / helfen

_____

4. das Kind / vieles / durch / die Schule / erlauben

_____

5. Ein gutes Kind / von / seine Eltern / zuhören

_____

6.   The Passive Voice in the Past Tense

The most common use of the passive voice is in the past tense. It is formed with the past tense of the auxiliary verb _werden_ followed by the past participle.

PAST TENSE OF **WERDEN**	
SINGULAR	PLURAL
ich wurde	wir wurden
du wurdest	ihr wurdet
er, sie, es wurde	sie wurden
Sie wurden	

+ past participle = passive voice
simple past tense

Der Originalfilm _Twister_ wurde im Jahre 1966 gedreht.

The original Twister _movie was filmed in 1966._

ÜBUNG G   **Berühmte Deutsche.** It's Monday. You're back in school and your history class is playing a trivia game to review contributions of famous Germans to history. Rewrite your notes into complete sentences so that you will be ready to answer your question when it's your turn. Two words that may help you are _erfinden_ (invent) and _entdecken_ (discover). Remember that the direct object of an active sentence becomes the subject of the passive sentence.

Alois Alzheimer	1906	die Alterskrankheit Alzheimers	zuerst identifiziert
Karl Benz und Gottfried Daimler	1885/86	der erste Verbrennungsmotor	erfinden
Mozart	1791	die Oper *Die Zauberflöte*	komponieren
Joseph Pulitzer	1911	der Pulitzer Preis	stiften (fund)
Erich Maria Remarque	1929	Im Westen nichts Neues	schreiben
Wilhelm Conrad Röntgen	1885	X-Strahlen	entdecken

EXAMPLE: Der Pulitzer Preis wurde 1911 von Joseph Pulitzer gestiftet.

1. _____

2. _____

3. _____

4. _____

5. _____

ÜBUNG H   **Entdeckungen und Erfindungen.** Now it's your turn. Your teacher has given your workgroup the name of several famous German-speakers. Their accomplishments are in a separate list. Draw arrows to match the creator to his accomplishment and write a passive voice sentence about 5 of the 11. You may have to research some of the names before you can complete this exercise.

der erste deutsche Reiseführer (veröffentlichen – publish)   Karl Baedeker

die Relativitätstheorie (entdecken)   Adolf und Rudolf Dassler

das Buch *Buddenbrucks* (schreiben)   Albert Einstein

die ersten Sportschuhe für Fußballer (machen)   Gabriel Daniel Fahrenheit

95 Thesen gegen den Papst (schreiben)   Friedrich Froebel

Bücher über nordamerikanische Indianer (schreiben)   Franz Kafka

der erste Kindergarten (gründen – establish)   Robert Koch

die Methode der Bakterienzilluskultur (erfinden)   Martin Luther

eine neue Nachrichtenagentur (gründen)   Thomas Mann

die Fahrenheit-Temperaturskala (erfinden)   Karl May

Die Verwandlung (schreiben)   Paul Julius Baron von Reuter

EXAMPLE: Die Fahrenheit -Temperaturskala wurde von Gabriel Daniel Fahrenheit erfunden.

1. _____

2. _____

3. _____

4. _____

5. _____

7.   Passive in the Present Perfect Tense

While used only seldom, the passive may also be used in the present perfect, past perfect and future perfect tenses.

PRESENT TENSE OF SEIN	
SINGULAR	PLURAL
ich bin	wir sind
du bist	ihr seid
er, sie, es ist	sie sind
Sie sind	

+ past participle + worden=
present perfect tense passive voice

Angela Merkel ist 2005 zur ersten deutschen Bundeskanzlerin gewählt worden.
Angela Merkel was elected the first female chancellor of Germany in 2005.

ÜBUNG I   **Die Bundeswahl.** Create sentences telling the story of the historical election in the Federal Republic of Germany in 2005 in which the first *Bundeskanzlerin* was elected. Prior to Angela Merkel the position of chancellor had always been held by a man. Use the present perfect tense.

EXAMPLE: diese historische Wahl / am 18. September 2005 / halten
Diese historische Wahl ist am 18. September 2005 gehalten worden.

1. an diesem Sonntag /Angela Merkel / zur ersten Bundeskanzlerin / wählen

_____

2. Ihr / keine klare Mehrheit / geben

_____

3. Eine Koalition / zwischen ihrer CDU / CSU Partei und der SPD Partie / schließen

_____

4. Am 22. November / Merkel und ihre Koalition im Bundestag / offiziell / wählen

_____

5. Als erstes / eine stärkere Krankenversicherung für das Volk / versprechen

_____

NOTE: The past perfect tense of a passive voice verb may be formed by using *waren* instead of *sein* as the auxiliary verb. The construction is seldom used.

Vor Angela Merkel war nie eine Frau zur Bundeskanzelerin gewählt worden.
Before Angela Merkel a woman had never been elected chancellor.

8.   Passive with Modal Verbs

The passive may be used with modal verbs in any tense. The pattern remains the same. The appropriate tense of the modals is used (see chapter 12) with the present participle followed by *werden*. The table below conjugates the verb *machen* (to make, do) with the modal *können* (can).

present tense:	**Das kann gemacht werden.**	*That can be done.*
past tense:	**Das konnte gemacht werden.**	*That could be done.*
future tense:	**Das wird gemacht werden können.**	*That will be able to be done.*

NOTE: There are patterns for the passive voice modal verbs in the perfect tenses but they are awkward and very seldom used.

ÜBUNG J   **Alles in Ordnung**. You're having a disagreement with your parents, who are finding fault with everything. Assure them that the situation can be corrected. Add three of your own.

EXAMPLE: Deine Schuhe sind schmutzig. / putzen   Sie können geputzt werden.
                   Dein Buch liegt auf dem Boden. / aufheben   Es kann aufgehoben werden.

1. Dein Hemd ist schmutzig. / umziehen

   _____

2. Deine Haare sind unordentlich. / kämmen

   _____

3. Dein Zimmer sieht furchtbar aus. / aufräumen

   _____

4. Deine Musik ist so laut. / leiser stellen

   _____

5. Dein T-Shirt ist schmutzig. / waschen

   _____

6. _____

7. _____

8. _____

9.   Special Uses of the Passive Voice

a. The Impersonal Passive with Introductory *es*

The passive may occur with the subject *es* implying that the verb applies to everyone. It usually implies permission or denial.

Es wurde laut musiziert. Es wird morgen gesungen.

There was loud music. There will be singing tomorrow.

NOTE: While used commonly, the introductory *es* is optional. Each of the above sentences can also be written without the *es*. There is a difference between "There is no smoking here." And "NO smoking here." The second is more forceful. Removing the *es* adds strength to the comment. The lack of *es* sends the message that the rule will be enforced. With *es*, the situation is simply being described.

Descriptive Statement:	**Es wird hier nicht geraucht.**	*There is no smoking here.*
More Forceful Statement:	**Hier wird nicht geraucht.**	*No smoking here.*

ÜBUNG K **Die Schilder**. Your school is hosting a German language festival. You are responsible for making signs. Change the following directions from your teacher into language for your signs using the impersonal passive.

EXAMPLE: Wir spielen Schach in der Bibliothek
Es wird in der Bibliothek Schach gespielt.

1. In der Mensa verkaufen sie keine alkoholischen Getränke.

   _____

2. Wir spielen Fußball in der Sporthalle.

   _____

3. Wir sprechen hier nur Deutsch.

   _____

4. Wir essen zu Mittag vegetarisch.

   _____

5. Wir geben kein Geld aus.

   _____

b. The False Passive

The passive is used more often in written rather than spoken German. It is often avoided by using the verb in the active voice and adding the subject *man* (one).

Passive:	**Wie wird diese Tür aufgemacht?**	*How is this door opened?*
False Passive:	**Wie macht man diese Tür auf?**	*How does one open this door?*

ÜBUNG L **Das Fragenspiel.** For a game of twenty questions you must make a list of six. These questions are for everyone and very vague, so you will use *man*.

EXAMPLE: Wie repariert man einen Computer?
            Wie schreibt man ein Buch?

1. _____

2. _____

3. _____

4. _____

5. _____

6. _____

CHAPTER 10
Subjunctive II – The Conditional Subjunctive

Verbs have three qualities that can be changed. They have *six tenses*: past and past perfect, present and present perfect, future and future perfect. They have *two voices*: active or passive. The final quality a verb can possess is *mood*; a verb is indicative or subjunctive. Most sentences are written in the indicative mood. If the verb expresses an unreal or contrary to fact condition, then the subjunctive mood is used.

> *If I were rich, I would buy a new Porsche. (But I'm not rich, so . . .)*
>
> *If I had a million dollars, I'd quit my job. (But I don't have a million dollars, so . . .)*

a. The sentences above are in the conditional subjunctive. They represent unreal, contrary to fact conditions. The speaker is not rich, nor is he going to buy a new Porsche, nor does she have a million dollars, nor will she quit her job. If adding a "but-statement" to negate the clause, as was done in the examples above, makes a true statement, then the verb is in the subjunctive mood.

> *If I were you, I'd talk to the teacher. (But I'm not you, so . . .)*
>
> *If I had my homework, I wouldn't need to talk to the teacher. (But I don't, so . . .)*

b. The subjunctive phrase is often translated into English using the word "would."

Ich hätte gern einen Kaffee. *I would like to have a coffee.* (Literally, I would have a coffee gladly.)

ÜBUNG A | **Wer spricht wohl?** Which one of the people listed below is speaking? Supply a possible speaker for each passage. Can you understand what each person is telling you?

ein Teenager – Arnold Schwarzenegger, als er Gouverneur Kandidat war – Beethoven – deine Klassensprecherin – J. K. Rowling – dein Lehrer

1. Als Gouverneur von Kalifornien würde ich Schulpflicht für Migrantenkinder einführen. Wir hätten keine Autosteuern mehr, und Parkanlagen wären allen freizugänglich.

   _____

2. Wenn ich ein zehntes Buch geschrieben hätte, wäre Harry darin erwachsen. Er hätte dann eine Hexenmeisterin geheiratet und 3 kleine Kinder gehabt.

   _____

3. Ich hätte eine zehnte Symphonie komponiert, wenn ich noch hätte hören können.

   _____

4. Weil ich meine Musik nicht so laut gespielt hatte, kam meine Mutter nicht in mein Zimmer herein.

   _____

5. Wenn ihr Alles verstanden hättet, dann hätten wir etwas Neues machen können.

_____

Bonus Question.

Ein Satz ist wahr. One of the sentences in the above exercise is true; it does not show an unreal, contrary to fact condition. Which one is it? _____

1.   *wären, hätten* and *würden*

The distinction between the indicative and the subjunctive is fading in spoken English. It is still strong and must be made in German. Any unreal condition, whether in English or German, is expressed using the subjunctive. The conditional subjunctive is formed using the past tense of the verb, adding personal verb endings and an umlaut if possible.

Wenn ich eine Million Euro(s) hätte . . .   *If I had a million euros . . .*   (But I don't, so . . .)

Wenn ich die Lehrerin wäre, . . .   *If I were the teacher . . .*   (But I'm not, so . . .)

The three most common subjunctives are *wären*, *hätten*, and *würden*.

CONJUGATION OF **SEIN** IN THE SUBJUNCTIVE II MOOD	
SINGULAR	PLURAL
ich wär – e *I would be, were*	**wir wär – en** *we would be, were*
du wär – est *you (informal) would be, were*	**ihr wär – et** *you (informal)would be, were*
er, sie, es wär – e *he, she, or it would be, were*	**sie wär – en** *they would be, were*
Sie wär – en *You (formal) would be, were*	

CONJUGATION OF **HABEN** IN THE SUBJUNCTIVE II MOOD	
SINGULAR	PLURAL
ich hätt – e *I would have*	**wir hätt – en** *we would have*
du hätt – est *you (informal) would have*	**ihr hätt – et** *you (informal) would have*
er, sie, es hätt – e *he, she, or it would have*	**sie hätt – en** *they would have*
Sie hätt – en *You (formal) would have*	

CONJUGATION OF **WERDEN** IN THE SUBJUNCTIVE II MOOD			
SINGULAR		PLURAL	
ich würd – e	*I would*	**wir würd –en**	*we would*
du würd – est	*you (informal) would*	**ihr würd – et**	*you (informal) would*
er, sie, es würd – e	*he, she, or it would*	**sie würd – en**	*they would*
Sie würd – en *You (formal) would*			

ÜBUNG B   **Eure Träume.** You and your friends are daydreaming about how ideal life could be. Express your dreams using the words *wenn* and *nur*. Together they mean "if only."

EXAMPLE: Thommy / will reich werden   Wenn Thommy nur reich wäre, . . .

1. Lena / ein Auto haben

   _____

2. Lauren und Micah / Klassensprecher sein

   _____

3. du, Jessica / viele CDs haben

   _____

4. wir / in der zwölften Klasse sein

   _____

5. Katherine / Millionärin sein

   _____

ÜBUNG C   **Und du?** Have you any daydreams you can express using *hätten* (would have) or *wären* (would be)? Write down 3 that you are willing to share with your class.

1. _____

2. _____

3. _____

2.   Conditional Clauses Using *würden*

The sentences in the above exercises are only half of a conditional sentence. The subjunctive *würden* (would) is used to supply the other half of the sentence. The infinitive completer goes to the end of the clause.

Wenn ich genug Zeit hätte, (dann) würde ich mit dir gehen.

If I had enough time, (then) I would go with you.

Wenn du älter wärest, (dann) würdest du ein Auto kaufen.

If you were older, (then) you would buy a car.

ÜBUNG D **Was würden wir tun?** Look at the dreams you and your classmates created in *Übung B*. What would everyone do if their dreams were to come true? Write sentences.

EXAMPLE: Wenn Thommy reich wäre, würde er mir ein tolles Geschenk kaufen.

1. _____
2. _____
3. _____
4. _____
5. _____

Bonus Questions:

If you're still willing to share your dreams with your classmates, then complete the sentences you created in *Übung C*.

1. _____
2. _____
3. _____

ÜBUNG E **Und deine Klassenkameraden?** Create interview questions for four of your classmates and one adult in the school asking them what they would do if . . . When you are done, ask them and write their answers under the questions.

EXAMPLE: Was würdest du tun, wenn du 500 Euros hättest?
Wenn ich 500 Euros hätte, (dann) würde ich viele Videospiele kaufen.
Was würden Sie tun, wenn sie Lehrerin wären?
Wenn ich Lehrerin wäre, würde ich den Schülern keine Tests mehr geben.

1. _____

   _____

2. _____

   _____

3. _____

   _____

4. _____

   _____

5. _____

_____

3.   Formation of the Subjunctive II in Strong Verbs

Using *würden* plus an infinitive completer to express a condition is typical of spoken German. There is a one word alternative that is preferred in more formal or written German. Its formation is easy. It uses the simple past tense of the verb and then adds the same personal endings as *würden*. It also adds an *umlaut* if possible.

Wenn ich noch 3 Euro(s) hätte, ginge ich ins Kino.

If I had 3 more Euros, I'd go to the movies.

Wenn er uns sähe, käme er mit ins Kino.

If he saw us, he'd come with us to the movies.

gehen, geht, ging, ist gegangen – to go

CONJUGATION OF **GEHEN** IN THE SUBJUNCTIVE II MOOD			
SINGULAR		PLURAL	
ich ging – e	*I would go*	**wir ging – en**	*we would go*
du ging – est	*you (informal) would go*	**ihr ging – et**	*you (informal) would go*
er, sie, es ging – e	*he, she, or it would go*	**sie ging – en**	*they would go*
Sie ging – en *You (formal) would go*			

sehen, sieht, sah, hat gesehen – to see

CONJUGATION OF **SEHEN** IN THE SUBJUNCTIVE II MOOD			
SINGULAR		PLURAL	
ich säh – e	*I would see*	**wir säh – en**	*we would see*
du säh – est	*you (informal) would see*	**ihr säh – et**	*you (informal) would see*
er, sie, es säh – e	*he, she, or it would go*	**sie säh – en**	*they would see*
Sie säh – en *You (formal) would see*			

NOTE: There are two verbs that form an exception to the *umlaut* rule. The modals *wollen* and *sollen* do not take an *umlaut* in the subjunctive.

ÜBUNG F   **Wenn ich nur . . .** You're juggling schoolwork, after school activities, and family responsibilities. You dream sometimes of being able to do something else. To get exercise creating the formal, written conditional, you choose to complete these sentences without using the words *wären*, *hätten* or *würden*.

EXAMPLE: Wenn ich nur das Wochenende frei hätte, fahren / mit euch / in die Berge
Wenn ich nur das Wochenende frei hätte, führe ich mit euch in die Berge.

1. Wenn meine Mutter nur hier wäre, müssen / ich / nicht / auf meinen Bruder / aufpassen

   _____

2. Wenn ich in dieser Klasse nur mehr lernte, bekommen / ich / bessere Noten

   _____

3. Wenn ich morgen kommen könnte, bringen / ich / meine Freundin

   _____

4. Wenn ich nur hungriger wäre, essen / ich / eine ganze Pizza

   _____

5. Wenn ich es jetzt machen könnte, . . .

   _____

| ÜBUNG G | **Was er täte, wenn er könnte.** You're home from school babysitting for your 10-year old sister. As is often the case, she is unhappy and telling you what she will do ONLY if she has to, wants to, is permitted to, etc. In the example below, *sähe* is more formal and usually reserved for written communication. *Würde . . . . sehen* is more casual and usually used when speaking. Create at least two formal sentences. |

EXAMPLE: Wenn ich es dürfte, jetzt / MTV / ansehen
Wenn ich es dürfte, sähe ich jetzt MTV an.
OR
Wenn ich es dürfte, würde ich jetzt MTV ansehen.

1. Nur wenn ich es müsste, helfen / ich / meine Mutter / mit dem Abwaschen

   _____

2. Nur wenn ich es dürfte, gehen / ich / mit / du / ins Kino

   _____

3. Nur wenn ich es wollte, anrufen / ich / Simon

   _____

4. Nur wenn ich es müsste, denken / ich / an + acc. / du

   _____

5. Nur wenn ich es sollte, essen / ich / Gemüse

   _____

6. Nur wenn ich es könnte, versprechen / ich / es / du

   _____

4.   Formation of the Subjunctive II in Weak Verbs

The formation of the conditional subjunctive for weak verbs is even easier than the strong verbs. The simple past tense is used with the same personal endings as above. No *umlaut* is added.

CONJUGATION OF **SPIELEN** IN THE SUBJUNCTIVE II MOOD			
SINGULAR		PLURAL	
ich spiel – te	*I would play*	**wir spiel –ten**	*we would play*
du spiel – test	*you (informal) would play*	**ihr spiel – tet**	*you (informal) would play*
er, sie, es spiel – te	*he, she, or it would play*	**sie spiel – ten**	*they would play*
Sie spiel – ten *You (formal) would play*			

Wenn es nicht regnete, spielte ich draußen.

If it weren't raining, I would play outside. (But it's not, so . . .)

ÜBUNG H   **Deine Entschuldigungen.** Your parents have given you a list of chores to do, but you can't seem to find anything you need. Tell your parents why you can't do what they ask.

EXAMPLE: Übe Klavier mindestens eine Stunde! (Musik)
Wenn ich meine Musik finden könnte, übte ich.
OR
Wenn ich meine Musik finden könnte, würde ich üben.

1. Putz dein Zimmer! (Staubsauger)

   _____

2. Spiel eine halbe Stunde mit deiner Schwester! (die Würfel)

   _____

3. Arbeite mit deinem Vater in der Garage! (Schuhe)

   _____

4. Mach dein eigenes Brotpaket! (Schinken)

   _____

5. Telefoniere mit deiner Großmutter! (Telefonnummer)

   _____

ÜBUNG I   **Die Pläne schmieden.** Your mother helps you find everything and soon the chores are done. It's time to go out. You're text messaging back and forth with your friends discussing what to do. You're unsure of certain conditions.

EXAMPLE: Wenn Thomas nur käme, dann hätten wir ein Auto.
          If only Thomas would come, then we'd have a car.

1. Wenn es nur nicht regnete, dann _____

2. Aber wenn wir Susanna einlüden, dann _____

3. Und wenn ich mein Fotoapparat mitbrächte, dann _____

4. Wenn es nicht so spät wäre, dann _____

5. Wenn ich Heike abholte, dann _____

| ÜBUNG J | **Was würdest du tun?** You had a great afternoon. Now imagine that your parents have gone out for the evening leaving you in charge of your younger sister. You're just putting her to bed when you hear what sounds like somebody breaking a window downstairs in the family room. Was would you do? Mention at least 5 things in the conditional subjunctive. |

_____

_____

_____

_____

_____

_____

_____

_____

5.   The Subjunctive II in the Past Tense

The past subjunctive is built on the past perfect form of the verb (*hatte geregnet*). The auxiliary verb *hatte* takes an *umlaut* and personal endings as in section one of this unit.

Present Indicative	**Es regnet.**	*It is raining.*
Present Subjunctive	**Wenn es regnete, . . .**	*If it were raining, . . .*
Simple Past Indicative	**Es regnete.**	*It was raining.*
Simple Past Subjunctive	**Wenn es geregnet hätte, . . .**	*If it had rained, . . .*

If the helping verb is *ist*, for example *ist gefahren*, then the past perfect indicative is *war gefahren* and the simple past subjunctive is *wäre gefahren*. The auxiliary verb *war* takes an *umlaut* and personal endings as in section one of this unit.

Wenn er gefahren wäre, (dann) wäre er nicht so spät gekommen.

If he had driven, (then) he wouldn't have come so late.

ÜBUNG K **Hätte sollen, hätte können, hätte werden!** Should have, could have, would have! Your friend Max is one of those people who always wish that they had done things differently. Using the cues below express what he wishes he had done last year in school.

EXAMPLE: mehr lernen / bessere Noten kriegen
Wenn er mehr gelernt hätte, hätte er bessere Noten gekriegt.

1. gut aufpassen / mehr lernen

_____

2. früher aufstehen / mehr Zeit haben

_____

3. früher ins Bett gehen / nicht immer müde sein

_____

4. immer zuhören / so viel verpassen

_____

5. mehr lesen / mehr lernen

_____

ÜBUNG L **Was hättest du besser machen sollen?** You pen pal wants to know what you think you should have done in the last year to make your life better. Write six sentence pairs to express what you wish you had done and what you would have gained had you done it. Do not only write about school.

EXAMPLE: Wenn ich mein Zimmer immer aufgeräumt hätte, hätte ich nicht so viel Ärger mit meinen Eltern bekommen.

1. _____
2. _____
3. _____
4. _____
5. _____
6. _____

CHAPTER 11

Subjunctive I – Indirect Speech

1. Definition of indirekte Rede

Direct speech, or *direkte Rede* in German, is set off from the rest of the sentence via quotation marks. The quotation marks signal to the listener that what follows is word for word exactly what the speaker said.

Johannes sagte seiner Lehrerin: „Steffi hat mich gehauen."

Johannes said to his teacher: "Steffi hit me."

When the teacher reported this incident to the principal, she told him what Johannes had said without using his exact words. This is called indirect speech (*indirekte Rede*) or the subjunctive I.

Johannes sagt, Steffi habe ihn gehauen.

Johannes said (that) Steffi had hit him.

Using the subjunctive I signals to the listener that the speaker is only reporting what has been told to her. She may or may not believe it.

2. The Formation of the Subjunctive I

Indirect speech is used to indicate what a speaker said without using his or her exact words. It is formed using the present tense of the verb and the subjunctive personal endings. There are no *umlauts* added and there is no difference between strong and weak verbs. The result is the equivalent of saying: "He or she said (that) . . . " or "It is said (that) . . . ".

Sie sagt, man habe ihr das Geld gestohlen.

She says (that) someone stole the money from her.

CONJUGATION OF **FINDEN** IN THE SUBJUNCTIVE I	
SINGULAR	PLURAL
ich find – e *I would find, found*	**wir find – en** *we would find, found*
du find – est *you (informal) would find, found*	**ihr find – et** *you (informal) would find, found*
er, sie, es find – e *he, she, or it would find, found*	**sie find – en** *they would find, found*
Sie find – en *You (formal) would find, found*	

NOTE: The rules for using the indirect speech in German are clear. Quoting someone without using his or her exact words requires the subjunctive I. An exception is often made in spoken German, but never if the speaker wants to cast doubt upon a statement made by another person. The subjunctive I sends a signal. It says: "These aren't my words. I'm only telling you what someone else said." The English equivalent adds the adverb "supposedly" or "allegedly."

> **Ihr Bruder habe die antike Vase zerbrochen.**
>
> *She says that (or supposedly, allegedly) her brother broke the antique vase.*

ÜBUNG A **Die Telefonnachrichten.** You have been helping out in the school office. Now the secretary has returned and you're giving her the phone messages you took. Herr Hardt isn't feeling well today. Frau Jones had to drive her husband to the airport. Susanna Hering's dog ate her homework. The principal will arrive an hour late. Petra Maier would like to bring an exchange student with her to school. And finally, according to the custodian, the heating system (*die Heizung*) isn't working. Some of these excuses may or may not be true. When you tell the secretary, make sure to use the indirect speech. This signals that you are only relaying what they said to you.

EXAMPLE: Herr Hardt hat angerufen. Er fühle sich heute nicht wohl.

1. Frau Jones hat angerufen. _____

2. Susanna Herings Mutter hat angerufen. _____

3. Der Rektor hat angerufen. _____

4. Petra Maier hat angerufen. _____

5. Der Hausmeister hat angerufen. _____

ÜBUNG B **Der Elternabend.** You and a classmate were behaving silly in class today. Unfortunately you forgot that parent-teacher conferences were this evening. Your teacher is reporting about your behavior to your mother. She has one version of the story, your mother apparently another. Fill in the conversation.

EXAMPLE: LEHRERIN: Thomas haut Steffi oft während der Pause.
MUTTER: Er sagte mir, Steffi haue ihn oft während der Pause.

1. LEHRERIN: Thomas schreibt oft die Antworten von Steffi ab.

   MUTTER: Er sagte mir, _____

2. LEHRERIN: Thomas provoziert Steffi oft.

   MUTTER: Er sagte mir, _____

3. LEHRERIN: Thomas spricht Steffi oft unverschämt an.

   MUTTER: Er sagte mir, _____

4. LEHRERIN: Steffi bringt jeden Tag ein Pausebrot, und Thomas klaut es ihr oft weg.

   MUTTER: Er sagte mir, _____

5. LEHRERIN: Thomas bekommt keine guten Noten bei mir

   MUTTER: Er sagte mir, _____

3.   The Subjunctive I of the Auxiliary Verbs

The three helping verbs *sein, haben* and *werden* follow the pattern above. Only *sein* has special forms in the subjunctive I that must be memorized.

CONJUGATION OF **SEIN** IN THE SUBJUNCTIVE I MOOD			
SINGULAR		PLURAL	
ich sei	*I am*	**wir sei – en**	*we are*
du sei – est	*you (informal) are*	**ihr sei – et**	*you (informal) are*
er, sie, es sei	*he, she, or it is*	**sie sei – en**	*they are*
***Sie* sei – en** *you (formal) are*			

CONJUGATION OF **HABEN** IN THE SUBJUNCTIVE I MOOD			
SINGULAR		PLURAL	
ich hab – e	*I would have*	**wir hab – en**	*we would have*
du hab – est	*you (informal) would have*	**ihr hab – et**	*you (informal) would have*
er, sie, es hab – e	*he, she, or it would have*	**sie hab – en**	*they would have*
Sie hab – en *You (formal) would have*			

CONJUGATION OF **WERDEN** IN THE SUBJUNCTIVE I MOOD			
SINGULAR		PLURAL	
ich werd – e	*I will*	**wir werd – en**	*we would*
du werd – est	*you (informal) will*	**ihr werd – et**	*you (informal) would*
er, sie, es werd – e	*he, she, or it will*	**sie werd – en**	*they would*
Sie werd – en *You (formal) would*			

ÜBUNG C   **Ich bin der Beste.** In your class there is a student who always maintains that he is the best. Write down what he has told you about himself and his class so you can show his statements to your friend. Use *meinen, glauben, sagen* and *behaupten* to vary your statements.

EXAMPLE: Ich bin der beste Fußballer in der Schule.
              Er meint, er sei der beste Fußballer in der Schule.

1. Ich bin der einzige Schüler mit einer Eins in Mathe. / meinen
_____

2. Ich werde in zwei Jahren Klassensprecher. / glauben
_____

3. Ich habe die besten Noten in der Klasse. / sagen
_____

4. Wir haben die schönsten Mädchen in unserer Mathestunden. / behaupten
_____

5. Unser Klassenlehrer ist sehr sympathisch. / sagen
_____

ÜBUNG D   **Eine Umfrage.** Ask several people in your family and circle of friends what their favorite activity is and write their answers for a class discussion tomorrow. Use the indirect speech to record their answers.

EXAMPLE: Mein Vater sagte, <u>er angele gerne mit seinen Freunden.</u>

1. Mein Geschichtslehrer behauptete, _____

2. Mein Mutter und Schwester meinten, _____

3. Meine beste Freundin sagte, _____

4. Unser Schulrektor meinte, _____

5. Mein sechsjähriger Bruder sagte, _____

ÜBUNG E   **Einige Fotos.** You have received some photos from your classmate who is on an exchange program in Austria. They show what she does every day. You're not sure if you believe everything she's telling you about her new life, so, when you show them to your friends, you use the indirect speech and the verb *behaupten* (to claim, maintain) or *berichten* (to report). Let them decide for themselves whether they believe her or not.

EXAMPLE: Sie behauptet, sie gehe jeden Tag schwimmen.
              OR
              Sie behauptet, sie schwimme jeden Tag.

1. _____

2. _____

3. _____

4. _____

5. _____

4.   Use of Tense in Subjunctive I

There are four tenses in indirect speech:

a. Present Tense

Er habe heute keine Zeit.
(He says that) he has no time today.

b. Present Perfect Tense

Er habe heute keine Zeit gehabt.
(He says that) he had no time today.

c. Future Tense

Er werde heute keine Zeit haben.
(He says that) he will not have any time today.

d. Future Perfect Tense

Er werde heute keine Zeit gehabt haben.
(He says that) he will not have had any time today.

ÜBUNG F | **Warum bist du nicht gekommen?** Many people did not show up for the **Klassenfete.** You asked them why. You must use your notes to write up a report for your *Klassensprecher* and use the *indirekte Rede* because you do not want anyone thinking that you accept these excuses.

EXAMPLE: Hansi – Ich habe gestern keine Zeit gehabt.
Hansi sagte, er habe gestern keine Zeit gehabt.
OR
Hansi sagte, dass er gestern keine Zeit gehabt habe.

1. Margot – „Ich bin zu meinen Großeltern gegangen."

   _____

2. Herr Marzipan – „Ich habe Fußball gespielt."

   _____

3. Marco – „Ich habe meine Hausaufgaben gemacht."

   _____

4. Luca – „Er hat eine Autopanne gehabt."

   _____

5. David – „Meine Mutter ist nicht zu Hause gewesen."

   _____

ÜBUNG G | **Ihre Entschuldigungen.** Some of your classmates claimed they couldn't go to the *Klassenfete* because they had do things at home. Use your notes to express what they said.

EXAMPLE: Hausarbeit machen müssen (Karl)
Karl sagte, er habe Hausarbeit machen müssen.

1. nicht alleine fahren dürfen (Maria)

   _____

2. nicht während der Woche ausgehen sollen (Benji)

   _____

3. seine kleine Schwester babysitten müssen (Charlie)

   _____

4. ihre Hausaufgaben machen müssen (Friede und Frank)

_____

5. seiner Schwester mit ihren Hausaufgaben helfen müssen (Stefan)

_____

5. The Subjunctive I in Archaic Expressions

There are a number of historical expressions that use the subjunctive I. This construction is archaic, i.e. it is no longer used unless the speaker is attempting to recreate the speech of times gone by. It's sufficient to recognize the construction.

Lang lebe der König. Möge er lang und glücklich leben.

Long live the king. May he live a long and happy life.

ÜBUNG H | **Ein Zeitungsartikel.** Sandrina Sopranisti, a famous operatic singer who graduated from your school seventeen years ago, has returned to perform with the school chorus. You've been asked to interview her for the school newspaper. She tells you all about her artistic lifestyle: how often she practices, what she eats, how much sleep she gets, what her family is like, where she will be performing, what her day looks like. She also tells you that she had once performed with the world famous Luciano Pavarotti. Write the article using the indirect speech rather than quoting her. Opera stars often lead exciting, flamboyant lives. Try to make yours as interesting as possible.

_____

_____

_____

_____

_____

_____

_____

_____

_____

_____

CHAPTER 12
Infinitive Constructions

1.   Verbs with an Infinitive Completer

a. Modal Verbs – Modal verbs set the pattern for all verb-infinitive completer constructions. The modal verbs are:

dürfen	darf	durfte	hat gedurft	*may, be permitted to*
können	kann	konnte	hat gekonnt	*can, be allowed to*
mögen	mag	mochte	hat gemocht	*like, like to*
müssen	muss	musste	hat gemusst	*must, have to*
sollen	soll	sollte	hat gesollt	*should*
wollen	will	wollte	hat gewollt	*want*

NOTE: When used in a sentence, the modal is the second element and the completer infinitive goes to the end of the sentence.

In Südbayern wollen wir die drei Schlösser von König Ludwig II sehen.

In Southern Bavaria we want to visit the three castles of King Ludwig II.

ÜBUNG A	**Wir wollen das Schloss Neuschwanstein besichtigen.** You and your parents are planning a trip to Southern Germany. Do some research on Southern Bavaria, particularly King Ludwig II and his castles. Look up the places on this list on the Internet. Use modals to express whether you think your parents should, must, should not, can, or cannot visit or see five of these *Sehenswürdigkeiten* (tourist attractions): *das Schloss Neuschwanstein, das Schloss Hohenschwangau, das Schloss Linderhof, der Starnberger See, München, die Herreninsel, der Chiemsee, die Michaelskirche (München), das Deutsche Museum.*

EXAMPLE: Ihr sollt die Herreninsel nicht verpassen.
            Ihr müsst doch die Herreninsel besichtigen.

1. sehen / sollen

_____

2. besichtigen / wollen

_____

3. nicht verpassen / dürfen

_____

4. anschauen / müssen

_____

5. besuchen / können

_____

6. eine Führung durch _____ machen / wollen

_____

| ÜBUNG B | **König Ludwig II.** You've decided that Ludwig II, often called "Crazy Ludwig" is interesting enough that you want to see the castles he created. Tell his story to your parents so that they will understand how these ornate castles came to be. Because you are telling the story, the verbs will be in the simple past tense. |

EXAMPLE: Ludwig /den Krieg gegen die Preußen / gewinnen / sollen.
          Ludwig sollte den Krieg gegen die Preußen gewinnen.

1. Als Dreizehnjähriger / er / eine Oper von Richard Wagner / sehr / mögen

_____

2. Als junger Mann / er / mehr Opern von Wagner / hören und lesen / wollen

_____

3. Aber dann / mit 18 Jahren / Ludwig / den Königsthron / aufsetzen / müssen

_____

4. Er / sein Volk / im Krieg / gegen die Preußen / führen / müssen

_____

5. Die Preußen waren zu stark. Er / den Krieg / nicht / gewinnen / können

_____

6. Nach dem Krieg / er / keine Politik mehr / machen / wollen

_____

| ÜBUNG C | **Die Geschichte geht weiter.** Ludwig was forced into a role he didn't want. He wanted to live in a Wagnerian world, one which would immerse him in music, Germanic folk heroes, and art. The Bavarian government expected him to rule. Continue your story telling your folks what the final outcome was. |

EXAMPLE: Er / sich / nur / mit Kunst und Musik / beschäftigen / wollen
          Er hat sich nur mit Kunst und Musik beschäftigen wollen.

1. Ludwig / drei neue Schlösser in französischen Stil / bauen / wollen

   _____

2. Alle Schlösser / Richard Wagner / ehren (honor) / sollen

   _____

3. Der Staat Bayern / die Kosten für Ludwigs Märchenschlösser / nicht / bezahlen / können

   _____

4. im Juni 1886 / Ludwig / einen Nachmittag / mit seinem Psychiater / verbringen / sollen.

   _____

5. Sie / auf dem Starnberger See / rudern / gehen / wollen.

   _____

6. Ludwig und sein Arzt / nicht / schwimmen / können / und / ertrinken

   _____

7. Ludwigs Tod / ein Unfall / gewesen / sein / sollen

   _____

Bonus Question:

Was meinst du? War Ludwigs Tod ein Unfall? Oder hat jemand ihn umgebracht? (umbringen = kill) Wenn ja, wer hat ihn umbringen wollen?

    b. Word order with modal verbs

When used in compound tenses (present perfect, past perfect, or future perfect), the word order for modals is VIM (verb-infinitive-modal). The auxiliary verb *haben* is the second element and the completer and the modal both go to the end of the sentence.

König Ludwig II hat ein viertes Schloss bauen wollen.

King Ludwig II wanted to build a fourth castle.

ÜBUNG D **Notizen über Bayerns König Ludwig II.** König Ludwig II planned many improvements for the Bavarian people, but he had many problems. The notes you took on your computer were formatted improperly. Correct this by matching the columns to write out what you learned about Ludwig II.

EXAMPLE: Ludwig II hat die Kultur in seinem Land fördern wollen.

Ludwig II / er		
die Kultur / in / sein Land		dürfen / geben
die Opern / von Wagner / immer		mögen / hören
nach Dezember 1865 / Wagner / kein Geld mehr		wollen / kämpfen
nicht gegen Preußen		dürfen / bauen
sein viertes Schloss / nicht		wollen / fördern
Sophie		sollen / heiraten

1. _____

2. _____

3. _____

4. _____

5. _____

| ÜBUNG E | **Was Ludwig wollte aber nicht konnte.** Ludwig II wanted to do so much for his people, but couldn't for one reason or another. Disappointed and unhappy, he retreated more and more into the world of art, stopped going to his capital city of Munich, and almost bankrupted the state of Bavaria by building overly ornate palaces. Combine the sentences to relate more about his life. |

EXAMPLE: Ludwig / nie / König / werden / wollen // aber / er / seinem Vater / auf den Thron/ nachfolgen (dative verb, *succeed*) / müssen
Ludwig hat nicht König werden wollen, aber er hat seinem Vater auf den Thron nachfolgen müssen.

1. Ludwig / hat / immer / auf dem Land / leben / wollen // aber / nach dem Tod seines Vaters / er / oft / in der Stadt München / sein / müssen

_____

2. er / einen Krieg gegen die Preußen / führen / müssen // aber er / ihn / nicht / gewinnen / können.

_____

3. er / die Großstadt / nicht mehr / besuchen / wollen // aber / er / oft / als König / hingehen / sollen

_____

4. er / Opern / von / Richard Wagner / immer / hören / wollen // und / seine Schlösser / wie Wagner-Opern / aussehen / sollen.

_____

5. Er / vier / Wagner Schlösser / bauen / wollen // aber / der Staat Bayern / nicht / dafür / zahlen / können

_____

6. Er / mit seinem Arzt / rudern gehen / sollen // aber / die zwei / nicht / schwimmen können.

_____

7. Seid Tod im Starnberger See / wie ein Unfall / aussehen / sollen // aber / vielleicht / sein Arzt / ihn / auch / töten / wollen.

_____

ÜBUNG F   **Was hat er tun wollen?** You've found a letter from "Crazy" King Ludwig II in which he describes his life. By the time he wrote it he'd already abandoned his governmental responsibilities and was spending his time (and the state's money) entertaining Wagner, building dream houses, and decorating them with images and symbols from Wagnerian operas. What are five things that you think he wanted to do during this "mad" period of his life?

EXAMPLE: Er hat Richard Wagner zu sich ins Schloss einladen wollen.

1. _____

2. _____

3. _____

4. _____

5. _____

NOTE: If the modal is used in a subordinating clause, the helping verb goes to the end of the clause and is placed before the completer infinitive and the modal. The word order VIM (verb-infinitive-modal) is maintained.

> **Er ist gestorben, bevor er sein viertes Schloss Falkenstein hat bauen können.**
> verb infinitive modal

> *He died before he could build Falkenstein, his fourth castle.*

ÜBUNG G   **Fragen über Ludwig.** You know much about Ludwig II. Now your friends are asking you questions, so that they will be able to answer Herr Marzipan's questions tomorrow in history class. If you know the answer to their questions, answer them as completely as possible. If not, reply to the questions below in the negative. You must answer positively in at least 2 of the 5 questions.

EXAMPLE: Weißt du, ob Ludwig erfolgreich hat regieren können?
Ludwig hat nicht gut regieren können. Er hat zu viel Geld ausgegeben.
OR
Nein, ich weiß nicht, ob Ludwig hat gut regieren können.

1. Weißt du, ob Ludwig den Krieg gegen die Preußen hat gewinnen können?

   _____

2. Weißt du, ob Ludwig Richard Wagner persönlich hat kennen lernen können?

   _____

3. Weißt du, wie viel der Staat hat für seine Schlösser hat ausgeben müssen?

   _____

4. Weißt du, ob Ludwig alle seine vier geplanten Schlösser hat bauen können?

   _____

5. Wusstest du, dass Ludwigs Arzt ihn vielleicht hat töten wollen?

   _____

c. Additional Verbs that can take an Infinitive Completer

Some verbs do not require, but often use, an infinitive to complete their meaning. The verb is the second element and the infinitive is placed at the end of its sentence or clause.

gehen   geht   ging   ist gegangen   *go*

Ludwig ging oft auf dem Starnberger See rudern.

Ludwig often went rowing on Lake Starnberg.

sehen   sieht   sah   hat gesehen   *see*

Er hat seine Gäste oft vom Schlossturm ankommen sehen.

He often saw his guests arriving from the castle tower.

hören   hört   hörte   hat gehört   *hear*

Er hat den Wasserfall hinter Schloss Neuschwanstein immer rauschen hören.

He always heard the waterfall rushing behind Neuschwanstein Castle.

helfen   hilft   half   hat geholfen   *help*

Heute helfe ich meiner Klasse ein Modell von Neuschwanstein bauen.

Today I am helping my class build a model of Neuschwanstein.

| ÜBUNG H | **Was er sah und hörte.** Imagine that you are Ludwig. You know that the members of your government are upset about your lifestyle and have been threatening to take action. You're alone in one of your castles. Suddenly you hear a noise and see a shape approaching in the shadows. Is your mind playing games on you, or is someone sneaking up on you? Using *hören* and *sprechen* with an infinitive completer, write down Ludwig's panicked thoughts. |

EXAMPLE: Ich höre ein Fenster brechen. Ich höre zwei Leute leise sprechen.

1. _____

2. _____

3. _____

4. _____

5. _____

| ÜBUNG I | **Gehen und helfen.** Ah, Ludwig is relieved. It's only his psychiatrist, who's become a friend by this time. In fact, he's come to invite Ludwig for an afternoon outing on the Starnberger See. What does he suggest? You'll have to fill in a lot of missing words for these clues to create logical sentences. |

1. helfen / deine Probleme lösen

_____

2. helfen / über deine Probleme / sprechen

_____

3. dann / gehen / See / rudern

_____

4. nächste Woche / Wagner / besuchen / gehen / wollen

_____

    d. _Lassen_ with an infinitive

      lassen   lässt   ließ   hat gelassen   _let, allow_

      Ludwigs Eltern ließen ihn oft nach München fahren.

      Ludwig's parents often allowed him to go to Munich.

NOTE: The verb _lassen_ is often used to denote that the speaker is having something done.

      Ludwig dekorierte seine Schlösser mit Schwänen.

      Ludwig decorated his castles with swans.

NOTE: The above statement implies that King Ludwig decorated the castles himself. Actually he hired theater set designers (_Bühnenbildausstatter_) to decorate his castles. The result was an ornateness and gimmickry that has made them famous throughout the world. He even had a grotto through which one could float on a swan boat.
The use of _lassen_ in the statements below makes it clear that Ludwig had someone decorate his castles for him as well as cut his hair.

      Ludwig ließ seine Schlösser mit Schwänen dekorieren.

      Ludwig had his castles decorated with swans.

      Ludwig lässt sich die Haare alle vier Wochen schneiden.

      Ludwig has his hair cut (literally lets the hair to him be cut) once a month.

| ÜBUNG J | **Ich lasse mir . . .** As a king, Ludwig had a lot of things done for him that you might or might now do yourself. Imagine that you are a king and live in a castle. What do you have done for you? Use _lassen_ as the verb in the second position. The completer infinitive goes to the end. |

EXAMPLE: Ich lasse mir jeden Abend ein Stück Kuchen bringen.
              Ich lasse mir mein Zimmer jeden Abend aufräumen.

1. _____

2. _____

3. _____

4. _____

5. _____

2.   Infinitive Constructions

a. *Um . . . zu*

Causality, why we do something, is often expressed in English by the words "in order to." German uses *um . . . zu* plus an infinitive.

Um seine Schlösser zu finanzieren, hat Ludwig Steuern von seinem Volk verlangt.

In order to finance his castles, Ludwig demanded taxes from his people.

Er hat Richard Wagner nach München eingeladen, um der Stadt eine kulturelle Wiedergeburt anzubieten.

He invited Richard Wagner to Munich, in order to offer a cultural rebirth to the city.

ÜBUNG K   **Why do you think that Ludwig and his visitors did the following?** Create sentences using the *um . . . zu* construction.

EXAMPLE: er / viel Geld ausgeben / / seine Schlösser / bauen
Er hat viel Geld ausgegeben, um seine Schlösser zu bauen.

1. Ludwig / prächtige Schlösser / bauen / wollen // Wagner / ehren

_____

2. Seine Regierung / mit / er / sprechen / wollen // sein Schlossbauerei / stoppen

_____

3. Ludwig / München / verlassen // das nicht mehr hören / müssen

_____

4. Ludwigs Psychiater / ihn / besuchen // auf dem See / mit / er / rudern / gehen

_____

5. Historiker / über Ludwigs letzten Tag / schreiben // die Kontroverse / „Tod oder Mord" / analysieren

_____

3.   *Ohne . . . zu*

A similar construction exists to express "without . . . -ing." The preposition *ohne*, without, introduces the clause, and the verb in the form of *zu* + infinitive goes to the end.

Ohne seinem Volk ein Wort zu sagen, begann Ludwig sein viertes Schloss zu bauen.

Without saying a word to his people, Ludwig began to build his fourth castle.

ÜBUNG L   **Du kannst gehen, nur wenn . . .** You're interested in Ludwig and his story now. In fact, it's been made into a musical called *Ludwig* that is playing in Munich. You've asked your parents for permission to go, but your father has some conditions. Reword his stipulations using an *ohne . . . zu* construction.

EXAMPLE: Deine Schwester muss mitgehen.
          Du kannst nicht gehen, ohne deine Schwester mitzunehmen.

1. Du musst deine Theaterkarte im Voraus kaufen.

    _____

2. Du musst einen Erwachsenen dabei haben.

    _____

3. Du musst mir sagen, wann du zurückkommst.

    _____

4. Du musst zuerst deiner Mutter in der Küche helfen.

    _____

5. Du musst eine gute Note morgen in deiner Klassenarbeit bekommen.

    _____

4.   *(An)statt . . . zu*

The final preposition to be used with a *zu* + infinitive construction is *(an)statt. Anstatt* and *statt* may be used interchangeably. Using either with *zu* plus the infinitive expresses "instead of . . . -ing."

Anstatt einen Tag am See zu verbringen, machen viele Touristen eine Schlossrunde.

Instead of spending a day at the lake, many tourists take a tour of the castles.

Anstatt zuerst nach Neuschwanstein zu fahren, wollen wir unsere Tour dort beenden.

Instead of going first to Neuschwanstein, let's end our tour there.

ÜBUNG M   **Der Freistaat Bayern.** Your friend has sent you an e-mail with suggestions for your trip to Bavaria. Write an answer e-mail and make other suggestions using *(an)statt.*

EXAMPLE: Wir fahren zuerst nach Neuschwanstein.   Statt zuerst nach Neuschwanstein zu fahren, sollen wir unsere Tour in München beginnen.

1. Wir können am See ein Picknick machen.

    _____

2. Wenn wir Neuschwanstein besuchen, können wir zu Fuß zur Marienbrücke gehen.

    _____

3. Und dann können wir das Schloss mit meiner Digitalkamera fotografieren.

    _____

4. Nach Neuschwanstein können wir Schloss Hohenschwangau besuchen.

   _____

5. Wir können in München übernachten.

   _____

ÜBUNG N | **Ich als König(in).** Imagine that you were a king or queen and did things like Ludwig. Write a fairy-tale about your time as royalty. Be sure to use at least five different types of verb completers to make your story interesting and authentic sounding. Use the narrative past tense.

Es war einmal ein(e) König(in) . . . . . .

   _____

   _____

   _____

   _____

   _____

   _____

   _____

   _____

   _____

Chapter 13
Genitive Case

1.   Showing Possession in German

In German there are two ways to show possession:

1. The most common method uses the word *von* with the dative.

    Das Buch von dem Mann liegt auf dem Tisch.

    The man's book (literally, the book of the man) is lying on the table.

    Das Buch von der Frau liegt daneben.

    The woman's book (literally, the book of the woman) is lying next to it.

2. The second method of showing possession is to use the genitive case. It is equivalent to the apostrophes in English.

    Das Buch des Mannes liegt auf dem Tisch.

    The man's book is lying on the table.

    Das Buch der Frau liegt daneben.

    The woman's book is lying next to it.

2.   The Formation of the Genitive

GENITIVE CASE DEFINITE AND INDEFINITE ARTICLES			
MASCULINE	FEMINIINE	NEUTER	PLURAL
des Mannes *of the man*	**der Frau** *of the woman*	**des Buches** *of the book*	**der Männer/Frauen/Bücher** *of the men, women, books*
eines Mannes *of a man*	**einer Frau** *of a woman*	**eines Buches** *of a book*	**meiner Männer/Frauen/Bücher** *of my men, women, books*

Masculine and neuter singular nouns take an –s or –es ending when used in the genitive. An –es is usually used instead of an –s when:

a. The noun is monosyllabic, i. e. it has only one syllable. **des Bildes**

b. The noun ends in –s, –ß, –x, or –z. **des Hauses, des Reflexes, des Netzes**

c. The noun ends in two consonants **des Buches**

The *–s* is usually added to the masculine and neuter singular genitive nouns when:

a. The noun ends in a vowel   **des Autos, des Sees**
b. The noun ends in a vowel followed by an *–h*   **des Schuhs, des Flohs**
c. The noun is the name of a person. (NO apostrophe!)   **Jessicas, Pauls**
d. The noun is foreign.   **des Museums**
e. The noun has more than one syllable and the last is unstressed. **des Kalenders**

The above aren't hard and fast rules, simply guidelines. Often the choice of *–s* or *–es* is left to the speaker. All dictionaries will list the genitive form for masculine and neuter nouns. Ex. *Buch n (e)s, –¨er* – book This means that the noun is neuter, can take either an *–s* or *–es* for the genitive, and pluralizes by *umlauting* the *u* and adding *–er*, *Bücher*.

NOTE: The use of an apostrophe to show possession, common in English, is starting to be used in Germany, particularly when the name of the possessor ends in *–s*, e.g. *Hans' Buch*. It is also not unusual to see Jessica's or Paul's in informal writing, although that is still considered incorrect in German.

| ÜBUNG A | **Superlative.** New Years is approaching and the genitive is popular. Magazines are all choosing their *Person des Jahres*. Your class is choosing their superlatives also. What titles would you give to the following? Use the genitive in your titles. |

EXAMPLE: die Lieblingssekretärin von dem Rektor.   die Lieblingssekretärin des Rektors.

1. der beste Lehrer in diesem Jahr

    _____

2. die beste Schülerin in dieser Woche

    _____

3. die Lieblingsmaskotte von der Schule

    _____

4. das freundlichste Mädchen in euerem Gymnasium

    _____

5. das beste Restaurant in euerer Stadt

    _____

| ÜBUNG B | **Die Filmtitel.** Your class is producing a film to highlight events of the past year. Several possible titles have been suggested. While OK, you feel, as script writer, that you would prefer a more formal title. Take the compound word suggestions and rewrite them breaking up the compound word and using the genitive case. |

EXAMPLE: Ein Epochenende   Das Ende einer Epoche

1. Die Klassenparodie _____

2. Das Jahresprojekt _____

3. Unsere Klassenerfolge _____

4. Das Tagesthema _____

5. Unser Klassenschnappschuss _____

ÜBUNG C **Das Wort des Tages.** Your principal is holding an assembly to recognize important achievements during the past year. Recreate a few from some of the word prompts below. The sentences will be in the present perfect tense, since the principal is recounting events that occurred during the last year.

EXAMPLE: die Mühe / unser Matheathleten / die Schule / der erste Preis / gewinnen
Die Mühe unserer Matheathleten hat der Schule den ersten Preis gewonnen.

1. Die Leistungen / unsere Fußballmannschaft / die Schule / in die Stadtliga / bringen

_____

2. Die unendliche Mühe / unsere Fakultät / die Schule / akademisch viel weiter/ bringen

_____

3. Die Spendenaktion / unser Elternverein / die Schule / ein Konzertflügel / finanzieren

_____

4. Schüler / unsere Schwesterschule in Indonesien / ihr erster Besuch hierher / machen

_____

5. Die Rektorin / das Nachbargymnasium / uns / zu ihrem Silvesterfest / einladen

_____

3. Genitive Prepositions

There are eight prepositions which take the genitive:

(an)statt	instead of	**diesseits**	this side of
auf Grund	as a result of	**inklusive**	including
infolge	because of	**während**	during
jenseits	that side of	***wegen**	on account of
***trotz**	in spite of		

*While written speech still requires the genitive, spoken German very often uses the dative after *trotz* and *wegen* rather than the genitive.

ÜBUNG D **Keine Berliner Reise mit der Klasse.** You are going to write a letter to your Oma who does not have e-mail. You need to correct some things you wrote her a few months ago. Use the notes below to express these changes.

EXAMPLE: trotz / mein Versuch / ich / keine / gute Noten / kriegen
Trotz meines Versuchs habe ich keine gute Note gekriegt.

1. infolge / meine schlechten Noten / ich / nicht /mit / die Klasse / nach / Berlin / dürfen / fahren (past tense)

   _____

2. während / die Zeit / ich / für / meine Klassenarbeiten / müssen / pauken (cram) (past tense)

   _____

3. wegen/ das Pauken / meine Ergebnisse / nicht so schlecht / sein (past tense)

   _____

4. anstatt / die Berlinreise / mit / die Klasse / zu machen / ich / jetzt / mit / Freunden / dürfen / reisen (present tense)

   _____

5. ich / diese Reise / nach Berlin / während / der Sommer / machen / dürfen (present tense)

   _____

| ÜBUNG E | **Der Silvesterabend.** Your school has been invited to attend the New Year's Eve party at the *Gymnasium* (high school) in the next town. You're meeting in an hour with their planning committee. As preparation for the meeting, create six statements that members of the committee might make. Each one of them should contain a different preposition from the list above.

EXAMPLE: Statt einer Band wollen wir nicht einen DJ haben?

1. _____
2. _____
3. _____
4. _____
5. _____
6. _____

| ÜBUNG F | **Die Silvesterfeiern.** You are chatting on IM with your pen pal in Germany. You're discussing the upcoming New Year's celebrations in your countries. There it's called Silvester after a pope who died on December 31, 335. Your pen pal is telling you what the traditions are like on his side of the Atlantic Ocean. Respond by telling him your New Year's Eve traditions.

EXAMPLE: Jenseits des Atlantiks (Deutschland) feiern wir dieses Jahr zu Hause.
Diesseits des Atlantiks gehen wir auf eine Fete im Nachbargymnasium.

1. Jenseits des Atlantiks schauen wir uns immer den Klassiker „Dinner for One" im Fernsehen an.

---

2. Jenseits des Atlantiks servieren wir meistens nur Partysnacks und trinken eine Sektbowle.

---

3. Jenseits des Atlantiks gibt es Feuerwerke um Mitternacht.

---

4. Jenseits des Atlantiks gießen wir Blei, um zu wissen was die Zukunft bringt.

NOTE: A popular Sylvester custom is to melt small chunks of lead (*Blei*) in a spoon held over a candle. When it is molten, it is poured quickly into a container of cold water. It hardens immediately into a unique shape. Participants try to decipher, much like a Rohrschach Test, what they see and infer from it their future for the coming year.

5. Jenseits des Atlantiks verschenken wir ein Marzipanschweinchen als Glücksbringer.

---

4. Adjectives Used with the Genitive

There is a group of adjectives that function as regular adjectives most of the time.

bedürftig	*needy, in need (of)*	**sicher**	*certain (of)*
bewusst	*aware (of)*	**verdächtig**	*suspected (of)*
gewiss	*certain (of)*	**wert**	*worth (of)*
schuldig	*guilty (of)*	**würdig**	*worthy (of)*

Der Mann ist verdächtig.   **Das schuldige Kind wird bestraft werden.**

The man is suspicious.   *The guilty child will be punished.*

NOTE: The words "suspicious" and "guilty" in the above examples are adjectives. They are unique, however, in that they can also be combined with the word "of."

Der Mann ist des Mordes schuldig.   *The man is guilty of the murder.*

Er ist der Hilfe eines Psychiaters bedürftig.   *He is in need of the help of a psychiatrist.*

War er der Strafe bewusst, bevor er die Tat beging?

Was he aware of the punishment, before he committed the deed?

When the word "of" is attached to their meaning, they become genitive adjectives. They follow a noun in the genitive case. In English one says: "The prizewinner is worthy of the honor." In German that sentence becomes *Der Preisgewinner ist der Ehre würdig*, literally "He is of the honor worthy."

Regular Adjective: **Der schuldige Mann wird sicher ins Gefängnis kommen.**
The guilty man will certainly land in prison.

Genitive Adjective: **Er ist des Mordes schuldig.**
He is guilty of the murder. (literally, he is of the murder guilty.)

ÜBUNG G   **Die Filmstunde.** Once again your film class is thinking about titles for your short film festival entries. You suggest using genitive adjective phrases as titles. You re-write the titles to demonstrate how dramatic they sound.

EXAMPLE: Hans ist schuldig. Er hat den Mann ermordet. Hans ist des Mordes schuldig!

1. Lisa braucht viel Liebe.

_____

2. Karl weiß sicher, dass seine Eltern ihn lieben.

_____

3. Man glaubt, dass Sylvester den Mord begangen hat.

_____

4. Er hat diese Ehre verdient.

_____

ÜBUNG H   **Die Klassensuperlativen.** You and your friends are creating a series of joke-superlatives relating to your class, your classmates, and things that have happened this year. What are your five suggestions? Use the genitive case in each one. Explain what you are reminded of when you make this suggestion.

EXAMPLE: Das beste Manöver der Fahrschule. Im April ist Kristen während der Fahrstunde gegen einen Baum gefahren.

1. _____
2. _____
3. _____
4. _____
5. _____

CHAPTER 14

Noun Review

1. Noun Attributes - Gender, Number and Case

Nouns have three attributes: gender, number and case. They are either masculine (*der*), feminine (*die*) or neuter (*das*).

Nouns are either *singular* or *plural*.

And, when used in a sentence, they are either in the *nominative, dative, accusative* or *genitive* case.

When working with a noun in a sentence it is important to identify its GNC. Only when the GNC is known can the correct article be chosen.

2. Noun Gender

The gender of a German noun is not intuitive, i.e. it does not always match the natural gender of the noun. For this reason the gender of all nouns must be memorized. There are a few rules that usually, not always, hold true.

a. Masculine nouns usually include:

1. Names of male humans and animals

der Athlet, die Athleten	*male athlete*	**(fem. = Athletin)**
der Kater, die Kater	*male cat*	**(fem. = Katze)**
der Pfau, die Pfauen	*peacock*	**(fem. = Pfauhenne)**
der Trainer, die Trainer	*coach*	**(fem. = Trainerin)**
der Vater, die Väter	*father*	

2. Names of the days, months, seasons and directions

der Januar, die Januare	*January*
der Montag, die Montage	*Monday*
der Nord(en), no plural	*north*
der Sommer, die Sommer	*summer*

3. Names of most storm or weather-related phenomena

der Blitz, die Blitze	*lightning*
der Donner, die Donner	*thunder*
der Eisregen, die Eisregen	*freezing rain*
der Front, die Fronten	*(weather) front*

der Grad, die Grade	*degree*
der Graupel, die Graupeln	*sleet*
der Hagel, die Hagel	*hail*
der Hoch- or Tiefdruck, no plural	*high or low pressure*
der Monsun, die Monsune	*monsoon*
der Nebel, die Nebel	*fog*
der Niederschlag, die Niederschläge	*precipitation*
der Orkan, die Orkane	*hurricane*
der Regen, die Regen	*rain*
der Schauer, die Schauer	*rain shower*
der Schnee, no plural	*snow*
der Smog, die Smogs	*smog*
der Sturm, die Stürme	*storm, gale-force winds*
der Tornado, die Tornados	*tornado*
der Wind, die Winde	*wind*
der Wirbelsturm, die Wirbelstürme	*tornado*

4. Names of most gems, stones and minerals

der Amethyst, die Amethyste	*amethyst*
der Diamant, die Diamanten	*diamond*
der Granit, die Granite	*granite*
der Marmor, die Marmore	*marble*
der Opal, die Opale	*opal*
der Saphir, die Saphire	*sapphire*
der Smaragd, die Smaragde	*emerald*
der Topas, die Topase	*topaz*

5. Nouns ending in *–ling*

der CD-Rohling, die CD-Rohlinge	*blank CD*
der Eindringling, die Eindringlinge	*gate crasher, invader*
der Feigling, die Feiglinge	*coward*
der Jüngling, die Jünglinge	*young man*
der Lehrling, die Lehrlinge	*apprentice*
der Liebling, die Lieblinge	*darling, dear*
der Pfifferling, die Pfifferlinge	*chanterelle (mushroom)*

6. Most nouns ending in *–s, –ß* or *–ss*

der Bus, die Busse	*bus*
der Fuchs, die Füchse	*fox*
der Fuss, die Füsse	*foot*
der Keks, die Kekse	*cookie*

der Kuss, die Küsse	*kiss*
der Riss, die Risse	*rip, tear*
der Schuss, die Schüsse	*shot*
der Stoß, die Stöße	*pile, batch*

7. Male nouns of agent, i.e. nouns ending in *–er* that are formed from a verb and name a person performing the action of that verb (*lehren* ⟶ *der Lehrer, die Lehrer* = teacher)

der Käufer, die Käufer	*male purchaser*
der Redner, die Redner	*male speaker*
der Sänger, die Sänger	*singer*
der Sportler, die Sportler	*sportsman*
der Tänzer, die Tänzer	*dancer*

8. Nouns which end in *–ismus, –ist* and *–or*

der Atheist, die Atheisten	*atheist*
der Globalismus, die Globalismen	*globalism*
der Idealismus, no plural	*idealism*
der Idealist, die Idealisten	*idealist*
der Realismus, no plural	*realism*
der Realist, die Realisten	*realist*
der Senior, die Senioren	*senior citizen*
der Tenor, die Tenöre	*tenor*

9. Nouns of one syllable that are formed from a principle part of a verb

der (Aus)tausch, no plural	*trade, exchange*
der Gang, die Gänge	*gait, hallway*
der Schein, die Scheine	*appearance*
der Schnitt, die Schnitte	*cut, slice*
der Tanz, die Tänze	*dance*

b. Feminine Nouns usually include

1. Nouns of two syllables ending in *–e*

die Farbe, die Farben	*color, paint*
die Tasche, die Taschen	*purse, pocket(book)*
die Woche, die Wochen	*week*
die Wolle, die Wollen	*wool*

2. Nouns ending in *–schaft* which has been added to one noun to form another

die Freundschaft, die Freundschaften	*friendship*
die Landschaft, die Landschaften	*countryside, landscape*
die Mannschaft, die Mannschaften	*team*

3. Nouns ending in *–ung* which has been added to a verb stem to form a noun

die Anschaffung, die Anschaffungen	*procurement*
die Formulierung, die Formulierungen	*formulation*
die Landung, die Landungen	*landing*
die Scheidung, die Scheidungen	*separation*

4. Nouns ending in *–heit* and *–keit* which have been added to an adjective to form a noun

die Schnelligkeit, die Schnelligkeiten	*speed*
die Faulheit, die Faulheiten	*laziness*
die Freundlichkeit, die Freundlichkeiten	*friendliness*
die Krankheit, die Krankheiten	*illness*
die Minderheit, die Minderheiten	*minority*
die Wahrheit, die Wahrheiten	*truth*

5. International nouns ending in *–ion*

die Globalization, no plural	*globalization*
die Mission, die Missionen	*mission*
die Nation, die Nationen	*nation*
die Revolution, die Revolutionen	*revolution*

6. Female nouns of agent formed by adding *–erin* to a male agent

die Lehrerin, die Lehrerinnen	*female teacher*
die Pilotin, die Pilotinnen	*female pilot*
die Berichterstatterin, die Berichterstatterinnen	*female newscaster*
die Schifahrerin, die Schifahrerinnen	*female skier*

7. Nouns ending in *–ei* or *–ie*

die Bäckerei, die Bäckereien	*bakery*
die Bücherei, die Büchereien	*library*
die Drogerie, die Drogerieen	*drug store*
die Fahrerei, no plural	*driving around, excess driving*
die Geographie, no plural	*geographie*
die Molkerei, die Molkereien	*dairy*
die Philosophie, die Philosophien	*philosophy*
die Spielerei, die Spielereien	*ridiculous games*

8. Nouns ending in *–ik*

die Fabrik, die Fabriken	*factory*
die Musik, die Musiken	*music*
die Physik, no plural	*physics*
die Problematik, no plural	*problemlatics*
die Technik, die Techniken	*technique*

9. Nouns ending in foreign suffixes (*–elle, –ette, –ine, –itis*, et al.)

die Aquarelle, die Aquarellen	*water color painting*
die Arthitis, no plural	*arthritis*
die Etikette, die Etiketten	*etiquette*
die Kriegsmarine, die Kriegsmarinen	*navy*
die Serviette, die Serviette	*table napkin*

10. Nouns of foreign origin ending in *–ät*. This ending is equivalent to the English *–ty*.

die Anonymität, no plural	*anonymity*
die Fakultät, die Fakultäten	*faculty*
die Minorität, die Minoritäten	*minority*

11. Numbers

die Eins, die Einsen	*one*
die Zwei, die Zweien	*two*

c. Neuter Nouns usually include

1. Nouns which end in the diminutive *–chen* or *–lein*. These two suffixes may be added along with an *umlaut* to most nouns and/or personal names to create the diminutive. When added to a noun, *–chen* and *–lein* equal the English *–y* (Bobby, Susie, et al.)

das Blümchen, die Blümchen	*little blossom, flower*
das Büchlein, die Büchlein	*little book*
das Fräulein, die Fräulein	*miss, unmarried young lady*
das Kindchen, die Kindchen	*little child*
das Mädchen, die Mädchen	*girl*
das Röslein, die Röslein	*small, mini rose*

2. Names of children and baby animals

das Baby, die Babys or Babies	*baby*
das Hündchen, die Hündchen	*puppy*
das Kätzchen, die Kätzchen	*kitten*
das Kind, die Kinder	*child*
das Mädchen, die Mädchen	*girl*
das Tierchen, die Tierchen	*little animal*

3. Collective nouns beginning with *Ge-*

das Gebäck, die Gebäcke	*pastry, baked goods*
das Gebäude, die Gebäude	*building*
das Gepäck, no plural	*luggage*
das Geräusch, die Geräusche	*noise*
das Geschwister, die Geschwister	*sibling*

das Gewitter, die Gewitter	*thunder and lightning storm*
das Gewicht, die Gewichter	*weight*

4. Nouns that end in *–nis*

das (Schul)zeugnis, die (Schul)zeugnisse	*report card*
das Bedürfnis, die Bedürfnisse	*need*
das Erlaubnis, die Erlaubnisse	*permission*
das Erlebnis, die Erlebnisse	*experience*
das Verhältnis, die Verhältnisse	*relationship*

5. Nouns that end in *–tum*

das Brauchtum, die Brauchtümer	*customs, traditions*
das Datum, die Daten	*date*
das Eigentum, die Eigentümer	*private property*
das Irrtum, die Irrtümer	*mistake, error*
das Wachstum, die Wachstümer	*growth*

6. Most nouns ending with the foreign suffixes *-ett, -il, -in, -ium, -ma, -ment,* and *-um.*

das Bankett, die Banketten	*banquet*
das Dogma, die Dogmen	*dogma*
das Kriterium, die Kriterien	*criterion*
das Museum, die Museen	*museum*
das Sonett, die Sonette	*sonnet*
das Studium, die Studien	*course of studies*

7. Numerical nouns, fractions, that always end in *–(s)tel* (-th in English)

das Drittel, die Drittel	*third*
das Viertel, die Viertel	*fourth*
das Fünftel, die Fünftel	*fifth*
das Siebtel, die Siebtel	*seventh*
das Zwanzigstel, die Zwanzigstel	*twentieth*
das Hundertstel, die Hundertstel	*hundredth*

NOTE: The above are fractions (one third, a fifth, etc.). The adjectival (ordinal) form of the number (third, fourth, fifth, etc.) is *erst-, zweit-, dritt-, viert-, fünft-, sechst-, siebt-, acht-, neunt-, zehnt-, elft-, zwölft-, dreizehnt-*. Below 20 a -t is added to the number to form an ordinal, *-tel* to form a fraction. Above 20 an *-st* is added to form an ordinal, *-stel* to a fraction: *zwanzigst-, einundzwanzigst-, dreißigst-, hundertst-*. Ordinals take adjective endings depending upon their use in the sentence. (See page 142).

8. Names of the Alphabet

das A, die As	*A*
das B, die Bs	*B*

ÜBUNG A   **Das Austauschprogramm.** Jennifer and James are two Americans who are in Germany on an exchange program. They have a number of stickers with nouns on them to help prepare them for things and situations they will encounter during their exchange. Unfortunately there are no articles with the nouns. Use the gender rules on pages 113–119 to fill in the articles.

EXAMPLE: _der_   Löffel

1. _____ Bäckerei

2. _____ Gebäck

3. _____ Häuschen

4. _____ Dose

5. _____ Gemütlichkeit

6. _____ Religion

7. _____ Arbeitsgemeinschaft

8. _____ Universität

9. _____ Reichtum

10. _____ Getränk

11. _____ Hähnchen

12. _____ Neuankömmling

13. _____ Quarz

14. _____ Hobby

15. _____ Bildnis

16. _____ Tornado

17. _____ Kuss

18. _____ Diskette

19. _____ Rollmops

20. _____ Erfrischung

ÜBUNG B   **Die Bruchzahlen.** Write the following fractions into German words.

1. 1/16 _____

2. 3/4 _____

3. 5/8 _____

4. 7/12 _____

5. 9/20 _____

6. 1/2 _____

7. 2/3 _____

8. 1/100 _____

3.   Noun Case

Nouns change their case depending upon their use in a sentence.

a. A noun is in the nominative case if:

1. It is the subject of the sentence, i.e. it performs the action of the verb.

Karnevalfestivitäten beginnen jedes Jahr offiziell am elften November um 11.11 Uhr.

Carnival festivities begin each year officially on Nov. 11th at 11:11 AM.

2. It follows a linking verb (verb of being) and is the same as the subject.

Der Donnerstag vor Karneval heißt Weiberfastnacht.

3. The noun is being directly spoken to.

Mein lieber Freund, wie feiern wir Karneval dieses Jahr?

My dear friend, how are we celebrating Carnival this year?

ÜBUNG C   **Der Karneval.** Jennifer and James visit Mainz, one of the premier Karneval cities of Germany. Fill in the blanks to understand their report. If you're unsure, write the GNC of each noun underneath it.

Mainz ist eine schön_____ Stadt am Rhein. D_____ Dom ist über eintausend Jahre alt. Wir

finden den Domplatz sehr schön. D_____ Gutenbergmuseum ist am Domplatz. D_____

alt_____ Drucker ist in dem Museum. D_____ Gutenbergstadt ist sehr interessant. D_____

Karneval heißt in Mainzer Dialekt Fassenacht.

b. The noun is in the dative case if

1. The noun is an indirect object, i.e. it is not preceded by a preposition and answers the question to whom, for whom or from whom or what.

2. The noun is the object of a dative verb. A list of dative verbs can be found on page 190.

3. The noun follows a dative preposition as its object. Dative prepositions include;

aus	*from, out of*
außer	*except for, besides*
bei	*at, near, at the home of*
*gegenüber	*across from, opposite*
mit	*with, by*
nach	*after, to, toward*
seit	*since (temporal), for*
von	*of, from, by*
zu	*to*

*gegenüber is usually used after its object

4. The noun follows a two-way preposition and shows location. It answers the question where.

an	*at, on, at the edge of, to*
auf	*at, to, on, on top of*
hinter	*behind*
in	*in, into*
neben	*next to, near*
über	*over, across, about, above*
unter	*under, among*
vor	*in front of, before, ago*
zwischen	*between*

5. The noun is followed by a dative adjective. A complete list of dative adjectives can be found on page 191.

c. The noun is in the accusative case if

1. The noun directly receives the action of the verb, i.e. it is the direct object of the sentence.

2. The noun follows an accusative preposition as its object.

**bis	*until, to, by*
durch	*through, by*
für	*for*
gegen	*against, for*
ohne	*without*

um   *around, for; at (time)*

*entlang   *along*

*entlang is often used after rather than before its object

**bis is often used in combination with a second preposition. If that is the case, the second preposition determines the case of its object.

3. The noun follows a two-way preposition and answers the question "where to."

4. The noun is not accompanied by a preposition and answers the question when or "how much." This is referred to as an adverbial objective.

ÜBUNG D   **Die Fastnacht.** You are interested in the celebration of *Fastnacht* in Mainz. You are doing some research online for a class presentation. Use your notes to write out your presentation.

EXAMPLE: D____ Tradition / von Fastnacht / vor / d____ 16. Jahrhundert / beginnen
Die Tradition von Fastnacht hat vor dem 16. Jahrhundert begonnen.

1. d____ modern____ Fastnacht / mit / d____ Gründung / von / d____ Mainzer *Carnevalsverein* (MCV) / in / d____ Jahr 1838 / anfangen

   _____

2. viel____ Leute / glauben // dass / Fastnacht / ein____ groß____, monatelang____ Party / sein

   _____

3. es / in / d____ Stadt Mainz / jeden Tag / viel____ Umzüge / geben

   _____

4. D____ Party / an / d____ Rosenmontag / mit / ein____ organizierten Umzug / anfangen

   _____

5. d____ Teilnehmer / an / d____ Umzüge____ / Narren (Fools) / heißen // und / sehr / bunt / angezogen / sein.

   _____

d. The Genitive Case

Nouns are in the genitive case if

1. The noun shows possession, i.e. it answers the question whose and is not part of a prepositional phrase.

2. The noun follows a genitive preposition as its object. Genitive prepositions include:

(an)statt	*instead of*
außerhalb	*outside of, with the exception of*
innerhalb	*within, inside of*
trotz	*in spite of, despite*
während	*during, in the course of*
wegen	*because of*

NOTE: In spoken German the dative case is increasingly replacing the genitive after the above prepositions. The genitive is still used in written expression, and is always used when showing possession.

| ÜBUNG E | **Die Fastnachtspläne.** You write your friend a short e-mail making suggestions for your planned *Fastnacht* celebrations. |

EXAMPLE: trotz / das schlechte Wetter / wir / mitmachen
Trotz des schlechten Wetters machen wir mit.

1. während / der Tag / wir / viele kleine Umzüge / sehen / können

   _____

2. letztes Jahr / Markus / innerhalb / eine Stunde / sechs verschiedene Umzüge / sehen

   _____

3. ich / trotz / meine Krankheit / zu den großen Umzügen / hingehen / dürfen

   _____

4. wegen / meine Krankheit / ich /aber / nicht zu spät / auf d_____ Strasse / dürfen / bleiben

   _____

5. außerhalb / ein kleines Husten / es / mir / gut / gehen

   _____

4.   Choosing the Correct Form of the Article

Once the GNC of a noun has been determined, the correct definite or indefinite article can be found in the tables below.

DEFINITE ARTICLES				
	SINGULAR			PLURAL
	MASCULINE	FEMININE	NEUTER	
NOMINATIVE	der	die	das	die
DATIVE	dem	der	dem	den + n
ACCUSATIVE	den	die	das	die
GENITIVE	des + (e)s	der	des + (e)s	der

INDEFINITE ARTICLES				
	SINGULAR			PLURAL
	MASCULINE	FEMININE	NEUTER	
NOMINATIVE	ein	eine	ein	keine
DATIVE	einem	einer	einem	keinen + n
ACCUSATIVE	einen	eine	ein	keine
GENITIVE	eines + (e)s	einer	eines + (e)s	keiner

ÜBUNG F **Die Fastnacht in Mainz.** Jennifer and James continue their story about Mainz and *Karneval*. Fill in the blanks with the correct endings.

D_____ Karneval in Mainz ist ein_____ groß_____ Fest. D_____ bunt_____ Umzüge

sind unglaublich. Jeder Narr trägt ein_____ Maske. D_____ Narren spielen Musik während

sie durch d_____ eng_____ Strassen marschieren. Narren auf d_____ Flößen (floats)

werfen d_____ Zuschauern Bonbons zu. D_____ glücklich_____ Zuschauer stehen auf

_____ Bürgersteig, fangen Bonbons, singen mit, und klatschen. Während ein_____ Umzug

lässt d_____ Polizei kein_____ Autoverkehr durchfahren. Es ist ein_____

wunderbar_____ Straßenfest.

ÜBUNG G **Ein Karnevalerlebnis.** Imagine that you were at a *Karneval* or *Fasching* celebration in Germany. Write a short story about what you saw and did. To get more information you may want to do an Internet search for the *Karneval* celebrations in Köln, Mainz, Bremen, or Aachen. Cities in the South with distinctive *Fasching* celebrations are Rottweil, Freiburg and München.

_____

_____

_____

_____

_____

_____

CHAPTER 15
Compound Words in German

1. Foreign Words in German

Languages have different conventions for creating new words. Over the years English has either just assimilated the foreign word into the language or created a new one from Greek, Latin, and sometimes French roots. German has traditionally turned to its own language. The difference is easy to see by examining terms within the medical profession.

Frauenarzt	*gynecologist*	**Krankenhaus**	*hospital*
Zahnärztin	*dentist*	**Krankenwagen**	*ambulance*

NOTE: Recent globalization has increased the number of foreign words being assimilated directly into German, but in almost all cases, a German-based equivalent has also been created. The DUDEN Verlag and more recently the Institut für Deutsche Sprache, both in Mannheim, are considered the authorities in determining spelling, gender, and proper pronunciation of the new words.

ÜBUNG A **Der Hausarzt.** Match names for the following health professionals in German. If you haven't had much experience with doctors, you may discover that the German is easier to understand than the English.

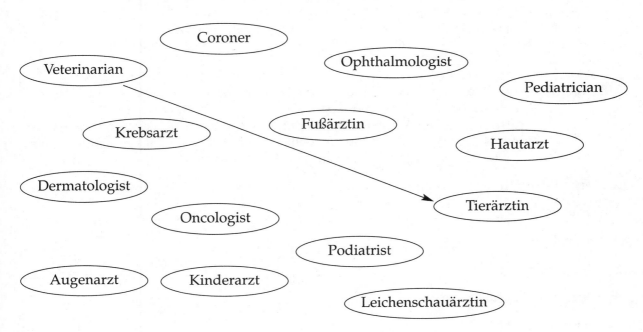

2.   Deciphering Compound Words

Compounding words, i.e. adding word or word stems together to form a new one, is common in German. The result is a long word, but one which readily conveys its meaning.

Sphygmomanometer ⟶ *sphygmo* = pulse in Greek

manus = hand in Latin

metron = a measure in Greek

er = agent-ending (agent = person doing action)

Bonus Question: What do you think a sphygmomanometer is? _____

Blutdruckmesser ⟶ *Blut* = blood in German
Druck = pressure in German
mess(en) = to measure in German
er = agent-ending

Bonus Question: What do you think a *Blutdruckmesser* is? _____

What is its article? _____

What is its plural? _____

Which word was easier to understand: "sphygmomanometer" or *Blutdruckmesser*? Which conveys better the function of a sphygmomanometer? Using compound nouns is often easier in German than in English. The last word in the compound determines its gender and the way it forms its plural.

Deciphering a compound word is just as easy. Words should be read from right to left, i.e. backwards. The genitive –s is often used as a connector. It translates as "of."

Bahn + hof + s + fund + büro⟶ *the lost and found office in the train station*
train   courtyard of   found/find office   *Bahnhofsfundbüro*
    train station   (lost and) found

ÜBUNG B   **Eine Wortschatzherausforderung.** You've accepted a vocabulary challenge. Without looking at a dictionary, write what you think these common words mean in English. A translation is not necessary, just a description of what the item is. Use your vocabulary as well as your knowledge of separable prefixes and their meanings. Guess what you think the article and plural will be.

EXAMPLE: Fundbüro   found office = lost and found   neuter   pl. = Fundbüros

1. Fernsprecher _____

2. Antibabypille _____

3. Klarsichtfolie _____

4. Feuerschutzalarmanlage _____

5. Tintenfisch _____

6. Stinktier _____

7. Lebensversicherung _____

8. Schulabschlussfeier _____

9. Selbstbildnis _____

10. Winterausverkauf _____

ÜBUNG C   **Du bist dran!** Now it's your turn. Create a single German word to express the following in English. Suggest an article and plural for your new word.

EXAMPLE: Interior Designer (*fem.*)   die Innenarchitektin, die Innenarchitektinnen

1. Newspaper article _____

2. Annual report _____

3. Cover charges _____

4. Motorcycle _____

5. World record _____

ÜBUNG D   **Ein Wettspiel.** With a partner or alone create 5 compound words that you think might be real words in German. Assign it an article and plural. Then look up the words in the dictionary or online or submit them to your teacher. How many did you get correct?

EXAMPLE: Jahresendefilmvorführung   End of the Year Film Showing

1. _____

2. _____

3. _____

4. _____

5. _____

3.   Creating a Noun from a Verb

a. Agents

An agent is someone who does something. Agents can be usually be created from German verbs by adding *–er* to the stem for a male or *–erin* for a female. If the vowel in a single-syllable verb stem can take an *umlaut*, it usually will.

kaufen	der Käufer	die Käuferin	*buyer, purchaser*
fahren	der Fahrer	die Fahrerin	*chauffeur*
angeben	der Angeber	die Angeberin	*braggart*
tun	der Täter	die Täterin	*the perpetrator, person who performed the act*

ÜBUNG E   **Was macht wer?** Create agents from the following verbs and write sentences using the new words.

EXAMPLE: backen   Der Bäcker kann ein gutes Graubrot backen.

1. denken _____

2. fressen _____

3. springen _____

4. sprechen _____

5. tragen _____

ÜBUNG F   **Die Berufe!** What would you call the following people?

EXAMPLE: Der Junge, der Schuhe im Flughafen putzt   Ein Schuhputzer

1. Der Mann, der Antiquitäten sammelt _____

2. Ein Vampir, der Blut saugt _____

3. Eine Frau, die das Wetter im Fernsehen voraussagt _____

4. Eine Frau, die das Geschirr im Restaurant spült _____

ÜBUNG G   **Die Tiere.** What do you think the following animals are called in English? Try to figure them out from the word "building blocks" rather than resorting to a dictionary.

1. Stinktier _____   6. der Menschenaffe _____

2. Schlaftier _____   7. der Hundertfüßer _____

3. Eisbär _____   8. das Nilpferd _____

4. Rennpferd _____   9. der Stachelschwein _____

5. Ameisenesser _____   10. die Klapperschlange _____

b. Gerunds

Many nouns in English are formed by adding –ing to the verb. The resulting -ing nouns are called gerunds and refer to the act of doing something.

(The act of) Eating too much is not healthy. **Zu viel Essen ist nicht gesund.**

(The act of) Running is a popular form of exercise nowadays. I like running.

Rennen ist heutzutage eine populäre Form der Übung. Ich mag Rennen.

Creating a gerund in German is even easier than in English. The infinitive of the verb is used as a neuter noun. When used in a sentence, the article *das* is often omitted.

rennen	**das Rennen**	*racing*
trinken	**das Trinken**	*drinking*
schneiden	**das Schneiden**	*cutting*
laufen	**das Laufen**	*running, walking*

ÜBUNG H | **Gesund leben macht fit.** For a health class project, you are making a list of activities which are good for students and those which are bad. This list will be posted in the health classes in your school. Using the word prompts, compile a list of activities you've noticed in your fellow students. Create a sentence for each that demonstrates whether you think the activity is positive or negative. When you are finished, add one healthy and one unhealthy activity to the list. Create sentences for the activities you add. Make sure you use the correct GNCs in all sentences.

EXAMPLE: Rauchen / deine Gesundheit / schaden   Rauchen schadet deiner Gesundheit

1. zu viel / Trinken / deine Reaktionszeit / verlangsamen

_____

2. grünes Gemüse / Essen / dein Körper / wertvoll / Vitamine / geben

_____

3. tägliches Joggen / fit / machen

_____

4. genug / Schlafen / deine Arbeit / in / die Schule / helfen

_____

5. Zu viel / unter / eine Sonnenlampe / Liegen / gefährlich / sein / können

_____

6. _____

7. _____

c. Single-Syllable Nouns from Verb Stems

The stem of many verbs can be used to create a masculine, single-syllable word. Usually such words can stand alone. Often they are used as building blocks in compound words.

> **fallen** ⟶ **der Fall**   fall   **Der Fall des dritten Reiches kam mit dem Tod von Hitler.**
> *The fall of the third Reich came with the death of Hitler.*
>
> **trinken** ⟶ **der Trank** potion **Romeo hat den Liebestrank getrunken.**
> *Romeo drank the love potion.*

NOTE: Verbs can be created from any of the principle parts of the verb.

| ÜBUNG I | **Den Verbstamm finden.** It is important, when deciphering long, German words, that one be able to recognize noun-from-verb constructions. What German words can you identify from the following German nouns? Circle the building blocks that come from verbs. What do you think the words mean? |

EXAMPLE: Fußgängerzone Foot +(go)+ er (agent) + zone = pedestrian zone

1. Ringkämpfer: Sumo Ringkämpfer haben einen massiven, runterhängenden Bauch.

   _____

2. Hörschwierigkeiten: Wegen Hörschwierigkeiten trägt er ein Hörgerät in jedem Ohr.

   _____

3. Zusammenbruch: Der finanzielle Zusammenbruch der Firma begann im Jahre 2004.

   _____

4. Soloflugstunden: Ein Pilot muss mindestens 30 Soloflugstunden, bevor er seinen Flugschein bekommen kann.

   _____

5. Terroristenangriff: Der schlimmste Terroristenangriff in neuester Zeit fand am 11.9. 2001 in New York City statt.

   _____

Bonus Question:

One of the longest and most famous compound words in German is:

Donaudampfschiffahrtsgesellschaftskapitaenskajütenschuhputzjunge

Can you guess what it means?

_____

CHAPTER 16
Adjectives and Adverbs
Ordinal Numbers
dasselbe vs. *das gleiche*

1.   Adjectives

An adjective is a word that modifies a noun. It agrees with that noun in gender, number and case (GNC).

Ich sah jenes tolle, farbenreiche Hundertwasser Haus in der malerischen Stadt Wien.
NSA   FSD

I saw that great, colorful Hundertwasser House in the picturesque city Vienna.

COMPARISON OF WEAK, STRONG, AND MIXED ADJECTIVE ENDINGS								
		SINGULAR					PLURAL	
		MASCULINE		FEMININE		NEUTER		
Nom	weak	der	alt-e	die	alt-e	das	alt-e	die alt-en
	mixed	ein	alt-er	eine	alt-e	ein	alt-es	keine alt-en
	strong		alt-er		alt-e		alt-es	alt-e
Dat.	weak	dem	alt-en	der	alt-en	dem	alt-en	den alt-en
	mixed	einem	alt-en	einer	alt-en	einem	alt-en	keinen alt-en
	strong		alt-em		alt-er		alt-em	alt-en
Acc.	weak	den	alt-en	die	alt-e	das	alt-e	die alt-en
	mixed	einen	alt-en	eine	alt-e	ein	alt-es	keine alt-en
	strong		alt-en		alt-e		alt-es	alt-e
Gen.	weak	des	alt-en	der	alt-en	des	alt-en	der alt-en
	mixed	eines	alt-en	einer	alt-en	eines	alt-en	keiner alt-en
	strong		alt-en		alt-er		alt-en	alt-er

a. Weak Adjective Endings

Adjectives sandwiched between a definite article (*der / die / das*) or a demonstrative adjective and a noun take weak adjective endings.

WEAK ADJECTIVE ENDINGS after a DEMONSTRATIVE ADJECTIVE			
	SINGULAR		PLURAL
	MASCULINE	FEMININE	NEUTER	
NOMINATIVE	dieser rot-e	diese rot-e	dieses rot-e	diese rot-en
DATIVE	diesem rot-en	dieser rot-en	diesem rot-en	diesen rot-en
ACCUSATIVE	diesen rot-en	diese rot-e	dieses rot-e	die jung-en
GENITIVE	diesen rot-en	dieser rot-en	dieses rot-en	dieser rot-en

Demonstrative adjectives include:

dieser – *this, these*   ***mancher** – *some*

jener – *that, those*   ***solcher** – *such a, such*

jeder (plural alle)–   **welcher** – *which*

each, every (plural all)   *used most often in plural

ÜBUNG A   **Das Hundertwasser Haus.** You're visiting Vienna and standing in front of the extremely colorful *Hundertwasser Haus*, one of Vienna's most famous tourist attractions. Supply the adjective endings that are missing.

D<u>as</u> bunt<u>e</u>, exotisch<u>e</u> Hundertwasser Haus liegt in d<u>em</u> ruhig<u>en</u> dritt<u>en</u> Bezirk dies_____

NSN   MSD

schön_____ Stadt Wien. D_____ bekannte Architekt von dies_____ exotisch_____ Haus heißt

Friedensreich Hundertwasser. In dies_____ ungewöhnlich_____ Haus gibt es 52 bunt_____

Wohnungen. All_____ Einwohner fühlen sich glücklich, dass sie in dies_____ herrlich_____,

weltbekannt_____ Bau leben dürfen. Manch_____ Einwohner leben seit d_____

erst_____Eröffnungstag am 15. Oktober 1986 in dies_____ kunstreich_____ Wohnung_____.

Dies_____ toll_____ Wohnung besteht aus Kurven und rund_____ Formen. Dass es fast ohne

ein_____ echt_____ Ecke gebaut wurde, macht d_____ künstlerisch_____ Haus eines d_____

beliebtest_____ Touristensehenswürdigkeiten in dies_____ herrlich_____ Stadt.

ÜBUNG B   **Friedensreich Hundertwasser.** The *Hundertwasser House* was really different! So colorful! You decide to do some research on this Viennese painter turned architect. Now take your notes and with the help of the tables above write good German sentences for your report.

EXAMPLE: Gemälde von d<u>em</u> berühmt<u>en</u> Künstler Friedensreich Hundertwasser hängen in d<u>em</u> weltbekannt<u>en</u> Kunsthaus Wien in d<u>er</u> Unter<u>en</u> Weißgerberstraße.

1. dies_____ / bekann_____ / Künstler / in / d_____ / österreichisch_____ / Hauptstadt / wurde geboren

   _____

2. jed_____ gut_____ Kunsthistoriker / wissen / dass / d_____ jung_____ Hundertwasser / 1949 / viel_____ Reisen / machen

   _____

3. er / 1952 / d_____ erst_____ Ausstellung / in d_____ Art Club Wien / haben

   _____

4. 1985 / ist / d_____ fantastisch_____, bunt_____ Hundertwasserhaus / in d_____ alt_____ / Hauptstadt / eröffnet wurden

   _____

5. manch_____ / von / d_____ / Gemälde_____man / noch / heute / in / d_____ fantastisch_____ Hundertwasserhaus / man / können / sehen

   _____

6. dies_____ begabt_____ Künstler / im Jahre 2000 / an Bord der „QE2" / auf d_____ Pazifischen Ozean / sterben

   _____

b. Mixed Adjective Endings

Adjectives which follow an indefinite article or possessive adjective take mixed adjective endings.

MIXED ADJECTIVE ENDINGS after an INDEFINITE ARTICLE			
	SINGULAR		PLURAL
	MASCULINE	FEMININE	NEUTER	
NOMINATIVE	ein alt-er	eine alt-e	ein alt-es	meine alt-en
DATIVE	einem alt-en	einer alt-en	einem alt-en	meinen alt-en
ACCUSATIVE	einen alt-en	eine alt-e	ein alt-es	meine alt-en
GENITIVE	eines alt-en	einer alt-en	eines alt-en	meiner alt-en

The words that follow this pattern (see list below) are *ein, kein,* and all the possessive adjectives.

ein	*a, an, one*	**sein**	*his*
kein	*none, not any, no*	**unser**	*our, ours*
mein	*my, mine*	**euer**	*your, yours (informal plural)*
dein	*your, yours (informal singular)*	**ihr**	*their, theirs*
sein	*its*	**Ihr**	*your, yours (formal)*
ihr	*her, hers*		

| ÜBUNG C | **Die Spanische Hofreitschule.** What fun! You were able to get tickets to see the evening performance of the Viennese Spanish Riding School, most commonly known as the Lipizzaner Horses. You took notes as soon as you got home for a report for your German class. Write the sentences for the report. |

EXAMPLE: Die spanisch___ Hofreitschule / ein___ klassisch___ Reitkunst / praktizieren
Die spanische Hofreitschule praktiziert eine klassische Reitkunst.

1. es / ein_____ wunderbar_____ Show / mit / d_____ elegant_____ Reiter _____ / auf

   ihr_____ weiß_____ Pferde_____ / sein

   _____

2. es / ein_____ beeindruckend_____ Programm / sein / / das / ein_____ elegant_____

   Harmonie / zwischen / ein_____ Reiter / und / sein_____ Pferd / zeigen

   _____

3. d_____ ganz_____ Programm / in / ein_____ prächtig_____ Barockhalle / in / Wien /
   stattfinden

   _____

4. Eintrittskarte / für gut_____ Plätze / an ein_____ Samstagabend / über 100 Dollar
   /können / kosten

   _____

5. ich / ein_____ wunderbar_____ Sitzplatz / haben

   _____

| ÜBUNG D | **Die Lipizzaner Pferde.** You were really impressed with the Lipizzaner horses. After you returned from the Spanish Riding School performance you looked up their story on the Internet. Your printed version got wet from a spilled glass of water. Fill in the blanks to make the report legible again. |

Im Jahre 1572 wurde eine Spanische Reitschule in Wien gegründet. D_____ Lipizzaner ist ein

Spanisch_____ Pferderasse. Deswegen heißt die Schule d_____ Spanisch_____ Reitschule.

Lipizzaner waren die beliebtest_____ Pferde zu der Zeit. 1735 war d_____ Bau von ein_____

schön_____ Barockhalle fertig. Die Winterreitschule existiert bis heute in dies_____ Gebäude.

Hier kann man immer ein_____ interessant_____ Programm mit d_____ Lipizzanern sehen.

| ÜBUNG E | **Die Lipizzaner in den USA.** You were amazed to discover that there are also Lipizzaner horses and a Spanish Riding School in the US. Fill in the blanks to discover more details. |

In d_____ USA gibt es auch jetzt ein_____ klassisch_____ Reitschule mit d_____

Lipizzaner_____. Am Ende d_____ Zweit_____ Weltkrieges haben d_____ amerikanisch_____

General Patton und d_____ österreichisch_____ Oberst Ottmar Hermann die Lipizzaner

zurück nach Wien geführt. Als Andenken daran hat die österreichisch_____ Regierung den

USA einig_____ Pferde geschenkt. Seit 1955 gibt es also in Florida die „Original Herrmann's

Royal Lipizzan Stallions of Austria" geführt immer noch von Ottmar Hermanns Familie. D

Pferde sind alle echt_____ Lipizzaner oder ihr_____ Fohlen. Also, wer nach Myakka City,

Florida hingeht, kann auch ein_____ echt_____ Lipizzaner Show sehen.

c. Strong Adjective Endings

Often adjectives stand alone before the noun with no *der* or *ein* word preceder. In that case, they take the strong adjective endings.

Seit mittelalterlicher Zeit gibt es in Wien einen Chor nur für junge,
FSD   MSA

männliche Sänger.
MPA

Since medieval times there has been a choir in Vienna only for young, male singers.

STRONG ADJECTIVE ENDINGS			
	SINGULAR		PLURAL
	MASCULINE	FEMININE	NEUTER	
NOMINATIVE	alt-er	alt-e	alt-es	alt-e
DATIVE	alt-em	alt-er	alt-em	alt-en
ACCUSATIVE	alt-en	alt-e	alt-es	alt-e
GENITIVE	alt-en	alt-er	alt-en	alt-er

ÜBUNG F | **Eine Tierumfrage.** After seeing the Lipizzaner you and your family discuss what kind of animals you like. Survey your family members and write down the results.

EXAMPLE: Meine Schwester mag weiße Kätzchen.

1. _____
2. _____
3. _____
4. _____
5. _____

| **ÜBUNG G** | **Die Uniform der Reiter.** You have written a description of the Lipizzaner riders. You need to polish the report by checking on the adjective endings and making sure that they are correct. |

EXAMPLE: Die Reiter tragen schön_____ Stiefel.

1. Die Reiter tragen eine Hose aus weiß_____ Hirschleder.

2. Der Oberteil von der Uniform ist aus braun_____ Stoff.

3. Die Stiefel sind aus schwarz_____ Leder.

4. In Wien hat jeder Reiter mindestens zwei schwarz_____ Zweispitzmützen.

5. Die Sporen sind aus verchromt_____ Stahl.

d. City Adjectives

Adjectives formed from the name of a city take an *-er* ending. They do not add additional endings regardless of their use in the sentence.

Die Wiener Sängerknaben singen heute Abend im Konzert mit der Prager Symphonie.

The Viennese Boys Choir is singing this evening in a concert with the Prague Symphony.

| **ÜBUNG H** | **Wo ist das?** Fill in the cities in the correct form. |

EXAMPLE: Die _____ Wolkenkratzer sind weltbekannt. / New York
Die New Yorker Wolkenkratzer sind weltbekannt.

1. Der _____ Bär ist ein Warenzeichen von der deutschen Hauptstadt. / Berlin

2. Wir haben ein Konzert mit den _____ Sängerknaben in den USA gehört. / Wien

3. Der _____ Dom ist über 1000 Jahre alt. / Köln

4. Tausende von Leuten besuchen den _____ Christkindlmarkt. / Nürnberg

5. Man kann bayrische Spezialitäten in dem berühmten _____ Hofbräuhaus essen. / München

2. Using the Adjective as a Noun

If the noun in the sentence is clearly understood without being mentioned (again), it may be eliminated. The correct adjective endings are put on all adjectives. The noun is eliminated and the last adjective before the eliminated noun is capitalized.

Das Wiener Kriminalmuseum ist eines der Besten ~~Kriminalmuseen~~ in der Welt.
                    NSN   NSN   NPG   FSD

The Viennese Museum of Crime is one of the best ~~museums of crime~~ in the world.

In the example above, the words crossed out are used to find the correct endings, but they are eliminated in the final sentence.

| **ÜBUNG I** | **Hat Wien eine gute Universität?** Your friend is asking you questions about Vienna. Answer her in the positive or negative following the patterns below. |

EXAMPLE: Hat Wien eine Universität? / gut
          Ja, sie hat eine sehr Gute. or Nein, sie hat keine.

1. Hat Wien einen Skiberg? / nein _____

2. Hat Wien ein Riesenrad? / sehr groß _____

3. Hat Wien ein Kunsthaus? / sehr gut _____

4. Hat Wien einen Fernsehturm? / nein _____

5. Hat Wien ein tibetanisches Restaurant? / nein _____

3.   Participles – Creating an Adjective from a Verb

A participle is an adjective or adverb created from a form of the verb. There are two ways to accomplish this in German.

a. The present participle is formed by adding *–d* and the appropriate adjective endings to the infinitive of the verb. It is translated into English by – *ing*.

schlafen = infinitive *to sleep* ⟶ **schlafend** = present participle *sleeping*
Schlafende Löwen brüllen nicht. Der brüllende Löwe im Tiergarten hatte Hunger.
Sleeping lions don't roar. The roaring lion in the zoo was hungry.

NOTE: The present participle modifies a noun. It is not part of a verb. "The lion is roaring" is translated as *Der Löwe brüllt.* "The roaring lion" is *der brüllende Löwe*.

| **ÜBUNG J** | **Der Tiergarten Schönbrunn.** in Vienna is the oldest zoo in the world. In 1752 it received its first visitors. While in the zoo you saw many animals. Use the verbs in the list to create present participles and match the present participle used as an adjective to the animal you saw. |

EXAMPLE: <u>Der schlafende</u> Löwe sah sehr niedlich aus.

spielen – fressen – schlafen – zwitschern – schwimmen – gähnen

1. Wir haben ein _____ Nilpferd gesehen und sehr gemocht.

2. Die _____ Affen waren sehr lustig.

3. Ein Mann hat die _____ Seerobben gefüttert.

4. _____ Kleinvögeln waren unheimlich laut.

5. Die Tierwärterin gab einem _____ Tiger rohes Fleisch zu fressen.

> **b.** The past participle, the third principle part of the verb (See chapter 2.) may be used as an adjective. It takes regular adjective endings. In weak verbs the translation into English is –ed. Strong verbs vary according to their third principle part.
>
> > **1.** Weak Verbs
> >
> > **besuchen** (infinitive)⟶ **besucht** (past participle) **visit**⟶ visited
> >
> > **Die meistbesuchte Touristensehenswürdigkeit in Wien ist der Tiergarten Schönbrunn.**
> >
> > *The most visited tourist attraction in Vienna is the Schönbrunn Animal Park.*
> >
> > **2.** Strong Verbs
> >
> > **beginnen** (infinitive)⟶ **begonnen** (past participle) **begin**⟶ begun
> >
> > **Das neubegonnene Wurmsuchenprogramm für Schulkinder ist sehr erfolgreich.**
> >
> > *The newly begun worm search program for school children is very successful.*

| ÜBUNG K | **Der Tiergarten Schönbrunn.** You had the opportunity to visit the zoo today. Fill in the blanks to discover more about it.

EXAMPLE: Im Tierpark gibt es zwei geschenkt<u>e</u> Pandabären von China und ein neugeboren<u>es</u> Elefantenbaby

1. anschauen: Das meist_____ Tier im Tiergarten ist der Elefant.

2. fotografieren: Die meist_____ Tiere in dem Tiergarten Schönbrunn sind die Pandabären.

3. anfliegen: Im Winter gibt es tausende _____ Wildvögel.

4. aufwachsen: Die im Zoo _____ Elefanten sind jetzt fast 30 Jahre alt.

5. bauen: Das 1999 _____ Regenwaldhaus ist eines der Besten der Welt.

4.   Adverbs

Adverbs modify a verb, an adjective, or another adverb. They answer the question "when," "how," "where" and "to what extent." They take no endings.

| ÜBUNG L | **Was die Tiere machen.** You are making up a matching game with cards to help teach your younger sister German. On the back of the cards you have written something about the animals whose pictures are on the other side. Now you need to add adverbs.

EXAMPLE: Der Löwe brüllt <u>sehr laut</u> .

1. Die Pinguine schwimmen _____.

2. Die zwei von China geschenkten Pandabären essen _____.

3. Das neugeborene Elefantenbaby flappt die Ohren _____.

4. Der Eisbär schläft _____.

5. Die Orang-Utans im Tiergarten Schönbrunn können _____ malen und zeichnen.

5.   Comparison of Adjectives and Adverbs

Adjectives and Adverbs have three forms. The positive (good), the comparative (used when comparing two things – better), and superlative (used when comparing more than two things – best).

POSITIVE, COMPARATIVE, AND SUPERLATIVE OF ADJECTIVES AND ADVERBS			
POSITIVE	COMPARATIVE	SUPERLATIVE	ENGLISH
intelligent	intelligenter	der intelligenteste am intelligentesten	intelligent
*alt	älter	der älteste am ältesten	old
*kurz	kürzer	der kürzeste am kürzesten	short
langsam	langsamer	der langsamste am langsamsten	long
schlecht	schlechter	der schlechteste am schlechtesten	bad, worse, worst
schnell	schneller	der schnellste am schnellsten	fast
toll	toller	der tollste am tollsten	super, great

*Adjectives and adverbs which take an *umlaut* in the comparative and the superlative include:

alt	*old*
arm	*poor*
dumm	*dumb*
gesund	*healthy*
groß	*big, tall*
jung	*young*
kalt	*cold*

krank	*sick*
klug	*clever*
lang	*long*
schwach	*weak*
stark	*strong*
warm	*warm*

NOTE: There are a few monosyllabic adjectives which do not take an *umlaut* in the comparative and the superlative forms: any word with *au* (*blau, faul, laut,* etc.) plus *bunt* (colorful), *falsch* (false), *froh* (happy, joyful), *klar* (clear), and *wahr* (true). Almost all others take an *umlaut*.

ÜBUNG M **Die Zootiere.** Using the animals from the zoo write out sentences using the three forms of the adverb or adjective.

EXAMPLE: schnell: Der Tiger läuft schnell. Der Leopard läuft schneller und der Gepard läuft am schnellsten.

1. schön: _____

2. klever: _____

3. interessant: _____

4. langsam: _____

5. toll: _____

POSITIVE, COMPARATIVE AND SUPERLATIVE OF IRREGULAR ADJECTIVES AND ADVERBS			
	COMPARATIVE	SUPERLATIVE	ENGLISH
bald	eher	am ehesten	*soon*
gern	lieber	am liebsten der liebste	*gladly* *the dearest*
groß	größer	am größten der größte	*big, large, tall* *the biggest*
gut	besser	am besten der beste	*good, better, best* *the best*
hoch	höher	am höchsten der höchste	*high* *the highest*
nah	näher	am nächsten der nächste	*near* *the nearest, next*
viel	mehr	am meisten der meiste	*much, more, most* *the most*

| **ÜBUNG N** | **Die Stadt wien ist eine der Schönsten der Welt.** Your Opa has visited Vienna many times and feels that it is the best city in the world. Complete the sentences using words he might use. |

EXAMPLE: Der Stephansdom ist einer der Schönsten (Döme is understood) in der Welt.

NOTE: When **ein** replaces a noun (one..) it must have the gender and number of the noun it replaces and its case is determined by its use in the sentence. In the sentence above, einer is MSN referring to the Stephansdom.

1. Die Schokoladentorte im Hotel Sacher ist / ein / best / in der Welt

   _____

2. Das Riesenrad im Prater ist / ein / hoch / in der Welt

   _____

3. Das Hundertwasserhaus ist / ein / kreativ / in der Welt

   _____

4. Die vier Gasbehälter von 1899 (Wiener Gasometer,) sind /schön / in Europa.

   _____

5. Das Gartenpalais Belvedere ist / ein / schön / in Europa

   _____

| **ÜBUNG O** | **Das Beste von Wien.** You have compiled a list of the biggest, best, etc. in Vienna. Use the notes you have taken to write out the sentences. |

EXAMPLE: die Staatsoper / das (alt) Gebäude / in der Ringstrasse
             Die Staatsoper ist das älteste Gebäude in der Ringstrasse.

1. Die (viel) Leute halten den Stephansdom für die (schön) Kirche der Welt.

   _____

2. Der (hoch) Turm in der Stadt Wien ist der Donauturm mit 230 Metern.

   _____

3. Das Riesenrad in dem Prater in Wien war lange Zeit das (groß) Riesenrad der Welt.

   _____

4. Die spanische Reitschule ist die (gut) Reitschule für klassischen Reitsport.

   _____

5. Die Touristen in Wien besuchen das Schloss Schönbrunn (gern).

   _____

6. Ordinal Numbers

Ordinal numbers are adjectives and take adjective endings. The ordinal numbers from 1–19 must be memorized. Numbers over 19 are easy. *–st* is added to the number plus the appropriate adjective ending. See table below.

ORDINAL NUMBERS					
first	**erster**	eleventh	**elfter**	twenty first	**einundzwanzigster**
second	**zweiter**	twelfth	**zwölfter**	twenty second	**zweiundzwanzigster**
third	**dritter**	thirteenth	**dreizehnter**	thirtieth	**dreißigster**
fourth	**vierter**	fourteenth	**vierzehnter**	fortieth	**vierzigster**
fifth	**fünfter**	fifteenth	**fünfzehnter**	fiftieth	**fünfzigster**
sixth	**sechster**	sixteenth	**sechzehnter**	sixtieth	**sechzigster**
seventh	**siebter**	seventeenth	**siebzehnter**	seventieth	**siebzigster**
eighth	**achter**	eighteenth	**achtzehnter**	eightieth	**achtzigster**
ninth	**neunter**	nineteenth	**neunzehnter**	ninetieth	**neunzigster**
tenth	**zehnter**	twentieth	**zwanzigster**	hundredth	**hundertster**

ÜBUNG P   **Die Feiertage.** Express the following dates in words.

EXAMPLE: Kinder freuen sich jedes Jahr auf den _____ Dezember, den Nikolaustag.

Kinder freuen sich jedes Jahr auf den sechsten Dezember, den Nikolaustag.

1. Der _____ Februar ist der Valentinstag.

2. Weihnachten ist am _____ Dezember.

3. Der _____ Februar kommt nur alle vier Jahre.

4. Die Iren tragen am _____ März grün.

5. Der letzte Tag im Januar ist der _____.

6. Ich habe am _____ Geburtstag.

7. *dasselbe* versus *das gleiche*

Both *der / die / dasselbe* and *der / die / das gleiche* translate into English as "the same." *Dasselbe* means "exactly the same." *Das gleiche* means "generally the same."

Mozart und Beethoven spielten in derselben Konzerthalle in Wien.

Mozart and Beethoven played in exactly the same concert hall in Vienna.

Wie üblich in den Zeiten, hatten sie die gleichen Perücken auf.

As was the custom in those days, they had the same wigs on.

NOTE: In the first sentence, they played in exactly the same hall. In the second sentence they both had the same wigs on, but not exactly the same one. Mozart did not borrow Beethoven's wig for the concert. He had the same style, possibly even same brand wig, but there are two different wigs in question. If he had had *dieselbe Perücke* on, they'd have been sharing one wig. An easy way to remember this is that *dieselbe* has an s, just like single. If a single person or thing is being discussed, *dieselbe* is correct. If it's general, *die gleiche* (starts with *g*) is used.

ÜBUNG Q	**Opas Wien.** Your Opa is talking about his last visit to Vienna. You answer his statements telling him that you often did the same thing as he did when he was in Vienna. Figure out if you should write a form of *derselbe* or *der gleiche*.

EXAMPLE: Ich habe in einem feinen Restaurant Kronprinz Rudolf gegessen.
Wir haben in demselben Restaurant gegessen.
Ich habe damals viel Sachertorte gegessen. Wir haben die gleiche Torte gegessen.

1. Ich habe in dem Hotel zur Kaffeemühle übernachtet.

   _____

2. Ich habe ein gutes Graubrot zum Frühstück gehabt.

   _____

3. Ich habe Bücher bei der Thalia-Buchhandlung in der Habsburger Hauptstraße gekauft.

   _____

4. Ich habe den Merian Reiseführer in Wien benutzt.

   _____

5. Ich habe Nathan der Weise von Lessing im Burgtheater gesehen.

   _____

ÜBUNG R	**Dein Stadtbesuch.** Now it is your turn to write about a city you have visited. Use as many adjectives as possible and make sure to write about the best or highest or biggest things in this city. Write at least ten sentences. If you prefer you could make up a story about a German, Swiss or Austrian city by using the Internet to get information.

EXAMPLE: Als ich München besucht habe, . . .

_____

_____

_____

CHAPTER 17
Verb-Preposition Combinations
wo(r)- and *da(r)-*Constructions

1. Verb-Preposition Combinations

Verbs are often used in combination with certain prepositions. The combination never varies. One always looks forward *to* something, works *on* something or suffers *from* something. The same is true for German verbs. Some of the more frequently-used combinations are listed below with their prepositions.

2. Verbs used with Dative Prepositions

a. An

arbeiten an + *dat.*	*work on something*
leiden an + *dat.*	*suffer from, be ill with*
leidet, litt, hat gelitten	
sterben an + *dat.*	*die of*
stirbt, starb ist gestorben	

b. Auf

bestehen auf + *dat.*	*insist upon*
besteht, bestand, hat bestanden	

c. Aus

bestehen aus + *dat.*	*consist of*
besteht, bestand, hat bestanden	
entnehmen aus + *dat.*	*take from, infer from*
entnimmt, entnahm, hat entnommen	
schließen aus + *dat.*	*conclude from, assume as a result as*
schließt, schloss, hat geschlossen	

ÜBUNG A | **Robert Koch (1843–1910).** One of the most famous physicians of the 19th century, German Robert Koch discovered the bacillus responsible for several diseases, most notably anthrax, tuberculosis, and cholera. He and his French contemporary Louis Pasteur are considered the two cornerstones of bacteriology even today. Transcribe your notes on this famous scientist.

EXAMPLE: im Jahre 1880 / viele Leute / Lungentuberkulose / sterben an
Im Jahre 1880 sind viele Leute an Lungentuberkulose gestorben.

1. Robert Koch / jahrelang / eine Heilmethode / arbeiten an

   _____

2. er / glauben // dass / Leute / nicht / die Todeskrankheit Lungentuberkulose / müssen / sterben an

   _____

3. er / seine Arbeit / entnehmen aus // dass / Bakterien / die Erreger / von Tuberkulose / sein

   _____

4. heutzutage / nur wenige Leute / diese Krankheit / leiden an

   _____

    d. Bei

sich bedanken bei + *dat.*	*thank, say thank you to someone*
stehen bei + *dat.*	*support someone, stand by someone*
steht, stand, hat gestanden	

    e. Mit

anfangen mit + *dat.*	*start something, begin with*
fängt an, fing an, hat angefangen	
aufhören mit + *dat.*	*stop doing something*
sich befassen mit + *dat.*	*take on, deal with*
rechnen mit + *dat.*	*count on something (to happen in the future)*
telefonieren mit + *dat.*	*talk with someone on the phone*
übereinstimmen mit + *dat.*	*agree with someone or something*
sich unterhalten mit + *dat.*	*converse with*
unterhält, unterhielt, hat unterhalten	
sich verloben mit + *dat.*	*become engaged to*

ÜBUNG B | **Tuberkulose heutzutage.** Thanks to the work of Koch and others TB is much less of a threat than it was years ago.

EXAMPLE: die Entdeckung / von / die Tuberkulosen-Erreger / eine neue Zeit / anfangen mit
Mit der Entdeckung von den Tuberkulosen-Erregern hat eine neue Zeit angefangen.

1. Koch / dann / die Erreger / von anderen Krankheiten / sich befassen mit

   _____

2. Viele Ärzte / Koch / übereinstimmen mit

   _____

3. Koch / andere Ärzte / sich unterhalten mit

   _____

4. sie / er / stehen bei

   _____

5. Robert Koch / 1905 / für diese Entdeckung / der Nobelpreis / erhalten

   _____

    f. Nach

sich erkundigen nach + _dat._	_inquire about_
fragen nach + _dat._	_ask about_
greifen nach + _dat._	_reach for, grasp for_
greift, griff, hat gegriffen	
riechen nach + _dat._	_smell of_
riecht, roch, hat gerochen	
schmecken nach + _dat._	_taste like_
streben nach + _dat._	_strive for_
suchen nach + _dat._	_look for, search for_

    ⎡ **ÜBUNG C** ⎤ **Die Forschung.** You're in class trying to understand scientific research similar to Koch's. Imagine a conversation between him and an assistant.

Zu viele Leute sterben __an__ Tuberkulose. Wir müssen _____ der Methode suchen, wie

die Krankheit sich verbreitet. Hier haben wir einen verdächtigen Fungus. Er riecht _____

Zwiebel und schmeckt _____ Spinat. Wir erkundigen uns _____ der Ursache von

Tuberkulose und streben immer _____ einem Heilmittel für die tödliche Krankheit.

    g. Von

abhängen von + _dat._	_depend upon_
hängt ab, hing ab, hat abgehangen	
denken von + _dat._	_think about (opinion)_
denkt, dachte, hat gedacht	
sich erholen von + _dat._	_recover from_
erzählen von + _dat._	_tell (a story) about_

halten von + *dat.*	*think about (opinion)*
hält, hielt, hat gehalten	
leben von + *dat.*	*live off, exist from*
sprechen von + *dat.*	*speak about (usually a reminiscence)*
spricht, sprach, hat gesprochen	
träumen von + *dat.*	*dream about*
etwas verstehen von + *dat.*	*know something practical, a skill*
versteht, verstand, hat verstanden	
etwas wissen von + *dat.*	*know something factual*
weiß, wusste, hat gewusst	

ÜBUNG D **Sigmund Freud (1856–1939).** A famous Austrian neurologist is the founder of modern-day psychoanalysis. His theories about dreams and the repression of desires are the foundation of modern psychology. Your friend has taken note for a class presentation about Freud. Help him write good German sentences.

EXAMPLE: Freud / meinen // dass / unsere Träume / eine Geschichte / uns / erzählen von
Freud meint, dass unsere Träume eine Geschichte von uns erzählt.

1. Viele / von / die damaligen Ärzte / seine Ideen / nicht viel /halten von

   _____

2. seine Patienten / ihre Träume / sprechen von

   _____

3. nur / Freud / eine Bedeutung / von / menschliche Träume / suchen nach

   _____

4. er / wollen / wissen // warum / wir / bestimmte Sachen / träumen von

   _____

5. er / immer / eine Antwort / greifen nach

   _____

h. Vor

Angst haben vor + *dat.*	*be afraid of*
hat, hatte, hat gehabt	
fliehen vor + *dat.*	*flee from*
flieht, floh, ist geflohen	
sich fürchten vor + *dat.*	*fear, be afraid of*
sich hüten vor + *dat.*	*guard (oneself) against*
retten vor + *dat.*	*save from*
warnen vor + *dat.*	*warn about*
zittern vor + *dat.*	*shake from (fear, the cold, etc.)*

i. Zu

beitragen zu + *dat.*	*contribute to*
trägt bei, trug bei, hat beigetragen	
gehören zu + *dat.*	*belong to*
gratulieren zu + *dat.*	*congratulate on*
herausfordern zu + *dat.*	*challenge someone to*
neigen zu + *dat.*	*lean toward, tend to*
zwingen zu + *dat.*	*force someone to*
zwingt, zwang, hat gezwungen	

ÜBUNG E   **Unsere Träume.** Your classmates were discussing their feelings about dreams and what they might mean. Use your notes, which got a little mixed up, to write about what they said. Make sure you use the correct case after the pronoun.

EXAMPLE: Wie kann man sich vor einer Neurose hüten?

Melanie hat keine Angst vor	die Traumanalyse
Michael und Maja fürchten sich vor	Angst
Wie kann man sich vor . . . hüten?	die Leute, die sich an ihre Träume nie erinnern
Wenn Janna aufwacht, zittert sie oft vor	Albträume
Manuela gehört zu	schlechte Träumen
Karla warnt alle vor	eine Neurose

1. Melanie hat keine Angst vor _____

2. Michael und Maja fürchten sich vor _____

3. Wie kann man sich vor . . . hüten? _____

4. Wenn Janna aufwacht, zittert sie oft vor _____

5. Mauela gehört zu _____

6. Karla warnt alle vor _____

3. Verbs Used with Accusative Prepositions

a. An

sich anpassen an + *acc.*	*conform to, adapt to*
denken an + *acc.*	*think about, keep in mind*
denkt, dachte, hat gedacht	
erinnern an + *acc.*	*remind*
sich erinnern an + *acc.*	*remember*

glauben an + *acc.*	*believe in*
schreiben an + *acc.*	*write to someone*
schreibt, schrieb, hat geschrieben	
teilnehmen an + *acc.*	*participate in*
nimmt teil, nahm teil, hat teilgenommen	

b. Auf

achten auf + *acc.*	*pay attention to*
antworten auf + *acc.*	*answer*
aufpassen auf + *acc.*	*watch out for*
deuten auf + *acc.*	*point to, often verbally*
sich freuen auf + *acc.*	*look forward to*
hoffen auf + *acc.*	*hope for*
hören auf + *acc.*	*listen to (behavior), obey*
sich konzentrieren auf + *acc.*	*concentrate on*
reagieren auf + *acc.*	*react to*
schießen auf + *acc.*	*shoot at*
schießt, schoss, hat geschossen	
verzichten auf + *acc.*	*deny oneself something, do without*
vorbereiten auf + *acc.*	*prepare for*
sich vorbereiten auf + *acc.*	*prepare (oneself) for*
warten auf + *acc.*	*wait for*
zählen auf + *acc.*	*count on (someone or something happening)*
zeigen auf + *acc.*	*point to (usually physically)*

c. Für

sich begeistern für + *acc.*	*be enthusiastic about*
sich entscheiden für + *acc.*	*decide for*
entscheidet, entschied, hat entschieden	
danken für + *acc.*	*thank for, say thank you for something*
halten für + *acc.*	*consider as, take for*
hält, hielt, hat gehalten	
sich interessieren für + *acc.*	*be interested in*
kandidieren für + *acc.*	*be in the running for an elected office*

ÜBUNG F	**Werner von Braun (1912–1977).** Werner von Braun is a famous German rocket scientist. After the war he was given the opportunity to leave Germany and come to the US. He did so and became known as the "Father of the American Space Program".

EXAMPLE: Am Ende des Krieges / Werner von Braun / eine Zukunft / in / die USA / sich entscheiden für
Am Ende des Krieges hat Werner von Braun sich für eine Zukunft in den USA entschieden.

1. in / die USA / er / eine Arbeit / an / ein Raumfahrtprogramm / sich freuen auf

   _____

2. er / gut / das Leben / in / die USA / sich anpassen an

   _____

3. am Anfang / er / die Raumfahrt / wollen / sich konzentrieren auf

   _____

4. er / aber / Raketen für das Militär / sich beschäftigen mit / müssen

   _____

5. er / nicht / die Arbeit / mit Militärraketen / sich begeistern für

   _____

6. ab 1959 / er / endlich / das Raumfahrtprogramm / dürfen / teilnehmen an

   _____

d. In

sich einmischen in + _acc._	_meddle into_
sich verknallen in + _acc._	_develop a crush on_
sich verlieben in + _acc._	_fall in love with_

e. Über

sich ärgern über + _acc._	_get angry about_
sich beschweren über + _acc._	_complain about (usually a formal complaint)_
denken über + _acc._	_think about, contemplate_
denkt, dachte, hat gedacht	
diskutieren über + _acc._	_discuss_
sich freuen über + _acc._	_be happy about, rejoice over_
sich informieren über + _acc._	_find out about, inform oneself about_
klagen über + _acc._	_complain about (usually informally)_
lachen über + _acc._	_laugh about_
nachdenken über + _acc._	_contemplate, think deeply about, ponder_
denken nach, dachten nach, hat nachgedacht	
sprechen über + _acc._	_speak about (formally, about facts, research)_
spricht, sprach, hat gesprochen	
spotten über + _acc._	_make fun of, mock_
urteilen über + _acc._	_make a judgment about, judge_
verfügen über + _acc._	_have access to something_

ÜBUNG G | **Von Braun und seine Zeit.** In a continuing discussion about Werner von Braun you decide to make a list of things he did or did not do while working for the US and NASA.

EXAMPLE: er / immer / ein Raumfahrtprogramm / denken über
            Er hat immer über ein Raumfahrtprogramm gedacht.

1. er / mit / seine Militär / die Möglichkeit / von solch einem Programm / diskutieren über

   _____

2. die Mitarbeiter / die Neinsager / sich ärgern über

   _____

3. trotzdem / sie / ihre Arbeit / mit Raketen / bei der Armee / sich freuen über

   _____

4. Im Jahre 1958 / er / und seine Mitarbeiter / endlich /mit / die Gründung / von NASA / / die notwendige Mittel / verfügen über

   _____

5. man / Werner von Braun / und / seine Arbeit / im Internet / sich informieren über/ können

   _____

    f. Um

sich bemühen um + *acc.*	*work toward something, strive for*
betteln um + *acc.*	*beg for*
sich bewerben um + *acc.*	*apply for*
bewirbt, bewarb, hat beworben	
gehen um + *acc.*	*concern, be about*
geht, ging, ist gegangen	
sich handeln um + *acc.*	*deal with, be about*
kämpfen um + *acc.*	*fight for*
konkurrieren um + *acc.*	*be in competition for*
sich kümmern um + *acc.*	*look after, take care of*
sich sorgen um + *acc.*	*worry about*
sich Sorgen machen um + *acc.*	*worry about*

ÜBUNG H | **Arnold Schwarzenegger (born July 30, 1947).** Schwarzenegger is a world famous Austrian-American who arrived in the USA in 1968 with little money and almost no knowledge of English. He was a body-builder, became a well-known film star and later a politician who was eventually elected as the 38th governor of California.

EXAMPLE: Arnold / immer / die Mittel / wollen / sich einmischen in
            Arnold wollte sich immer in die Politik einmischen.

1. Am Anfang / er / seine Karriere / sich Sorgen machen um

   _____

2. aber / bald / alle Kritiker / positiv / seine Filme / sprechen über

   _____

3. er / nicht mehr / seine Zukunft und Anerkennung / kämpfen um

   _____

4. 2003 / er / der Gouverneurposten in Kalifornien / sich bemühen um

   _____

5. er / sein Gewinn / sich freuen über

   _____

4.   _wo(r)_-Constructions

Asking a question using one of these verb-preposition combinations is easy. The prefix _wo-_ is added to the preposition to create an interrogative. If the preposition starts with a vowel, then _wor-_ is added.

für was ⟶ **wofür**   _what for, why_

mit was ⟶ **womit**   _with what_

Wonach suchte Robert Koch?   _What was Robert Koch looking for?_

Woran arbeitete Werner von Braun?   _What did Werner von Braun work on?_

| ÜBUNG 1 | **Einige Fragewörter.** You are preparing a celebrity interview. Fill the correct interrogative into these sentences. |

EXAMPLE: Worauf freuen Sie sich meistens?

1. _____ ärgern Sie sich?

2. _____ geht es in Ihrem neuen Film?

3. _____ leidet der Hauptcharakter in dem Film?

4. _____ beschäftigen Sie sich in Ihrer Freizeit?

5. _____ machen Sie sich am meisten Sorgen?

6. _____ denken Sie, wenn Sie allein sind?

7. _____ träumen Sie abends?

8. _____ haben Sie am meisten Angst?

9. _____ verzichten Sie, wenn Sie Diät machen?

10. _____ vorbereiten Sie sich im Moment?

NOTE: The above *wo(r)*-construction can only be used if the expected answer is a thing or a clause. If it is a person, then an interrogative pronoun must be used. See page 163. The interrogative pronouns *wem* (dative) or *wen* (accusative) are used to create similar questions if the expected answer is a person.

ÜBUNG J   **Das Interview geht weiter.** Your interview is continuing, but you are now asking more personal questions. Fill in the preposition with the correct interrogative pronoun *wem* or *wen*.

EXAMPLE: <u>In wen</u> haben Sie sich verliebt?

1. Die Bambi-Preise kommen bald. _____ begeistern Sie sich?

2. Sie dürfen wählen. _____ entscheiden Sie sich?

3. _____ haben Sie sich als Kind zuerst verknallt?

4. Sie tragen einen neuen Ring. _____ sind Sie verlobt?

5. _____ klagen Sie sich am meisten?

6. Sie sind weit von zu Hause. _____ sehnen Sie sich am meisten?

7. _____ spotten Sie meistens, wenn Sie lachen wollen?

8. _____ sprechen Sie morgen bei der Bambi-Verleihung?

5.   *da(r)-* Constructions

A similar construction is available when making a statement. In this case *da-* and *dar-* would be used instead of *wo-* or *wor-*. English once used this construction frequently. Remnants remain in the words thereby, therefore, therewith, thereupon, thereafter, etc. Rather than mention the object of a preposition, the prefix "there" was added to the preposition taking the place of its direct object.

German accomplishes the same goal with *da-* and *dar-*.

with it	*damit*	under it	*darunter*
for it	*dafür*	on top of it	*darauf*

Ich habe einen Bambi gewonnen. Ich komme damit nach Hause.

ÜBUNG K   **Das Interview geht weiter.** Your celebrity is telling you about the film that won her a Bambi in 2002. Rewrite her words using a *da-* or *dar-* construction to substitute for the prepositional phrase.

EXAMPLE: In dem Film bekam ich eine Bambi-Verleihung. Darin spielte ich eine Diva.

1. Ich habe so oft über dieses Thema diskutiert.

---

2. Der Film beschäftigt sich mit einem Skandal.

_____

3. Die Diva wird für eine Mörderin gehalten.

_____

4. Die Polizei wartet auf ein das Resultat eines DNA-Tests.

_____

5. In der Wartezeit verliebte die Diva sich in ein außerirdisches Wesen.

_____

6. Dieses Wesen rettete sie vor einem großen Erdbeben.

_____

7. Sie litt an Durst, und es hat eine Quelle frischen Wassers gefunden.

_____

8. Dort gab es ein wunderschönes Haus, in dem sie lange lebten.

_____

NOTE: The object of the preposition is not always a noun. Sometimes it is a full clause. When that is the case, the preposition is completed with the prefix _da-_ (or _dar_) and then the subordinate clause is added. The _da-_ construction is often translated in English with the phrase "the fact that."

Noun Object of Preposition:　　**Ich kann mich auf meine Mutter verlassen.**
I can depend upon my mother.

Clause Object of Preposition:　　**Ich kann mich darauf verlassen, dass meine Mutter kommt.**
I can depend upon the fact that my mother is coming.

Noun Object of Preposition:　　**Die Mutter sorgt sich um ihr Kind.**
The mother worries about/cares about her child.

Clause Object of Preposition:　　**Die Mutter sorgt sich darum, dass ihr Kind gesund isst.**
Mother worries about/takes care, that her child eats well.

ÜBUNG L　　**Das Interview ist beendet.** Your interview is coming to a close. You found the diva-alien love story rather absurd, but the Bambi nominating committee didn't. It was nominated for Best Picture. You interview your celebrity about her preparations for the big red-carpet event.

EXAMPLE:　Glauben Sie jetzt an außerirdische Wesen?　dass / sie / existieren
Ja, ich glaube daran, dass sie existieren.

1. Womit rechnen Sie? dass / wir / mindestens / einen Preis / gewinnen

_____

2. Worauf hoffen Sie? dass / wir / alle / in allen drei Kategorien / gewinnen

_____

3. Worauf freuen Sie sich? dass / wir / alle / auf der Bühne / stehen / werden

_____

4. Wofür werden Sie sich dann bedanken? dass / die Fans / so treu / bleiben

_____

5. Womit beginnt Ihre Dankrede? dass / ich / meiner Mutter / danken

_____

6. Womit schließt Ihre Dankrede ab? dass / ich den Fans / danken

_____

ÜBUNG M | **Du wirst berühmt.** You too will become famous some day. Write sentences using *da-* constructions and clauses to indicate what you do or avoid doing to work towards a good future. Use your imagination and think also of things that people have said to you. Choose three verbs from this chapter to complete the exercise on your own.

EXAMPLE: aufpassen auf   Ich passe immer darauf, dass ich nie meine Freunde vergesse.

1. sich bemühen um   _____

2. sich informieren über   _____

3. danken für   _____

4. _____

5. _____

6. _____

ÜBUNG N | **Eine berühmte Persönlichkeit.** Choose someone from history whom you admire. Write at least six sentences about this person using at least four of the verb preposition combinations in this chapter. The person you write about should be of German, Swiss, or Austrian descent.

_____

_____

_____

_____

_____

_____

CHAPTER 18
Pronouns and Relative Clauses

1.   Pronouns

A pronoun substitutes for a noun. It agrees with the word it replaces in gender and number. Its case is determined by its use in the sentence.

Der Film „Triumph des Willens" von Leni Riefenstahl ist weltbekannt. Kennst du ihn?
MSN   MSA

The film „Triumph des Willens" by Leni Riefenstahl is known worldwide. Do you know it?

NOTE: The pronoun agrees with the grammatical gender of the noun, which is not always the same as its natural gender. In the sentence above, *Film* is a masculine noun; therefore the masculine pronoun must be used. Literally the translation reads: "The film is well known. Do you know him?"

PRONOUNS				
	NOMINATIVE	DATIVE	ACCUSATIVE	GENITIVE
SINGULAR				
I /me	ich	mir	mich	There is no genitive pronoun. The genitive translates into "of me/him, etc. It is replaced by the possessive pronoun my/mine/his (see below)
you (informal)	du	dir	dich	
he/him	er	ihm	ihn	
she/her	sie	ihr	sie	
it	es	ihm	es	
you (formal)	Sie	Ihnen	Sie	
PLURAL				
we/us	wir	uns	uns	
you informal	ihr	euch	euch	
they/them	sie	ihnen	sie	
you formal	Sie	Ihnen	Sie	

ÜBUNG A | **Leni Reifenstahl.** Riefenstahl was one of modern Germany's most famous film directors, photographers and writers. Complete the second sentence using a pronoun.

EXAMPLE: Leni Reifenstahl wurde 1902 in Berlin geboren. __Sie__ zog im Jahre 1920 nach Zeuthen um.

1. Leni hat Malerei und Zeichnen an der Berliner Kunstakademie studiert, aber _____

   wollte nicht Zeichnerin werden. _____ gefiel das Tanzen viel mehr.

2. Dann hatte sie Probleme mit ihrem Vater. Er hat _____ geärgert, weil _____ es seiner Tochter verbot, Tanzstunden zu nehmen.

3. Leni verließ also 1921 das Haus von ihren Eltern. Jetzt konnte _____ tanzen lernen.

4. Von 1921 bis 1923 hat sie bei der russischen Tänzerin Eugenie Eduardowa Ballet gelernt.

   Von _____ hat sie viel gelernt.

5. Ihre Ballettkarriere dauerte bis 1923. Eine Knieverletzung endete _____.

6. Sie hat „Der Berg des Schicksals", einen Film über zwei Bergsteiger, gesehen.

   _____ faszinierte _____.

ÜBUNG B | **Leni wird Schauspielerin.** Leni found the film about mountain climbing so compelling, that she decided to move to the Alps to learn the skills. Fill in the pronouns.

Leni lebte ein Jahr in den Alpen. Danach suchte Arnold Fanck, den Regisseur von dem Film,

auf und fragte _____, ob _____ in seinem nächsten Film mitspielen dürfe. Er war fasziniert

von _____ und sagte sofort ja. Der Film hieß *Der heilige Berg* und war ein sofortiger Erfolg.

Leni mochte Fanck und hatte noch mehrere Filme mit _____ gemacht. In _____ hat _____

Bergsteigerinnen und Skifahrerinnen gespielt. Es gab keine so athletische Schauspielerin wie

_____. Dann kam einer der entscheidendsten Tage in ihrem Leben. Im Jahre 1933 lernte

_____ Adolf Hitler kennen. _____ fand _____ auch faszinierend. _____ fragt _____, ob

_____ einen kurzen Dokumentarfilm für _____ machen konnte. Das war das Ende ihrer

Schauspielkarriere und der Anfang ihrer Karriere als Regisseurin.

ÜBUNG C   **Was weißt du über Leni Riefenstahl?** You are leading a class discussion about Leni Riefenstahl and her film career. What do you ask the named person(s)? Then write their answer using pronouns rather than repeating the noun. Remember the difference between *kennen* and *wissen*.

EXAMPLE: Margot / den Film *Sieg des Glaubens*
 DU: Margot, kennst du den Film *Sieg des Glaubens*?
 MARGOT: Nein, ich kenne ihn nicht. or Ja, ich kenne ihn.

1. David und Delia / die Geburtsstadt von Leni Reifenstahl

 DU: _____

 DAVID UND DELIA: _____

2. Herr Marzipan / ihr erster Film

 DU: _____

 HERR MARZIPAN: _____

3. Anna / die Schule, wo Leni Kunst studierte

 DU: _____

 ANNA: _____

4. David und Delia / das Kino in Berlin, wo Riefenstahlfilme gezeigt werden

 DU: _____

 DAVID UND DELIA: _____

5. Dagmar / wo Leni das Bergsteigen gelernt hat

 DU: _____

 DAGMAR: _____

2.   Possessive Pronouns

The possessive adjective with strong adjective endings may be used as a pronoun.

Reifenstahl hatte ihre Lieblingsszene in dem Film, und ihr Regisseur hatte seine.
                    FSA   FSA

Reifenstahl had her favorite scene in the movie, and her director had his.

Ich habe meinen Lieblingsfilm von Riefenstahl und Sie haben Ihren.
             MSA   MSA

I have my favorite Riefenstahl film and you have yours.

POSSESSIVE PRONOUNS			
	SINGULAR		PLURAL
	MASCULINE	FEMININE	NEUTER	
NOMINATIVE	**mein-er**	**mein-e**	***mein-es**	**mein-e**
DATIVE	**mein-em**	**mein-er**	**mein-em**	**mein-en**
ACCUSATIVE	**mein-en**	**mein-e**	***mein-es**	**mein-e**
GENITIVE	Genitive means "of the, of my, etc." While there is a possessive adjective (**das Buch seines Vaters**), there is no possessive pronoun in the genitive case.			

NOTE:
*When used as a pronoun, the *–e* is optional in spoken German.
Das Buch ist seins or *seines.*

ÜBUNG D | **Riefenstahl als Sportlerin.** Reifenstahl became an avid skier and mountain climber. Complete the ideas with a possessive pronoun.

EXAMPLE: Herr Marzipan hat seine Lieblingsfilme und ich habe ___Meine___.

1. Leni Reifenstahl hatte ihre Lieblingsschiberge und Arnold Fanck hatte _____.

2. Sie hatte ihren Lieblingsberg zum Steigen und ihr Regisseur hatte _____.

3. Sie ist auf ihren Schiern gelaufen und ich auf _____.

4. Reifenstahl hat Respekt durch ihre sportlichen Leistungen gefunden und die olympischen

    Sportler durch _____.

5. Herr Marzipan hat seinen Lieblingswinterport und wir haben _____.

3.   Relative Clauses Introduced by a Relative Pronoun

A relative pronoun introduces a relative clause, which is a clause that modifies a noun. In the sentence below, the entire clause *that made Leni controversial* modifies *Film.*

Der Film, der Leni kontrovers machte, war *Triumph des Willens.*

The Film, that made Leni controversial, was The Triumph of the Will.

A relative clause tells more about a person, place or thing. It answers the question "which one" after a noun. In the sentences below the director made several films. The logical question is: "Which director?" The relative clause answers that question for the reader. It's the director who made the film *Triumph of the Will.*

No relative clause: **Die Regisseurin hat mehrere Filme gemacht.**

With relative clause: **Die Regisseurin, die den Film *Triumph des Willens*, drehte, hat mehrere Filme gemacht.**

The relative clause answers the question "which one." It is introduced by a relative pronoun (see table below) and comes immediately after the noun it refers to. The relative pronoun, translated as "who," "whom," or "whose," introduces the relative clause and the finite verb is at the end.

RELATIVE PRONOUNS				
	SINGULAR			PLURAL
	MASCULINE	FEMININE	NEUTER	
NOMINATIVE	der	die	das	die
DATIVE	dem	der	dem	denen
ACCUSATIVE	den	die	das	die
*GENITIVE	dessen	deren	dessen	deren

*The genitive is used if the relative pronoun translates as "whose"

Anton Flack ist der Regisseur, der Leni Riefenstahl ihre erste Chance gab.
           MSN   MSN

Anton Flack is the director who gave Leni Riefenstahl her first chance.

Wo ist die Frau, deren Filme so gut sind?
         FSN   FSG

Where is the woman, whose films are so good?

Der letzte Bergfilm, in dem sie spielte, hieß *SOS-Eisberg*.
        MDN   MSD

The last mountain movie, in which she acted, was called SOS-Iceberg.

The pronoun introduces the relative clause and throws the verb to the end of its clause. It agrees with the word it is replacing in gender and number. Its case is determined by its use in the sentence.

ÜBUNG E **Lenis Filme.** You are writing a report about your recent studies of German film and Leni Reifenstahl. You did some research online and took notes in very simple German. Now combine your simple sentences into complex ones using relative pronouns.

EXAMPLE: Leni Reifendstahl ist eine deutsche Filmmacherin. Sie wurde in Berlin geboren.
          Leni Reifendstahl, die in Berlin geboren wurde, ist eine deutsche Filmmacherin.

1. Ich sah einen Film. Der Film war sehr interessant.

   _____

2. Der Film heißt _Triumph des Willens_. Ich mag diesen Film sehr.

   _____

3. Der Mann ist mein Deutschlehrer. Er hat den Film empfohlen.

   _____

4. Wir sahen auch andere Filme. Ihre Themen waren ganz anders.

   _____

5. Leni Reifenstahl wollte in den USA Filme machen. Sie war nach dem Krieg sehr kontrovers.

   _____

| ÜBUNG F | **Ihr Nachkriegsleben.** The next part of your report has to do with Reifenstahl's life after the war. Here you also have to join sentences with relative pronouns to make them interesting and well written. You will have to use the genitive pronoun. |

EXAMPLE: Reifenstahl wurde in der Nachkriegzeit verachtet. Ihr Leben war schwer.
  Reifenstahl, deren Leben schwer war, wurde in der Nachkriegzeit verachtet.

1. Ihre Filme wurden verboten. Die Themen waren vielleicht zu propagandisch.

   _____

2. Ihre Freunde haben ihr geholfen. Die Freunde waren zu der Zeit weltweit.

   _____

3. Im Jahre 1972 machte sie eine olympische Fotoreportage. Die Fotos haben Reifenstahl wieder Anerkennung gewonnen.

   _____

4. In den 70ziger Jahren machte sie viele Reisen. Das Ziel war oft Afrika.

   _____

5. 1973 veröffentlichte sie das Buch _Die Nuba_. Die Fotos haben sie als Fotografin berühmt gemacht.

   _____

6. Ihr letztes Fotobuch hieß _Wunder unter Wasser_. Die Bilder hat sie alle beim SCUBA-Tauchen gemacht.

   _____

7. Ihren 100. Geburtstag feierte sie mit Siegfried und Roy in Las Vegas. Ihre Show mit wilden Tigern ist weltbekannt.

   _____

4. Relative Clauses Introduced by Prepositions

The relative clause is often introduced by a preposition. The relative pronoun then becomes the object of the preposition. The pronoun takes the gender and number of the noun it refers to, and its case is determined by the preposition it follows.

Kennst du den Lehrer, mit dem wir den Film gesehen haben?
  MSN   MSD

Do you know the teacher, with whom we saw the film?

ÜBUNG G | **Notizen von deiner Filmklasse.** You took notes from your film class on your computer. Transcribe them combining sentences using prepositions and relative pronouns.

EXAMPLE: Das ist der Film. Ich habe oft von dem Film oft gesprochen.
            Das ist der Film, von dem ich oft gesprochen habe.

1. Ihr letzter Film war über die Unterwasserwelt. Ich habe von dem Film gehört.

   _____

2. Ihr hundertster Geburtstag fand am 22. August 2002 in Las Vegas statt. Bei dem Geburtstag haben viele berühmte Stars mitgefeiert.

   _____

3. Zwei von den Stars heißen Siegfried und Roy. Sie war mit den Stars befreundet.

   _____

4. Die Tiger sind Albinotiere. Die deutschen Domteure (animal trainers) Siegfried und Roy arbeiten mit den Tigern.

   _____

5. Reifenstahl hatte auch viele Freunde bei der Geburtstagfeier gehabt. Unter den Freunden befanden sich Filmstars, afrikanische Freunde, und amerikanische Filmfans.

   _____

5. Relative Clauses Introduced by a *wo(r)*-Construction

In the above exercises, the relative clause was introduced by a preposition followed by a relative pronoun. If the noun to which the relative pronoun refers is a person, the preposition plus pronoun must be used. However, if the noun to which the relative pronoun refers is a thing, the preposition may be completed with *wo-* or *wor-* (see page 153) and the relative pronoun may be eliminated. The English translation is "which."

Hier ist das Zimmer, in dem unsere Filmstunde stattfindet.

Here is the room in which our film studies class takes place.

OR

Hier ist das Zimmer, worin unsere Filmstunde stattfindet.

In the above example, since a room is a thing and not a person, it is not necessary to use a relative pronoun. Either *in dem* or *worin* would be an acceptable introduction to the relative clause.

ÜBUNG H   Your cousin from Berlin is visiting your school and is excited by your film class. You want to give her a tour in German so you wrote out a script and now you must look up the correct *wo*-construction for your sentences.

EXAMPLE: Hier ist die Bushaltestelle, <u>wobei</u> wir aussteigen sollen.

1. Hier ist der Eingang, _____ wir gehen müssen.

2. Das Lehrbuch, _____ wir viel lesen müssen, heißt *Filme und Filmemacher*.

3. Raum 212 im ersten Stock ist der Raum, _____ wir die Filme anschauen.

4. Wir haben viele alte Filmrollen, _____ man sehr sorgfältig umgehen muss.

5. Hier ist unsere DVD/CD-Sammlung. Wir haben 201 Audio CDs, _____ wir auch DVDs haben.

6.   Relative Clauses which Refer to a Location

If the relative clause refers to a location rather than a person or a thing, it is also not necessary to use a relative pronoun-preposition combination. The single word *wo* can introduce the clause, as long as the noun to which it refers specifies a location. If the noun to which it refers is the proper name of a city, state, country, continent, etc., then wo must be used.

Die Stadt, wo Leni Reifenstahl studierte, heißt Berlin.

The city where Leni Riefenstahl studied is called Berlin.

Hier ist der Raum, wo die Schüler, die sich für Film interessieren, sich treffen.

Here is the room, where students who are interested in film meet.

Germans use both constructions in order to vary their spoken and written language, i.e. sometimes they use the preposition with the relative pronoun to introduce a relative clause. Other times they use *wo, wo-* or *wor-*. In the examples below, both sentences below are correct.

Dort drüben ist das Kino, wo viele Premieren stattfinden.

Dort drüben ist das Kino, in dem viele Premieren stattfinden.

| **ÜBUNG I** | **Deine Fotos.** You've collected some photos and drawings to use for your movie script about two people who meet in a city in Germany. Describe each location and what is happening using the relative pronoun *wo*. |

EXAMPLE: Sie treffen sich hier zum ersten Mal.
Die Stadt, wo sie sich zum ersten Mal treffen, heißt Berlin.

1. Das Mädchen wohnt in diesem Haus mit ihrer alten Mutter. Es hat die Adresse Apfelstraße 14.

_____

2. Die Schule heißt das Keller-Gymnasium. Der Junge ist in der zehnten Klasse.

_____

3. Das Kino heißt das Palast Kino. Das Paar will in diesem Filmhaus einen Film sehen.

_____

4. Der Park hat schöne Wege. Das Paar spaziert hier gerne.

_____

5. Die Bushaltestelle ist an der Ecke. Der Junge wartet stundenlang hier.

_____

7.   The Relative Pronoun *was*

Often the relative pronoun refers to the whole clause and not to an individual element in that clause.

Der Junge wollte mit dem Mädchen ausgehen, was die Mutter für unmöglich hielt.
The boy wanted to go out with the girl, which the mother thought impossible.

Werner hat vier Filme diese Woche angesehen, was er doch wunderbar findet.
Werner saw four films this week, which he finds wonderful.

In both the sentences above the relative pronoun was refers to the whole clause. What the mother thought impossible was the idea that the boy would go out with the girl and what Werner finds wonderful is the fact that he saw four films this week.

| ÜBUNG J | **Was?** What do your family members and relatives think about the following ideas? Use *was* to introduce the clause in which you write what they think. Vary your answers. |

EXAMPLE: In der Filmstunde sehen wir viele Filme. Was denkt dein Vater?
         In der Filmstunde sehen wir viele Filme, was mein Vater gut findet.

1. Viele von diesen Filmen sind auf Deutsch. Wie reagiert deine Deutschlehrerin?

   _____

2. Oft müssen wir samstags ins Kino gehen. Was sagt deine Schwester dazu?

   _____

3. Es kostet uns viel Geld. Was meint deine Oma?

   _____

4. Wir diskutieren die Filme stundenlang. Und dein Bruder. Was sagt er?

   _____

5. Ich möchte auch Film an der Uni studieren. Wie gefällt das deiner Mutter?

   _____

8.   Using the Relative Clause

The relative clause, more than any other German construction, adds flavor and life to a narrative. It defines and describes people, places and things.

Simple Sentence: **Der ältere Junge will mit dem Mädchen ausgehen.**
                                       The older boy wants to go out with the girl.

Sentence with Relative Clause: **Der ältere Junge, den die Mutter wirklich nicht gern hat, will mit dem Mädchen ausgehen.**
                                       The older boy, whom the mother really does not like, wants to go out with the girl.

The second sentence takes a straightforward, dry sentence and gives it a personality.

ÜBUNG K   **Junge lernt Mädchen kennen.** You're writing a film story proposal for your film class in German. Your teacher has told you to write about things you know. You've finished the basic outline. Now you have to add flavor. Add at least one relative clause to each sentence, so that the end result is a unified, interesting story with personality. You may add additional elements or sentences in creating your story.

1. Der Junge kam in das Zimmer.

   _____

2. Er sah das Mädchen.

   _____

3. Der Junge wollte mit dem Mädchen in den Park gehen.

   _____

4. Ihre Mutter war in dem Zimmer.

   _____

5. Die Zwei gingen dorthin.

   _____

6. Am Samstag sahen sie sich in der Stadt.

   _____

7. Jetzt.....

   _____

CHAPTER 19

Negation
doch – Review
Flavor Words
Exclamations

1. Negation

One of the most common ways of answering a question in the negative is to use the word *nein*.

War Johanna Spyri eine deutsche Autorin? Nein, sie war eine schweizerische Autorin.

Very often the *nein*-statement is combined with one containing the word *nicht* or *kein*.

Nein, sie ist keine deutsche Autorin. or **Nein, sie ist nicht eine deutsche Autorin.**

Both of the above sentences mean the same. One negates the noun with the adjective *kein*. The other negates the verb with the adverb *nicht*. A good writer will use both to add variety to his or her German.

a. Negation with *kein*

Kein modifies the noun it negates and translates into "no" (quantity), "none," "not any," "not a," "or not an." It negates and also denotes absence of the noun it modifies.

Johanna Spyri, die Autorin von *Heidis Lehr- und Wanderjahre*, hatte keine Töchter, nur einen Sohn.
Johanna Spyri, the author of Heidi *had no (not any) daughters, only a son.*

Heidi hat kein Geld.	*Heidi has no money (and never had any).*
Heidi hat kein Geld mehr.	*Heidi no longer has any money (although she did have some.)*

NOTE: In the first sentence above *kein* was used alone in the sentence. Johanna Spyri never had any daughters, only sons. In the second, it was used in combination with *mehr*. Adding *mehr* after the noun communicates that the subject once satisfied what the verb says, but no longer. Heidi had money at one point, but no longer has any.

Heidi war eine Waise (an orphan). Sie hatte keine Eltern mehr.
Heidi was an orphan. She no longer had any parents.

| ÜBUNG A | **Heidi kommt auf die Alm.** You're reading the story of Heidi to your younger sister and she interrupts you with questions. Answer them in the negative using a form of *kein*. Add *mehr* after the noun if it is appropriate. If you are unfamiliar with Johanna Spyri's novel about Heidi, you can find the book in the children's section of the library or online. |

EXAMPLE: Wo ist Heidis Mutter? Heidi hat keine Mutter mehr.

1. Wo ist Heidis Haus? _____

2. Wo sind Heidis Eltern? _____

3. Hat Heidi einen Hund? _____

4. Hat der Alm-Onkel (Alm-Öhi) eine Frau? _____

5. Hat Heidis Tante Dede Kinder? _____

6. Hast du einen von den Heidi-Filmen gesehen? _____

b. Negation with nicht

Another common method of negating a German sentence is using *nicht*, which is usually placed immediately before the word, phrase or clause it negates. The verb must remain the second element in the sentence. Therefore, if *nicht* negates the verb, it follows it or, in very short sentences, goes to the end of the sentence.

Heidis Großvater lebt mit zwei Söhnen auf der Alm.

            ∧

         nicht

Heidi's grandfather does not live with two sons on the Alm.

| ÜBUNG B | **Heidi lernt ihren Großvater kennen.** Heidi is on the Alm now and meeting her grandfather, the Alm-Öhi, for the first time. Decide what is being negated and position the word nicht in each sentence where you think it belongs. Then write the sentence in a correct format. |

EXAMPLE:

    Die Tante will, dass Heidi am Ende des Nachmittags mit ihr zurückgeht.

        ∧   ∧

    nicht   or   nicht

    Correction: Die Tante will, dass Heidi bei dem Alm-Öhi bleibt.

1. Der Alm-Öhi lebt mit seinem Sohn Tobias auf der Alm.

    _____

2. Die kleine Heidi hat ihren Großvater jeden Sommer besucht. Sie kannte ihn gut. (2x nicht)

    _____

3. Bei ihrem Großvater schläft Heidi auf einer weichen Matratze neben der Küche.

    _____

4. Der Junge, der die Ziegen für den Alm-Öhi hütet, heißt Josef.

    _____

5. Heidi geht jeden Tag mit Peter nach Frankfurt.

    _____

| ÜBUNG C | **Nicht oder kein?** Negate the following sentences. You decide whether to use *nicht, nicht....mehr, kein* or *kein... mehr*. |

EXAMPLE: Heidi lebt bei ihrer Mutter.   Heidi lebt nicht mehr bei ihrer Mutter.

1. Heidi hat Angst vor den Ziegen. _____

2. Peters Großmutter kann Heidi sehen. _____

3. Ihre Tante Dede liebt sie. _____

4. Sie lebt unglücklich dort mit dem Alm-Öhi. _____

5. Jeden Tag kommen Liebesgrüße von der Tante Dede. _____

    c. Negation Words

        Certain words negate an expression without the use of *kein* or *nicht*. They are:

nie / immer	*never / always*
***niemand / *jemand**	*no one / someone*
nirgendwo / irgendwo	*nowhere / somewhere*
nichts / etwas	*nothing / something*
niemals / immer	*never / always*

        niemand and *jemand* are pronouns. They take an *–em* ending in the dative and an *–en* in the accusative. There is no genitive and they take no endings in the nominative.

| ÜBUNG D | **Heidi auf der Alm.** You're continuing the story of Heidi with your little sister. She's having a hard time imaging that a little girl can be so alone. She continues to interrupt with questions that you must answer. Answer them using the words of negation above. |

1. Aber wer liebte Heidi am Anfang? _____

2. Wie oft kam die Tante zu Besuch? _____

3. Was hatte Heidi, als sie auf die Alm kam? _____

4. Und wo hätte sie wohnen können, wenn nicht bei dem Alm-Öhi? _____

5. Wann wollte sie nach Frankfurt? _____

d. Doch

Doch is a negation when a positive reaction is expected. (See page 62.)

Heidis Vater liebte sie nicht. Doch, aber er ist gestorben, als sie 2 Jahre alt war.
Heidi's Father didn't love her. Yes he did, but he died when she was 2 years old.

Doch may also be added to a sentence to show incredulity, i.e. to show that the speaker can't completely believe what she's saying herself. It adds emotion and urgency to a factual statement.

Dede will sie doch nicht wegnehmen?   **Doch, sie will sie wegnehmen.**
Dede certainly doesn't want to take her away?   Yes she does; she wants to take her away.

The following exercise uses *doch* in both these functions. The first sentence uses the *doch* that signals incredulity. The second contradicts the first speaker, answering in the positive when a negative answer is expected. The best translation for *doch* is a word very seldom used in today's English: "indeed."

ÜBUNG E | **Doch.** Your little sister is totally lost in the story. As it continues and Dede comes back to take Heidi to Frankfurt, she's almost as upset as Heidi and her grandfather were. She's jumping to conclusions that may or may not be correct. React to her emotional exclamations.

EXAMPLE: DEINE SCHWESTER: Das kann doch nicht Tante Dede sein?
Du: Doch, das ist Tante Dede.

1. SCHWESTER: Aber sie kann Heidi nicht mitnehmen wollen!

   Du: _____

2. SCHWESTER: Aber Heidi muss doch nicht mitgehen!

   Du: _____

3. SCHWESTER: Aber will der Alm-Öhi sie doch nicht behalten?

   Du: _____

4. SCHWESTER: Aber Heidi wird es doch nicht bei der neuen Familie in Frankfurt mögen!

   Du: _____

5. SCHWESTER: Vermisst sie doch nicht ihren Großvater und ihr Leben auf der Alm?

   Du: _____

2.   Flavor Words – *aber, denn, doch, halt, ja, mal*

Doch is a so-called flavor word or particle. Other flavor words are *aber, denn, halt, ja,* and *mal*. Used more often in spoken than in written German, they are among the most difficult elements for a non-native speaker to master. They have no literal meaning, but they add flavor; they add urgency and emotional content to a sentence.

Flavorless, factual sentence:	**Heidi liebt ihren Großvater.**
Sentence that conveys emotional content:	**Heidi liebt aber ihren Großvater.**
	Heidi liebt doch ihren Großvater.
Flavorless, factual sentence:	**Sie fuhr mit der Tante nach Frankfurt.**
Sentence that conveys emotional content:	**Sie fuhr aber (or doch) mit der Tante nach Frankfurt.**

a. Aber and Doch

The literal translation of *aber* is "but" and *doch* is "indeed." When added for flavor, they add urgency and emotion. They encourage the speaker to pay attention and react quickly.

Ich will aber (*or* doch) nicht!	*But I don't want to!*
Mein Name ist aber (*or* doch) nicht Schulz!	*But my name isn't Schulz.*
Das ist aber (*or* doch) nicht fair!	*But that isn't fair.*
Das ist aber (*or* doch) nicht meine Mutter!	*But that isn't my mother!*

ÜBUNG F	**Heidi spricht mit Klara.** Heidi enjoys her friend Klara's company in Frankfurt, but misses her grandfather and her friends on the Alm. She discusses her feelings with Klara. Insert flavor words *doch* or *aber* to emphasize how strongly each girl feels about the topic.

EXAMPLE: Klara: Aber Heidi, du hast es viel besser hier. or Heidi, du hast es viel besser hier.
                                        ∧   ∧
                                      doch   doch or aber

1. KLARA: Aber Heidi, es ist Winter. Es ist zu kalt in den Alpen.

2. HEIDI: Ja, Klara, der Himmel im Winter ist am schönsten.

3. KLARA: Du hast dort zu wenig zu essen.

4. HEIDI: Der Großvater macht den besten Schweizer Käse.

5. KLARA: Ich werde dich vermissen.

6. HEIDI: Du kannst mich im Sommer besuchen.

7. KLARA: Dann sollst du Geschenke für alle mitnehmen.

8. HEIDI: Danke vielmals. Du bist so nett zu mir gewesen.

b. Denn – shows impatience but also the knowledge that something is going to happen.

Flavorless, factual sentence:	**Wo ist sie?**
Sentence that conveys emotional content:	**Wo ist sie denn?**
Flavorless, factual sentence:	**Kann sie nicht schneller kommen?**
Sentence that conveys emotional content:	**Kann sie denn nicht schneller kommen?**

ÜBUNG G **Warum kommt sie denn nicht?** Peter is waiting impatiently for Heidi to return to the mountains. He's at the train station and it seems as if her train will never come. Write 5 thoughts that are running through his head. In each, use the word *denn, aber,* or *doch* to signal how excited he is.

1. _____

2. _____

3. _____

4. _____

5. _____

c. *Halt* means "simply" and minimizes a request or an accomplishment.

Peters Großmutter:	Heidi, hab vielen Dank für die wunderbaren Geschenke.
Heidi:	Großmutter, das sind halt weiße Brötchen, die du gut kauen kannst.

Heidi has brought white rolls from Frankfurt to Peter's grandmother, who has difficulties chewing the more robust farmer's bread in the mountains. Heidi downplays her generosity by stating that they are "simply" white rolls.

ÜBUNG H **Es ist halt so.** All the participants are modest about their part in Klara's recovery. What do they say they did?

EXAMPLE: Herr Stresemann / hierher schicken   Ich habe Klara halt hierher geschickt.

1. Heidi / ermuntern _____

2. Alm-Öhi / gut füttern _____

3. Peter / die Hand geben _____

4. Heidi und Peter / auf die Alm schieben _____

5. Klara / einen Fuß vor den Anderen setzen _____

d. *Mal* softens a statement. Translated literally as "sometime" or "time," it is often used in commands and suggestions.

Command:	**Komm her!** (*said to a misbehaving, annoying child*)
Softened Command:	**Komm mal her!** (*said to an unhappy crying child*)
Suggestion:	**Wollen wir sie besuchen?**
	Let's visit her. Shall we visit her?
More Casual Suggestion:	**Wollen wir sie mal besuchen?**
	Let's visit her (sometime).

Bonus Question:
Place the following three statements in the order of most urgent (1) to least urgent (3).
Komm her! _____ **Komm mal her!** _____ **Komm doch her!** _____

ÜBUNG I   **Heidi und Peter bringen Klara das Laufen bei.** Heidi has returned to the Alm and Klara has come to visit for the summer. Peter and Heidi help her learn to walk again. Use appropriate flavor words, including *mal, doch, aber, denn* and *halt* to give their words more impact. Several words may work for each space. Each adds a different flavor to the sentence. Be able to explain what you wanted to accomplish with your choice of word.

EXAMPLE: Du kannst es __doch__ . Steh __mal__ langsam auf!

1. PETER: Gib mir _____ deine Hand!

2. KLARA: Ich kann _____ nicht. Ich habe Angst.

3. HEIDI: Du brauchst _____ keine Angst zu haben. Wir helfen dir _____.

4. PETER: Mach's _____! Du brauchst _____ vor dem Stuhl aufzustehen.

5. KLARA: Ich versuche aufzustehen. Warum kann ich es _____ nicht?

6. HEIDI: Du brauchst _____ ein bisschen Übung. Ich helfe dir _____.

    e. *Ja* reinforces a statement gently. It signals that the speaker is sincere in what he's saying.

      Statement: **Heidi, du darfst morgen nach Hause fahren.**

      Compassionate Statement: **Heidi, du darfst ja morgen nach Hause fahren.**

ÜBUNG J   **Klaras Vater kommt.** Klara's father comes and the children are excited to show him Klara's accomplishment. Insert the word *ja* in each sentence where you think it belongs.

EXAMPLE: Peter: Klar, guck mal! Er kommt!
                                      ^
                                    ja

1. Herr Stresemann: Aber Klara, du siehst so gesund und glücklich aus!

2. Klara: Ich bin es auch, Vater. Ich will dir etwas zeigen. (Use **ja** 2x.)

3. Herr Stresemann: Klara, was machst du denn? Du sollst aufpassen!

4. Peter: Herr Stresemann, gucken Sie sie mal an! Sie kann laufen.

5. Alm-Öhi: Ja, Herr Stresemann, Ihre Klara ist wieder gesund.

6. Herr Stresemann: Klara, du kannst laufen!

ÜBUNG K | **Geschafft!** Your sister is excited. Klara not only stood up, she walked! Your sister couldn't wait to tell everyone the story at dinner. Write 5 sentences containing flavor words that she used in telling the tale.

EXAMPLE: Sie ist doch aufgestanden und hat ja drei Schritte genommen.

1. _____

2. _____

3. _____

4. _____

5. _____

ÜBUNG L | **Heidis Lehr- und Wanderjahre.** Your sister enjoyed the story so much that you've decided to write your own copy. Tell Heidi's story in your own words, using your best German. Remember to use sentences with more than one clause. Use relative clauses and subordinate clauses. Add some direct and indirect quotes. Where possible, use some flavor words to add emotional content.

_____

_____

_____

_____

_____

_____

_____

_____

_____

_____

_____

_____

_____

Continue on a separate sheet of paper if you need more room.

3.   Exclamations

Exclamations are short, self-contained, explosive statements that show emotion: anger, disappointment, surprise, excitement, fear, et al. They can be fun to use and add authenticity to one's German. An exclamation is always followed by an exclamation point.

A list of common exclamations in German include: (The English translations are approximate and do not always carry the same emotional import as the original German.)

Ach!	*Oh!*
Ach du armes Kindchen!	*You poor baby.*
Ach du dickes Ei!	*Oh my goodness.*
Ach du grüne Neune!	*Oh my goodness.*
Ach du liebes Bisschen!	*Oh my goodness.*
Ach du meine Güte!	*Oh my goodness.*
Ach du Lieber!	*Oh my goodness.*
Ach du Schande!	*What a shame.*
Ach so!	*Ah, so that's how it is.*
Alle Neune!	*Right on target!*
Aha!	*Aha!*
Aua!	*Ouch!*
Bah!	*Bah!*
Donnerwetter!	*Man!*
Halli Hallo!	*Hi!*
Hallo!	*Excuse me (getting someone's attention)*
Hoppla!	*Whoops!*
Hurra!	*Hooray!*
Igitt!	*Yuck!*
Juhu!	*Yoohoo!*
Mensch!	*Man!*
Mist!	*Drats!*
Na!	*Well!*
Na also!	*I told you so.*
Na bitte!	*I ask you!*
Na dann!	*Get on with it!*
Na freilich!	*Of course!*
Na klar!	*Of course!*
Na schön!	*OK (giving in)*
Na so was!	*Such a thing! Unbelievable!*
Na und?	*And now?*

O Graus!	*Dreadful. Horrible.*
Oje!	*Oh my. (negative)*
Pfui!	*Ick!*
Pfui Teufel!	*Ugh!*
Pscht!	*Shh...*
Quatsch!	*Ridiculous!*
Schade!	*Too bad! What a pity.*
Scheibenkleister!	*Drats!*
Verflixt!	*Rats!*

Appendix – Grammar Reference Tables

1. Weak Verbs – Conjugation

		ACTIVE VOICE	PASSIVE VOICE	SUBJUNCTIVE I	SUBJUNCTIVE II
hören – to hear					
PRESENT TENSE	ich	höre	**werde** gehört	höre	hörte alternative: **würde** hören
	du	hörst	**wirst** gehört	hör**est**	hör**test** alternative: **würdest** hören
	er, sie, es	hört	**wird** gehört	höre	hörte alternative: **würde** hören
	wir	hören	**werden** gehört	hören	hörten alternative: **würden** hören
	ihr	hört	**werdet** gehört	hör**et**	hör**tet** alternative: **würdet** hören
	sie, Sie	hören	**werden** gehört	hören	hörten alternative: **würden** hören
PAST TENSE	ich	hörte	**wurde** gehört	hörte	**hätte** gehört alternative: **würde** gehört **haben**
	du	hörtest	**wurdest** gehört	hörtest	**hättest** gehört alternative: **würdest** gehört **haben**
	er, sie, es	hörte	**wurde** gehört	hörte	**hätte** gehört alternative: **würde** gehört **haben**
	wir	hörten	**wurden** gehört	hörten	**hätten** gehört alternative: **würden** gehört **haben**
	ihr	hörtet	**wurdet** gehört	hörtet	**hättet** gehört alternative: **würdet** gehört **haben**
	sie, Sie	hörten	**wurden** gehört	hörten	**hätten** gehört alternative: **würden** gehört **haben**

		ACTIVE VOICE	PASSIVE VOICE	SUBJUNCTIVE I	SUBJUNCTIVE II
FUTURE TENSE	ich	**werde** hören	**werde** gehört **werden**	**werde** hören	
	du	**wirst** hören	**wirst** gehört **werden**	**werdest** hören	
	er, sie, es	**wird** hören	**wird** gehört **werden**	**werde** hören	
	wir	**werden** hören	**werden** gehört **werden**	**werden** hören	
	ihr	**werdet** hören	**werdet** gehört **werden**	**werdet** hören	
	sie, Sie	**werden** hören	**werden** gehört **werden**	**werden** hören	
PRESENT PERFECT TENSE	ich	**habe** gehört	**bin** gehört **worden**	**habe** gehört	
	du	**hast** gehört	**bist** gehört **worden**	**habest** gehört	
	er, sie, es	**hat** gehört	**ist** gehört **worden**	**habe** gehört	
	wir	**haben** gehört	**sind** gehört **worden**	**haben** gehört	
	ihr	**habt** gehört	**seid** gehört **worden**	**habet** gehört	
	sie, Sie	**haben** gehört	**sind** gehört **worden**	**haben** gehört	
PAST PERFECT TENSE	ich	**hatte** gehört	**war** gehört **worden**		
	du	**hattest** gehört	**warst** gehört **worden**		
	er, sie, es	**hatte** gehört	**war** gehört **worden**		
	wir	**hatten** gehört	**waren** gehört **worden**		
	ihr	**hattet** gehört	**wart** gehört **worden**		
	sie, Sie	**hatten** gehört	**waren** gehört **worden**		

		ACTIVE VOICE	PASSIVE VOICE	SUBJUNCTIVE I	SUBJUNCTIVE II
FUTURE PERFECT TENSE	ich	**werde** gehört **haben**	**werde** gehört **worden sein**	**werde** gehört **haben**	
	du	**wirst** gehört **haben**	**wirst** gehört **worden sein**	**werdest** gehört **haben**	
	er, sie, es	**wird** gehört **haben**	**wird** gehört **worden sein**	**werde** gehört **haben**	
	wir	**werden** gehört **haben**	**werden** gehört **worden sein**	**werden** gehört **haben**	
	ihr	**werdet** gehört **haben**	**werdet** gehört **worden sein**	**werdet** gehört **haben**	
	sie, Sie	**werden** gehört **haben**	**werden** gehört **worden sein**	**werden** gehört **haben**	
IMPERATIVE	du	Hör(e)!	Werde gehört!		
	wir	Hören wir!	Werden wir gehört!		
	ihr	Hört!	Werdet gehört!		
	sie, Sie	Hören Sie!	Werden Sie gehört!		

2.   Strong Verbs (Auxiliary Verb = *haben*)

		ACTIVE VOICE	PASSIVE VOICE	SUBJUNCTIVE I	SUBJUNCTIVE II
tragen, trägt, trug, hat getragen – to wear or carry **(hat)**					
PRESENT TENSE	ich	trag**e**	**werde** getragen	trag**e**	trüg**e** alternative: **würde** tragen
	du	tr**ä**gst	**wirst** getragen	trag**est**	trüg**est** alternative: **würdest** tragen
	er, sie, es	tr**ä**gt	**wird** getragen	trag**e**	trüg**e** alternative: **würde** tragen
	wir	trag**en**	**werden** getragen	trag**en**	trüg**en** alternative: **würden** tragen
	ihr	trag**t**	**werdet** getragen	trag**et**	trüg**et** alternative: **würdet** tragen
	sie, Sie	trag**en**	**werden** getragen	trag**en**	trüg**en** alternative: **würden** tragen
PAST TENSE	ich	trug	**wurde** getragen	trug**e**	**hätte** getragen alternative: **würde** getragen **haben**
	du	trug**st**	**wurdest** getragen	trug**est**	**hättest** getragen alternative: **würdest** getragen **haben**
	er, sie, es	trug	**wurde** getragen	trug**e**	**hätte** getragen alternative: **würde** getragen **haben**
	wir	trug**en**	**wurden** getragen	trug**en**	**hätten** getragen alternative: **würden** getragen **haben**
	ihr	trug**t**	**wurdet** getragen	trug**et**	**hättet** getragen alternative: **würdet** getragen **haben**
	sie, Sie	trug**en**	**wurden** getragen	trug**en**	**hätten** getragen alternative: **würden** getragen **haben**

		ACTIVE VOICE	PASSIVE VOICE	SUBJUNCTIVE I	SUBJUNCTIVE II
FUTURE TENSE	ich	**werde** tragen	**werde** getragen **werden**	**werde** tragen	
	du	**wirst** tragen	**wirst** getragen **werden**	**werdest** tragen	
	er, sie, es	**wird** tragen	**wird** getragen **werden**	**werde** tragen	
	wir	**werden** tragen	**werden** getragen **werden**	**werden** tragen	
	ihr	**werdet** tragen	**werdet** getragen **werden**	**werdet** tragen	
	sie, Sie	**werden** tragen	**werden** getragen **werden**	**werden** tragen	
PRESENT PERFECT TENSE	ich	**habe** getragen	**bin** getragen **worden**	**habe** getragen	
	du	**hast** getragen	**bist** getragen **worden**	**habest** getragen	
	er, sie, es	**hat** getragen	**ist** getragen **worden**	**habe** getragen	
	wir	**haben** getragen	**sind** getragen **worden**	**haben** getragen	
	ihr	**habt** getragen	**seid** getragen **worden**	**habet** getragen	
	sie, Sie	**haben** getragen	**sind** getragen **worden**	**haben** getragen	
PAST PERFECT TENSE	ich	**hatte** getragen	**war** getragen **worden**		
	du	**hattest** getragen	**warst** getragen **worden**		
	er, sie, es	**hatte** getragen	**war** getragen **worden**		
	wir	**hatten** getragen	**waren** getragen **worden**		
	ihr	**hattet** getragen	**wart** getragen **worden**		
	sie, Sie	**hatten** getragen	**waren** getragen **worden**		

		ACTIVE VOICE	PASSIVE VOICE	SUBJUNCTIVE I	SUBJUNCTIVE II
FUTURE PERFECT TENSE	ich	**werde** getragen **haben**	**werde** getragen **worden sein**	**werde** getragen **haben**	
	du	**wirst** getragen **haben**	**wirst** getragen **worden sein**	**werdest** getragen **haben**	
	er, sie, es	**wird** getragen **haben**	**wird** getragen **worden sein**	**werde** getragen **haben**	
	wir	**werden** getragen **haben**	**werden** getragen **worden sein**	**werden** getragen **haben**	
	ihr	**werdet** getragen **haben**	**werdet** getragen **worden sein**	**werdet** getragen **haben**	
	sie, Sie	**werden** getragen **haben**	**werden** getragen **worden sein**	**werden** getragen **haben**	
IMPERATIVE	du	Trag(e)!	Werde getragen!		
	wir	Tragen wir!	Werden wir getragen!		
	ihr	Tragt!	Werdet getragen!		
	sie, Sie	Tragen Sie!	Werden Sie getragen!		

3.   Strong Verbs (Auxiliary Verb = *sein*)

		ACTIVE VOICE	SUBJUNCTIVE I	SUBJUNCTIVE II
gehen, geht, ging, ist gegangen – to go **(ist)**				
PRESENT TENSE	ich	gehe	gehe	ginge alternative: **würde** gehen
	du	gehst	gehest	gingest alternative: **würdest** gehen
	er, sie, es	geht	gehe	ginge alternative: **würde** gehen
	wir	gehen	gehen	gingen alternative: **würde** gehen
	ihr	geht	gehet	ginget alternative: **würdet** gehen
	sie, Sie	gehen	gehen	gingen alternative: **würden** gehen
PAST TENSE	ich	ging	ginge	**wäre** gegangen alternative: **würde** gegangen **sein**
	du	gingst	gingest	**wärest** gegangen alternative: **würdest** gegangen **sein**
	er, sie, es	ging	ginge	**wäre** gegangen alternative: **würde** gegangen **sein**
	wir	gingen	gingen	**wären** gegangen alternative: **würden** gegangen **sein**
	ihr	gingt	ginget	**wäret** gegangen alternative: **würdet** gegangen **sein**
	sie, Sie	gingen	gingen	**wären** gegangen alternative: **würden** gegangen **sein**

		ACTIVE VOICE	SUBJUNCTIVE I	SUBJUNCTIVE II
FUTURE TENSE	ich	**werde** gehen	**werde** gehen	
	du	**wirst** gehen	**werdest** gehen	
	er, sie, es	**wird** gehen	**werde** gehen	
	wir	**werden** gehen	**werden** gehen	
	ihr	**werdet** gehen	**werdet** gehen	
	sie, Sie	**werden** gehen	**werden** gehen	
PRESENT PERFECT TENSE	ich	**bin** gegangen	**sei** gegangen	
	du	**bist** gegangen	**sei(e)st** gegangen	
	er, sie, es	**ist** gegangen	**sei** gegangen	
	wir	**sind** gegangen	**seien** gegangen	
	ihr	**seid** gegangen	**sei(e)t** gegangen	
	sie, Sie	**sind** gegangen	**seien** gegangen	
PAST PERFECT TENSE	ich	**war** gegangen	**wäre** gegangen	
	du	**warst** gegangen	**wärest** gegangen	
	er, sie, es	**war** gegangen	**wäre** gegangen	
	wir	**waren** gegangen	**wären** gegangen	
	ihr	**wart** gegangen	**wäret** gegangen	
	sie, Sie	**waren** gegangen	**wären** gegangen	
FUTURE PERFECT TENSE	ich	**werde** gegangen **sein**	**werde** gegangen **sein**	
	du	**wirst** gegangen **sein**	**werdest** gegangen **sein**	
	er, sie, es	**wird** gegangen **sein**	**werde** gegangen **sein**	
	wir	**werden** gegangen **sein**	**werden** gegangen **sein**	
	ihr	**werdet** gegangen **sein**	**werdet** gegangen **sein**	
	sie, Sie	**werden** gegangen **sein**	**werden** gegangen **sein**	
IMPERATIVE	du	Geh(e)!		
	wir	Gehen wir!		
	ihr	Geht!		
	sie, Sie	Gehen Sie!		

4. Strong Verbs – List of Principal Parts

		PRINCIPAL PARTS OF STRONG VERBS		
INFINITIVE	PRESENT TENSE THIRD PERSON SINGULAR	PAST TENSE FIRST AND THIRD PERSONS SINGULAR	PAST PARTICIPLE WITH AUXILIARY VERB	ENGLISH MEANING
backen	bäckt	backte (buk)	hat gebacken	bake
befehlen	befiehlt	befahl	hat befohlen	command
beginnen	beginnt	begann	hat begonnen	begin
beißen	beißt	biss	hat gebissen	bite
bergen	birgt	barg	hat geborgen	hide, protect
betrügen	betrügt	betrog	hat betrogen	betray, deceive
biegen	biegt	bog	hat/ist gebogen	bend, turn
bieten	bietet	bot	hat geboten	offer
binden	bindet	band	hat gebunden	tie, bind
bitten	bittet	bat	hat gebeten	request, plea
blasen	blast	blies	hat geblasen	blow
bleiben	bleibt	blieb	ist geblieben	stay, remain
braten	brät	briet	hat gebraten	roast, fry
brechen	bricht	brach	hat gebrochen	break
brennen	brennt	brannte	hat gebrannt	burn
bringen	bringt	brachte	hat gebracht	bring
denken	denkt	dachte	hat gedacht	think
dringen	dringt	drang	hat/ist gedrungen	press forward
dürfen	darf	durfte	hat gedurft	may, be allowed to
empfehlen	empfiehlt	empfahl	hat empfohlen	recommend
erschrecken	erschrickt	erschrak	ist erschrocken	be startled
essen	isst	aß	hat gegessen	eat
fahren	fährt	fuhr	hat/ist gefahren	ride, drive
fallen	fällt	fiel	ist gefallen	fall
fangen	fängt	fing	hat gefangen	catch
findet	findet	fand	hat gefunden	find
fliegen	fliegt	flog	hat/ist geflogen	fly
fliehen	flieht	floh	ist geflohen	flee
fließen	fließt	floss	ist geflossen	flow
fressen	frisst	fraß	hat gefressen	eat (animal), devour

INFINITIVE	PRESENT TENSE THIRD PERSON SINGULAR	PAST TENSE FIRST AND THIRD PERSONS SINGULAR	PAST PARTICIPLE WITH AUXILIARY VERB	ENGLISH MEANING
frieren	friert	fror	hat/ist gefroren	freeze
gebären	gebärt	gebar	hat geboren	give birth to
geben	gibt	gab	hat gegeben	give
gedeihen	gedeiht	gedieh	ist gediehen	grow, thrive
gehen	geht	ging	ist gegangen	go, walk
gelingen	gelingt	gelang	ist gelungen	succeed
gelten	gilt	galt	hat gegolten	be valid
genießen	genießt	genoss	hat genossen	enjoy
geschehen	geschieht	geschah	ist geschehen	happen
gewinnen	gewinnt	gewann	hat gewonnen	win
gießen	gießt	goss	hat gegossen	pour
gleichen	gleicht	glich	hat geglichen	resemble
gleiten	gleitet	glitt	ist geglitten	glide, slide
graben	gräbt	grub	hat gegraben	dig
greifen	greift	griff	hat gegriffen	grasp, grab
haben	hat	hatte	hat gehabt	have
halten	hält	hielt	hat gehalten	hold, stop
hängen	hängt	hing	hat gehangen	hang
hauen	haut	haute	hat gehauen	cut
heben	hebt	hob	hat gehoben	life, raise up
heißen	heißt	hieß	hat geheißen	be called
helfen	hilft	half	hat geholfen	help
kennen	kennt	kannte	hat gekonnt	know, be acquainted with
klingen	klingt	klang	hat geklungen	sound
kneifen	kneift	kniff	hat gekniffen	pinch
kommen	kommt	kam	ist gekommen	come
können	kann	konnte	hat gekonnt	can, be able to
kriechen	kriecht	kroch	ist gekrochen	crawl
laden	lädt	lud	hat geladen	load
lassen	lässt	ließ	hat gelassen	let, leave, allow
laufen	läuft	lief	ist gelaufen	run, walk

INFINITIVE	PRESENT TENSE THIRD PERSON SINGULAR	PAST TENSE FIRST AND THIRD PERSONS SINGULAR	PAST PARTICIPLE WITH AUXILIARY VERB	ENGLISH MEANING
leiden	leidet	litt	hat gelitten	suffer
lesen	liest	las	hat gelesen	read
liegen	liegt	lag	hat gelegen	lie
mahlen	mahlt	mahlte	hat gemahlen	grind
meiden	meidet	mied	hat gemieden	avoid
messen	misst	maß	hat gemessen	measure
misslingen	misslingt	misslang	ist misslungen	fail
mögen	mag	mochte	hat gemocht	like, like to
müssen	muss	musste	hat gemusst	must, have to
nehmen	nimmt	nahm	hat genommen	take
nennen	nennt	nannte	hat genannt	name
pfeifen	pfeift	pfiff	hat gepfiffen	whistle
preisen	preist	pries	hat gepriesen	praise
raten	rät	riet	hat geraten	advise, guess
reiben	reibt	rieb	hat gerieben	rub
reißen	reißt	riss	hat/ist gerissen	rip, tear
reiten	reitet	ritt	hat/ist geritten	ride (an animal)
rennen	rennt	rannte	ist gerannt	run
riechen	riecht	roch	hat gerochen	smell
ringen	ringt	rang	hat gerungen	wrestle
rufen	ruft	rief	hat gerufen	call
salzen	salzt	salzte	hat gesalzen	salt
saufen	säuft	soff	hat gesoffen	drink (animal)
schaffen	schafft	schuf	hat geschaffen	create, accomplish
scheiden	scheidet	schied	hat/ist geschieden	separate
scheinen	scheint	schien	hat geschienen	shine, seem
schieben	schieb	schob	hat geschoben	shove, push
schießen	schießt	schoss	hat geschossen	shoot
schlafen	schläft	schlief	hat geschlafen	sleep
schlagen	schlägt	schlug	hat geschlagen	hit, beat
schleichen	schleicht	schlich	ist geschlichen	creep
schließen	schließt	schloss	hat geschlossen	close, end

INFINITIVE	PRESENT TENSE THIRD PERSON SINGULAR	PAST TENSE FIRST AND THIRD PERSONS SINGULAR	PAST PARTICIPLE WITH AUXILIARY VERB	ENGLISH MEANING
schmeißen	schmeißt	schmiss	hat geschmissen	throw out, chuck
schmelzen	schmilzt	schmolz	hat/ist geschmolzen	melt
schneiden	schneidet	schnitt	hat geschnitten	cut
schreiben	schreibt	schrieb	hat geschrieben	write
schreien	schreit	schrie	hat geschrien	scream, shout
schreiten	schreitet	schritt	ist geschritten	stride
schweigen	schweigt	schwieg	hat geschwiegen	be silent
schwimmen	schwimmt	schwamm	hat/ist geschwommen	swim
schwingen	schwingt	schwang	hat geschwungen	swing
sehen	sieht	sah	hat gesehen	see
sein	ist	war	ist gewesen	be
senden	sendet	sandte	hat gesandt	send, deploy
singen	singt	sang	hat gesungen	sing
sinken	sinkt	sank	hat gesunken	sink
sitzen	sitzt	saß	hat gesessen	sit
sollen	soll	sollte	hat gesollt	should, supposed to
spinnen	spinnt	span	hat gesponnen	be silly, tell tall tales
sprechen	spricht	sprach	hat gesprochen	speak
springen	springt	sprang	ist gesprungen	jump, spring
stechen	sticht	stach	hat gestochen	stick, prick
stehen	steht	stand	hat gestanden	stand
stehlen	stiehlt	stahl	hat gestohlen	steal
steigen	steigt	stieg	ist gestiegen	climb
sterben	stirbt	starb	ist gestorben	die
stinken	stinkt	stank	hat gestunken	smell bad
stoßen	stößt	stieß	hat/ist gestoßen	bump, push
streichen	streicht	strich	hat gestrichen	stroke, pet, paint
streiten	streitet	stritt	hat gestritten	quarrel, argue
tragen	trägt	trug	hat getragen	carry, wear
treffen	trifft	traf	hat getroffen	meet
treiben	treibt	trieb	hat getrieben	drive
trinken	trinkt	trank	hat getrunken	drink

INFINITIVE	PRESENT TENSE THIRD PERSON SINGULAR	PAST TENSE FIRST AND THIRD PERSONS SINGULAR	PAST PARTICIPLE WITH AUXILIARY VERB	ENGLISH MEANING
tun	tut	tat	hat getan	do
verbieten	verbietet	verbot	hat verboten	forbid
verderben	verdirbt	verdarb	hat/ist verdorben	spoil
vergessen	vergisst	vergaß	hat vergessen	forget
verlieren	verliert	verlor	hat verloren	lose
verzeihen	verzeiht	verzieh	hat verzogen	forgive
wachsen	wächst	wuchs	ist gewachsen	grow
waschen	wäscht	wusch	hat gewaschen	wash
weichen	weicht	wich	ist gewichen	yield
weisen	weist	wies	hat gewiesen	point
werben	wirbt	warb	hat geworben	advertise
werden	wird	wurde	ist geworden	become, will
werfen	wirft	warf	hat geworfen	throw
wiegen	wiegt	wog	hat gewogen	weigh
wissen	weiß	wusste	hat gewusst	know (a fact)
wollen	will	wollte	hat gewollt	want, want to
ziehen	zieht	zog	hat gezogen	pull
zwingen	zwingt	zwang	hat gezwungen	force

5.   Dative Verbs

The following verbs take dative direct objects.

abraten, rät ab, riet ab, hat abgeraten (von + *dat.*)   *advise against*

ähneln   *resemble*

antworten   *answer*

ausweichen, weicht aus, wich aus, ist ausgewichen   *avoid, get out of the way*

begegnen   *meet*

beistehen, steht bei, stand bei, hat beigestanden   *support, stand behind*

beitreten, tritt bei, trat bei, ist beigetreten   *join*

bekommen   *agree with (food)*

danken   *thank*

dienen   *serve*

drohen   *threaten*

einfallen, fällt ein, fiel ein, ist eingefallen	*occur*
entgegenkommen, kommt entgegen, kam entgegen, ist entgegengekommen	*come towards*
folgen (ist)	*follow*
gehorchen	*obey*
gehören	*belong to*
gelten, gilt, galt, hat gegolten	*be meant for*
gleichen, gleicht, glich, hat geglichen	*be the same as, resemble*
gratulieren	*congratulate*
helfen, hilft, half, hat geholfen	*help*
imponieren	*impress*
nachahmen	*mock, ape, copy*
passen	*fit*
schaden	*harm*
schmeicheln	*flatter*
trauen	*trust*
vertrauen	*have trust or confidence in*
wehtun, tut weh, tat weh, hat wehgetan	*hurt*
widersprechen, widerspricht, widersprach, hat widersprochen	*contradict*
zuhören	*listen to*

6.   Reflexive Verbs

sich ärgern	*get angry*
sich ändern	*change*
sich anziehen	*dress*
sich ausziehen	*undress*
sich umziehen	*change clothes*
sich bedanken (bei + *dat.*) (für + *acc.*)	*thank (someone) (for)*
sich beeilen	*hurry*
sich befinden	*be located*
sich benehmen	*behave*
sich beschäftigen (mit + *dat.*)	*occupy oneself (with)*
sich beschweren (über + *acc.*)	*complain (about)*
sich bewegen	*move*
sich bewerben (um + *acc.*)	*apply (for)*
sich entscheiden	*decide*
sich erholen	*recuperate*
sich erkälten	*catch a cold*

sich erinnern (an + *acc.*)	remember
sich entschuldigen (bei + *dat.*) (für + *acc.*)	apologize (to someone) (for something)
sich freuen (auf + *acc.*)	look forward to
sich freuen (über + *acc.*)	be happy about
sich fühlen	feel (health)
sich gewöhnen (an + *acc.*)	get used (to)
sich interessieren (für + *acc.*)	be interested (in)
sich irren	err
sich schämen	be ashamed
sich setzen	sit down
sich treffen (mit + *dat.*)	meet (with)
sich unterhalten (mit + *dat.*)	entertain, converse (with)
sich verabreden (mit + *dat.*) (für + *acc.*)	make a date (with someone) (for (time))
sich verabschieden (von + *dat.*)	say good-bye (to)
sich vorstellen	introduce oneself
sich umdrehen	turn around
sich verlieben (in + *acc.*)	fall in love (with)
sich verloben (mit + *dat.*)	get engaged (to)

7.   Definite and Indefinite Articles

DEFINITE ARTICLES			
	SINGULAR		PLURAL
	MASCULINE	FEMININE	NEUTER	
NOMINATIVE	der	die	das	die
DATIVE	dem	der	dem	den
ACCUSATIVE	den	die	das	die
GENITIVE	des	der	des	der

INDEFINITE ARTICLES			
	SINGULAR		PLURAL
	MASCULINE	FEMININE	NEUTER	
NOMINATIVE	ein	eine	ein	keine
DATIVE	einem	einer	einem	keinen
ACCUSATIVE	einen	eine	ein	keine
GENITIVE	eines	einer	eines	keiner

8.   Adjective Endings

COMPARISON OF WEAK, STRONG, AND MIXED ADJECTIVE ENDINGS

| | | SINGULAR | | | PLURAL |
	MASCULINE	FEMININE	NEUTER	
Nom. weak	der alt-e	die alt-e	das alt-e	die alt-en
mixed	ein alt-er	eine alt-e	ein alt-es	keine alt-en
strong	alt-er	alt-e	alt-es	alt-e
Dat. weak	dem alt-en	der alt-en	dem alt-en	den alt-en
mixed	einem alt-en	einer alt-en	einem alt-en	keinen alt-en
strong	alt-em	alt-er	alt-em	alt-en
Acc. weak	den alt-en	die alt-e	das alt-e	die alt-en
mixed	einen alt-en	eine alt-e	ein alt-es	keine alt-en
strong	alt-en	alt-e	alt-es	alt-e
Gen. weak	des alt-en	der alt-en	des alt-en	der alt-en
mixed	eines alt-en	einer alt-e	eines alt-en	keiner alt-en
strong	alt-en	alt-er	alt-en	alt-er

German-English Vocabulary

Abbreviations used in this glossary

acc. – accusative

dat. – dative

pl. – plural

prep. dat./prep. acc. – preposition which takes the dative/accusative case

s.o. – some one

s.t. – something

v.t. – transitive verb (verb that can take a direct object and usually uses haben to form the perfect tenses)

v.i. – intransitive verb (verb that cannot take a direct object and usually uses sein to form the perfect tenses)

sep. – separable prefix verb

A

das A, *pl.* **-s** A

abbiegen, biegt ab, bog ab, hat abgebogen *sep.* turn into (a street)

der Abend, *pl.* **-e** evening

abends evenings

die Abendvorführung, *pl.* **-en** performance

aber but

abfahren, fährt ab, fuhr ab, ist/hat abgefahren *sep.* to depart

abhängen, hängt ab, hing ab, hat abgehangen von (+ *dat.***)** *sep.* to depend upon

abholen *sep.* to pick up

ablesen, liest ab, las ab, hat abgelesen *sep.* to read off

abnehmen, nimmt ab, nahm ab, hat abgenommen *sep.* to take off, lose weight

abraten, rät ab, riet ab, hat abgeraten von dat *sep.* to advise someone against something

abschießen, schießt ab, schoss ab, hat abgeschossen von (+ *dat.***)** *sep.* to shoot off (of something)

abschließen, schließt ab, schloss ab, hat abgeschlossen *sep.* to lock up

absehen, sieht ab, sah ab, hat abgesehen von (+ *dat.***)** *sep.* to disregard

abspringen, springt ab, sprang ab, hat abgesprungen to jump off

das Abwaschen, *pl.* **-** washing up, doing dishes

acht eight

achten auf (+ *acc.***)** to pay attention to

afrikanisch African

akademisch academic

das Albinotier, *pl.* **-e** albino animal

alkoholisch alcoholic

allein alone

alles everything

die Alm, *pl.* **-en** Alpine pasture

der Alm-Onkel, *pl.* **-** Alm Uncle

die Alpen Alps

der Alpinskier, *pl.* **-** or **Alpinschier** Alpine skier

als when (single event in the past); as

alt old

die Alterskrankheit, *pl.* **-en** Alzheimers, old age-related disease

der Ameisenesser, *pl.* **-** anteater

der Amethyst, *pl.* **-e** amethyst

an at, on, at the edge of, to

an Bord on board (a ship)

an(statt) . . . zu instead of

analysieren to analyze

anbieten bietet an, bot an vat angeboten *sep.* to offer

das Andenken, *pl.* **-** souvenir

andere other, different

(sich) ändern to change oneself

die Anerkennung, *pl.* **-en** recognition

anfahren, fährt an, fuhr an, ist/hat angefahren *sep.* drive towards something, knock something over, go at someone (verbally)

der Anfang, *pl.* **-ˇe** beginning

anfangen, fängt an, fing an, hat angefangen mit (+ *dat.***)** *sep.* to start something, begin (with)

anfliegen, fliegt an, flog an, ist angeflogen *sep.* to approach by air

der Angeber, *pl.* **-** braggart

angeln to fish

Angst haben, hat, hatte, hat gehabt vor (+ *dat.***)** to be afraid (of)

die Angst, **ˇe** worry, anxiety

anhaben, hat an, hatte an, hat angehabt *sep.* to have on, wear

anhalten, hält an, hielt an, hat angehalten *sep.* to stop (a vehicle or motion)

ankommen, kommt an, kam an, ist angekommen *sep.* to arrive

anmachen *sep.* to turn on

(sich) anmelden *sep.* to register oneself

annehmen, nimmt an, nahm an, hat angenommen *sep.* to assume

die Anonymität anonymity

(sich) anpassen an (+ *acc.***)** *sep.* to conform to, adapt to

anprobieren *sep.* to try on

anrufen, ruft an, rief an, hat angerufen *sep.* to call up

die Anschaffung, *pl.* **-en** procurement, acquisition

anschauen *sep.* to look at; watch

ansehen, sieht an, sah an, hat angesehen *sep.* to look at

anstatt . . . zu instead of . . . (verb) + ing

anstecken *sep.* to infect someone

sich anstecken *sep.* to catch an illness from *s.o.*

antik antique

die Antiquität, *pl.* **-n** antique

die Antwort, *pl.* **-n** answer

antworten auf (+ *acc.***)** to answer (something)

(sich) anziehen, zieht sich an, zog sich an, hat sich angezogen *sep.* get dressed, put something on

der Apfel, *pl.* **-ˇ** apple

der Apfelkuchen, *pl.* **-** apple cake

der Apfelsaft, *pl.* **-ˇe** apple juice

die Aquarelle, *pl.* **-n** watercolor painting

die Arbeit, *pl.* **-en** work

arbeiten an (+ *dat.***)** to work (on something)

die Arbeitsgemeinschaft, *pl.* **-en** work group

der Archäologe, *pl.* **-n** archeologist

der Ärger, *pl.* **-** annoyance

ärgerlich annoying

(sich) ärgern über (+ *acc.***)** to get angry (about)

arm poor

der Arm, *pl.* **-e** arm

der Arme, *pl.* **-n** poor man

die Armbrust, *pl.* **-ˇe** crossbow

die Armee, *pl.* **-n** army

arrogant arrogant

die Arthitis arthritis

der Arzt, *pl.* **-ˇe** male doctor

der Atheist, *pl.* **-en** atheist

der Athlet, *pl.* **-en** male athlete

die Athletin, *pl.* **-nen** female sports figure

der Atlantik Atlantic

die Atmosphäre, *pl.* **-n** atmosphere

auch also

auf at, to, on, on top of

auf Grund as a result of

aufbauen *sep.* to build up

auffahren, fährt auf, fuhr auf, ist aufgefahren *sep.* to drive up to, start up

auffallen, fällt auf, fiel auf, ist aufgefallen *sep.* stand out, be conspicuous

aufführen *sep.* to perform

aufgeben, gibt auf, gab auf, hat aufgegeben *sep.* to give up

aufheben *sep.* to lift (up)

aufhören mit (+ *dat.***)** *sep.* to stop doing (something)

auflösen *sep.* to solve

aufmachen *sep.* to open

aufpassen auf (+ *acc.***)** *sep.* to watch out (for), pay attention (to)

aufräumen *sep.* to tidy up

aufschließen, schließt auf, schloss auf, hat aufgeschlossen *sep.* to unlock

aufschreiben, schreibt auf, schrieb auf, hat aufgeschrieben *sep.* to write down

aufstehen, steht auf, stand auf, ist aufgestanden *sep.* to stand up, get up from bed

auftreten tritl auf, trat auf, ist aufgetreten *sep.* to appear; to step out

aufwachen, wacht auf, wachte auf, ist aufgewacht *sep.* to wake up (naturally)

aufwachsen, wächst auf, wuchs auf, ist aufgewachsen *sep.* to grow up

aufwecken *sep.* to wake (someone) up

der Augenarzt, *pl.* -¨e opthamalogist, eye doctor

aus *prep. dat.* from, out of

ausatmen *sep.* to exhale

ausbrechen, bricht aus, brach aus, ist ausgebrochen aus (+ *dat.*) *sep.* to break out (of something)

ausdrucken *sep.* to print out

ausfahren, fährt aus, fuhr aus, ist ausgefahren *sep.* to exit; to drive out

ausfallen, fällt aus, fiel aus, ist ausgefallen wegen (+ *gen*) *sep.* to be canceled (because of)

ausführen *sep.* to walk (a dog)

ausfüllen *sep.* to fill out

ausgeben, gibt aus, gab aus, hat ausgegeben *sep.* to spend (money)

ausgehen, geht aus, ging aus, ist ausgegangen *sep.* to go out

ausgraben, gräbt aus, grub aus, hat ausgegraben *sep.* to dig up

aushelfen, hilft aus, half aus, hat ausgeholfen *sep.* to help out

auslassen, lässt aus, ließ aus, hat ausgelassen *sep.* to let out

auslegen, legt aus, lag aus, hat ausgelegen *sep.* to lay out

ausmachen *sep.* to turn off

auspacken *v.t., sep.* to unpack

ausprobieren *sep.* to try out

ausreichen *sep.* to be enough

(sich) ausruhen *sep.* to relax

ausschließen schließt aus , schloss aus, hat aus geschlossen *sep.* to conclude from, assume as a result as

aussehen, sieht aus, sah aus, hat ausgesehen nach (+ *dat.*) *sep.* to look like, resemble

außer except for, besides

außerhalb outside of, with the exception of

außerirdische extraterrestrial

aussteigen, steigt aus, stieg aus, ist ausgestiegen *sep.* to get out, climb out

der Austausch trade, exchange

austragen, trägt aus, trug aus, hat ausgetragen to deliver

auswählen *sep.* to choose

auswerten *sep.* to evaluate

(sich) ausziehen, zieht sich aus, zog sich aus, hat sich ausgezogen *sep.* to undress

das Auto, *pl.* -s car

die Autobiografie, *pl.* -n autobiography

die Autopanne, *pl.* -n car breakdown

der Autor, *pl.* -en male author

die Autorin, *pl.* -nen female author

die Autosteuer, *pl.* -n automobile tax

das Autoverkehr traffic

B

das B, *pl.* -s B

das Baby, *pl.* -s or **die Babies** baby

babysitten, babysittet, babysittete, hat gebabysittet to babysit

der Babysitter, *pl.* - babysitter

backen, bäckt, backte (or buk), hat gebacken to bake

der Bäcker, *pl.* - baker

die Bäckerei, *pl.* -en bakery

das Bad, *pl.* -¨er bath, swimming pool, bathroom

baden swim, bathe

(sich) baden bathe

die Bahn train

die Bakterie, *pl.* -n bacteria

bald soon

das Ballett, *pl.* -e ballet

der Bambi-Preis, *pl.* -e European media award

die Bambi-Verleihung Bambi award ceremony

die Band (rock) band

die Bank, -en, *pl.* -¨e bank; bench

das Bankett, *pl.* -en banquet

der Banksicherheitsdienst, *pl.* -e bank security staff

der Bär, *pl.* -¨en bear

die Barockhalle, *pl.* -n Baroque hall

der Bau, *pl.* -ten (or *pl.* -e) building

der Bauch, *pl.* -¨e abdomen; stomach

bauen to build

das Bauerei, *pl.* -en building s.t.

der Baum, -¨e tree

Bayern Bavaria

bayrisch Bavarian

der Beamte, *pl.* -n official

(sich) bedanken bei (+ *dat.*) to thank, say thank you to someone

(sich) bedanken bei (+ *dat.*) / für (+ *acc.*) to thank, say thank you (to someone) / (for something)

die Bedeutung, *pl.* **-en** meaning

das Bedürfnis, *pl.* **-se** need

bedürftig needy, in need (of)

(sich) beeilen to be in a hurry

beeindruckend impressive

beenden to end

(sich) befassen mit *dat.* to take on, deal with

befehlen, befiehlt, befahl, hat befohlen to command

(sich) befinden, befindet sich, befand sich, hat sich befunden to be located

(sich) befreunden to make friends

begabt gifted

begehen, begeht, beging, hat begangen to commit (an act)

(sich) begeistern für (+ *acc.***)** to be enthusiastic (about)

begeistert enthusiastic

beginnen, beginnt, begann, hat begonnen to begin, start

begraben, begräbt, begrub, hat begraben to bury

behalten, behält, beheilt, hat behalten to keep

behaupten to maintain; assert

bei *prep. dat.* at, near, at the home of

beibringen, bringt bei, brachte bei, hat beigebracht *sep.* to teach (*s.o.* something)

beide both

beifahren, fährt bei, fuhr bei, ist beigefahren *sep.* to ride as front seat passenger, ride shotgun

beifügen *sep.* to add (something)

das Bein, *pl.* **-e** leg

beistehen, steht bei, stand bei, hat beigestanden *sep.* to stand with *s.o.*, support *s.o.*

beitragen, trägt bei, trug bei, hat beigetragen zu (+ *dat.***)** *sep.* to contribute (to)

beitreten, tritt bei, trat bei, ist beigetragen *sep.* to join

bekannt known

bekommen, bekommt, bekam, hat bekommen to receive

beliebt beloved

(sich) bemühen um (+ *acc.***)** to work (toward something), strive (for)

(sich) benehmen, benimmt sich, benahm sich, hat sich benommen to behave

benutzen to use

bereiten to prepare

der Berg, *pl.* **-** mountain

der Bergsteiger, *pl.* **-** male mountain climber

die Bergsteigerin, *pl.* **-nen** female mountain climber

die Berichterstatterin, *pl.* **-nen** female newscaster

die Berlinreise, *pl.* **-n** trip to Berlin

berühmt famous

(sich) beschäftigen mit (+ *dat.***)** to occupy oneself (with)

beschränken auf (+ *acc.***)** to limit (to)

beschützen vor (+ *dat.***)** to protect (against)

(sich) beschweren über (+ *acc.***)** to complain about (usually a formal complaint)

besichtigen to take a look around

besonders especially

besser better

best best

bestehen, besteht, bestand, hat bestanden auf (+ *dat.***)** to insist (upon)

bestehen aus (+ *dat.***)** to consist of

bestehlen, bestiehlt, bestahl, hat bestohlen to rob (someone)

bestimmt definite, definitely

der Besuch, *pl.* **-e** visit

besuchen *v.t.* to visit

beten to plead, pray

betrügen um (+ *acc.***)** to cheat someone out of something, betray

das Bett, *pl.* **-en** bed

betteln um (+ *acc.***)** to beg (for)

bevor before

(sich) bewegen to move, stir

(sich) bewerben, bewirbt sich, bewarb sich, hat sich beworben um (+ *acc.***)** to apply (for)

bewusst aware (of)

bezahlen to pay

bezahlt paid

(sich) beziehen, bezieht sich, bezog sich, hat sich bezogen auf (+ *acc.***)** to refer (to)

der Bezirk, *pl.* **-e** district

der Biathlonwettkampf, *pl.* **-̈e** biathalon competition

die Bibliothek, *pl.* **-en** library

(sich) biegen, biegt sich, bog sich, hat sich gebogen to bend

bieten, bietet, bat, hat geboten to offer

das Bild, *pl.* **-er** picture

das Bildnis, -se portrait

binden, bindet, band, hat gebunden to bind

bis *prep. acc.* until; up to

bisschen a little

(sich) blamieren to embarrass oneself

blasen, bläst, blies, hat geblasen to blow

das Blei lead

bleiben, bleibt, blieb, ist geblieben to stay, remain

der Blitz, *pl.* **-e** lightning

das Blümchen, - little blossom, flower

das Blut blood

der Blutdruckmesser, *pl.* **-** syphgmomanometer

das Bobrennen bobsled racing

der Bobsport bob sledding

der or das Bonbon, *pl.* **-s** pieced candy

das Boot, *pl.* **-e** boat

böse angry

der Boxer, *pl.* **-** boxer

braten, brät, briet, hat gebraten to roast (food)

brauchen to need

das Brauchtum, *pl.* **-¨er** customs, traditions

braun brown

brechen, bricht, brach, hat gebrochen to break

(sich etwas) brechen, bricht, brach, hat gebrochen to break (a body part)

brennen, brennt, brannte, hat gebrannt to burn, be on fire

die Brille, *pl.* **-n** eyeglasses

bringen, bringt, brachte, hat gebracht to bring

die Bronzmedaille, *pl.* **-n** bronze medal

das Brötchen, *pl.* **-** roll

der Bruder, *pl.* **-¨** brother

brüllend roaring

brünette brunette

das Buch, *pl.* **-¨er** book

die Bücherei, *pl.* **-en** library

die Buchhandlung, *pl.* **-en** book store

das Büchlein, *pl.* **-** little book

bügeln to iron

die Bühne, *pl.* **-n** stage

der Bühnenbildausstatter, **-** set designer

die Bundeskanzlerin, *pl.* **-nen** female chancellor

die Bundesmeisterin, *pl.* **-nen** female national champion

der Bundestag Lower House of Parliament

bunt colored, colorful

das Burgtheater, *pl.* **-** Imperial Court Theater

der Bus, *pl.* **-se** bus

die Bushaltestelle, *pl.* **-n** bus stop

der CD-Rohling, *pl.* **-e** blank CD

die Chance, *pl.* **-n** chance

der Chor, *pl.* **-¨e** choir

der Christkindlmarkt, *pl.* **-¨e** Christmas market

der Computer, *pl.* **-** computer

D

da since (causal, reason)

dabei there; thereby

der Dadaismus Dadism

damals then, at that time

die Dame, *pl.* **-n** woman; lady

damit so that; with it

danach after that

daneben next to it

danken für (+ *acc.*) to thank for, say thank you for something

die Dankrede, *pl.* **-n** thank you speech

dann then, at that time

darauf on it; on them

darum for it; that's why

dass that

dasselbe, derselbe, dieselbe the same

das *Dat*.um, die *Dat*.en date

dauern to last; take time to

die Decke, *pl.* **-n** tablecloth; cover

dein your (fam.)

dekorieren to decorate

denken von (+ *dat.*) denkt, dachte, hat gedacht think about (opinion)

denken, denkt, dachte, hat gedacht an (+ *acc.*) / über (+ *acc.*) think (about) / contemplate

das Denkmal, *pl.* **-¨er** monument

denn because

deswegen for that reason, on account of that

determiniert determined

deuten auf (+ *acc.*) to point (to)

deutsch German (adj.)

der Dezember, *pl.* **-e** December

der Diamant, *pl.* **-en** diamond

der Diamantenring, *pl.* **-e** diamond ring

die Diät, *pl.* **-en** diet

der Dichter, *pl.* **-** poet

dienen to serve

der Dienstag, -e Tuesday

diesseits this side of

die Digitalkamera, *pl.* **-s** digital camera

die Diskette, -n diskette

diskutieren über (+ *acc.*) to discuss, talk about

(sich) distanzieren von (+ *dat.*) distance oneself from

der DJ, *pl.* **-s** DJ

doch but; yet; indeed

das Dogma, die Dogmen dogma

der Dokumentarfilm, *pl.* **-e** documentary film

der Dom, *pl.* **-e** cathedral

der Domplatz, *pl.* **-¨e** cathedral square

der Donner, *pl.* - thunder

der Donnerstag, *pl.* -e Thursday

dort there

die Dose, *pl.* -n tin can

das Drama, die Dramen drama

draußen outside

drei three

dreizehn thirteen

dringen, dringt, drang, hat gedrungen to urge; put pressure on

das Drittel, *pl.* - third

die Drogerie, *pl.* -en drug store

drüben over there

der Drucker, *pl.* - printer

du you *fam.*

dumm dumb

durch *prep. acc.* through; by

durchfahren, fährt durch, fuhr durch, ist durchgefahren *sep.* to drive through

dürfen, darf, durfte, hat gedurft may, to be permitted to

der Durst thirst

(sich) duschen to take a shower

die DVD/CD-Sammlung, *pl.* -en DVD/CD collection

E

echt real; pure; really

die Ecke, *pl.* -n corner

der Egoist, *pl.* -en egoist

ehemalig former

die Ehre, *pl.* -n honor

ehren to honor

das Eid, *pl.* -e oath

eigen own

das Eigentum, *pl.* -"er private property

(sich) eignen zu (+ *dat.*) be suitable as

einatmen *sep.* to inhale

(sich etwas) einbilden *sep.* to imagine something (that's usually not correct)

einblasen, bläst ein, blies ein, hat eingeblasen *sep.* to blow into

einbrechen, bricht ein, brach ein, hat eingebrochen *sep.* to break in

der Eindringling, *pl.* -e burglar

einfahren, fährt ein, fuhr ein, ist eingefahren *sep.* to enter; to drive into

einfallen, fällt ein, fiel ein, ist eingefallen (+ *dat.*) *sep.* to occur to someone

einführen in (+ *acc.*) *sep.* introduce something into an environment

der Eingang, *pl.* -"e entrance

einige a few

einkaufen *sep.* to shop

einladen, lädt ein, lud ein, hat eingeladen *sep.* to invite

(sich) einmischen in (+ *acc.*) *sep.* to meddle in

einpacken *sep.* to pack

die Eins one

einschlafen, schläft ein, schlief ein, ist eingeschlafen *sep.* to fall asleep

einsteigen, steigt ein, stieg ein, ist eingestiegen *sep.* to get in, climb in

eintausend a thousand

eintragen, trägt ein, trug ein, hat eingetragen *sep.* to register, enter

eintreten, tritt ein, trat ein, ist eingetreten *sep.* to step in; enter (movement)

die Eintrittskarte, *pl.* -n ticket (to enter)

der Einwohner, *pl.* - inhabitant

einzig only; unique

das Eis ice cream

der Eisbär, *pl.* -en polar bear

der Eisberg, *pl.* -e iceberg

die Eishockeymannschaft, *pl.* -en ice hockey team

das Eishockeyspiel, *pl.* -e ice hockey game

der Eiskunstlauf figure skating

die Eiskunstlaufhalle, *pl.* -n indoor skating rink

der Eisregen freezing rain

der Eisschnelllauf speed skating

ekelhaft nauseating

elegant elegant

die Eltern parents

der Elternabend, *pl.* -e parent-teacher night

der Elternverein, *pl.* -e parent-teacher association

empfehlen, empfiehlt, empfahl, hat empfohlen to recommend

empfinden empfindet, empfand, hat empfunden to feel; sense

(sich) empören to become indignant, become enraged

das Ende, *pl.* -n end

enden to end

endlich finally

das Endspiel, *pl.* -e final game in a sports competition

entdecken to discover

die Entdeckung, *pl.* -en discovery

entlang along

entnehmen, entnimmt, entnahm, hat entnommen (aus + *dat.*) take from, infer from

(sich) entscheiden, entscheidet sich, entschied sich, hat sich entschieden für/gegen (+ *acc.*) decide (for/against)

(sich) entschuldigen bei (+ *dat.***) / für (+** *acc.***)** to excuse oneself; to apologize to *s.o.* for

die Entschuldigung, *pl.* **-en** excuse; apology

entweder . . . oder either . . . or

die Epoche, -n epoch

er he; it (*masc.*)

das Erdbeben earthquake

die Erde, -n earth

erfinden, erfindet, erfand, hat erfunden to invent

die Erfindung, *pl.* **-en** invention

der Erfolg, -e success

erfolgreich successful

die Erfrischung, *pl.* **-en** refreshment

(sich) ergeben, ergibt sich, ergab sich, hat sich ergeben aus (+ *dat.***)** to result (from)

das Ergebnis, *pl.* **-se** result

(sich) erholen von (+ *dat.***)** to recuperate/recover (from)

(sich) erinnern an (+ *acc.***)** to remember

erinnern an (+ *acc.***)** to remind (about)

die Erinnerung, *pl.* **-en** memory

(sich) erkälten to catch a cold

die Erkältung, *pl.* **-en** cold

(sich) erkundigen nach (+ *dat.***)** to inquire (about)

erlauben to allow

das Erlaubnis, *pl.* **-se** permission

erleben to experience

das Erlebnis, *pl.* **-se** experience

ermuntern to encourage

eröffnen to open (ceremoniously)

der Eröffnungstag, *pl.* **-e** opening day

der Erreger, *pl.* **-** germ

errichten to erect

erschießen, erschießt, erschoss, hat erschossen to shoot (dead)

erst first, just

ertrinken, ertrinkt, ertrank, ist ertrunken to drown

erwachsen to grow up

der Erwachsene, *pl.* **-n** adult

erzählen von (+ *dat.***)** to tell (a story) about

essen, isst, aß, hat gegessen *v.t.* to eat

das Esspaket, *pl.* **-e** snack pack

die Etikette, *pl.* **-n** etiquette

der Euro, *pl.* **-s** Euro (currency)

das Europa Europe

existieren to exist

exotisch exotic

F

die Fabrik, *pl.* **-en** factory

der Fahnenträger, *pl.* **-** flag bearer

fahren, fährt, fuhr, ist/hat gefahren to ride, drive

der Fahrer, *pl.* **-** chauffeur

die Fahrerei driving around, excess driving

die Fahrschule, *pl.* **-en** driving school

die Fahrt, *pl.* **-en** trip

die Fakultät, *pl.* **-en** faculty

der Fall, *pl.* **-ˮe** fall; case

fallen, fällt, fiel, ist gefallen to fall

falten to fold

die Familie, *pl.* **-n** family

der Fan, *pl.* **-s** fan (as in sports)

fantastisch fantastic

die Farbe, *pl.* **-n** color; paint

färben to color; to paint

fast almost

die Fastnacht carnival atmosphere; celebration the day before Ash Wednesday

faszinieren to fascinate

die Faulheit laziness

der Favorit, *pl.* **-en** favorite

feiern to celebrate

der Feiertag, *pl.* **-e** holiday

der Feigling, *pl.* **-e** coward

fein fine

das Fenster, *pl.* **-** window

fern far; at a distance

fernsehen to watch TV

das Fernsehen, - television

der Fernsehturm, *pl.* **-ˮe** TV tower

der Fernsprecher, *pl.* **-** telephone

fertig ready; finished

fest firm

das Fest, *pl.* **-e** party

festhalten, hält fest, hielt fest, hat festgehalten an (+ *dat.***)** *sep.* hold onto tightly

festlegen *sep.* to establish, set firm

feststellen *sep.* to determine

der Feuerschutzalarm, *pl.* **-e** fire alarm

das Feuerwerk, *pl.* **-** fireworks

der Film, *pl.* **-e** film

der Filmfan, *pl.* **-s** film fan

das Filmhaus, *pl.* **-ˮer** movie theater

die Filmmacherin, *pl.* **-nen** female film maker

der Filmregisseur, *pl.* **-e** movie director

die Filmrolle, *pl.* **-n** movie part

der Filmstar, *pl.* **-s** film star

die Filmstunde, *pl.* **-n** class on movie-making

der Filmtitel, *pl.* **-** film title

finanzieren to finance

finden, findet, fand, hat gefunden *v.t.* to find

der Finger, *pl.* **-** finger

der Fingernagel, *pl.* **-ˮ** fingernail

die Firma, die Firmen company

fit fit

das Fleisch meat

fliegen, fliegt, floh, ist geflagen to fly

fliehen, flieht, floh, ist geflohen vor (+ *dat.***)** to flee (from)

fließen, fließen, fließt, floss, ist geflossen to flow

der Floh, *pl.* **-¨e** flea

das Floß, *pl.* **-¨e** raft

die Flöte, *pl.* **-n** flute

der Flughafen, *pl.* **-¨n** airport

der Flugplan, *pl.* **-¨e** flight plan; schedule

das Flugprogramm, *pl.* **-e** flight lessons

der Flugschein, *pl.* **-e** plane ticket

die Flugschule, *pl.* **-n** flight school

föhnen to blow dry

folgen to follow

die Form, *pl.* **-en** form; shape

die Formulierung, *pl.* **-en** formulation

fort forth

fortfahren, fährt fort, fuhr fort, ist fortgefahren *sep.* to continue, drive on

fortgehen, geht fort, ging fort, ist fortgegangen *sep.* to go on

das Fotoalbum, die Fotoalben photo album

der Fotoapparat, *pl.* **-e** camera

das Fotobuch, *pl.* **-¨er** picture book; photo album

fotografieren *v.t.* to photograph

die Fotografin, *pl.* **-nen** female photograher

das Fotomodel, *pl.* **-s** photo model

die Fotoreportage, *pl.* **-n** photojournalism

die Frage, *pl.* **-n** question

fragen nach (+ *dat.***)** to ask (about)

französisch French

die Frau, *pl.* **-en** woman

der Frauenarzt, *pl.* **-¨e** male gynecologist

das Fräulein, *pl.* **-** Miss, unmarried young woman

frei free

die Freiheit, *pl.* **-en** freedom

der Freitagabend, *pl.* **-e** Friday evening

die Freizeit leisure time

freizugänglich free of entry charge; open to the public

fressen, frisst, fraß, hat gefressen to eat (for animals)

(sich) freuen auf (+ *acc.***)** to look forward (to)

(sich) freuen über (+ *acc.***)** be happy (about)

der Freund, *pl.* **-e** male friend

die Freundin, *pl.* **-nen** female friend; girlfriend

freundlich friendly

die Freundlichkeit, *pl.* **-en** friendliness

die Freundschaft, *pl.* **-en** friendship

der Frieden, *pl.* **-** peace

frieren, friert, fror, hat gefroren to freeze

frisch cool; fresh

froh happy

der Front, *pl.* **-en** (weather) front

früh early

das Frühstück, *pl.* **-e** breakfast

der Fuchs, *pl.* **-¨e** fox

fühlen to feel

(sich) fühlen to feel (health)

führen to lead

die Führung, *pl.* **-en** guided tour; leadership

fünf five

das Fünftel, *pl.* **-** fifth

der Fungus, die Fungi fungus

für *prep. acc.* for

furchtbar terrible

(sich) fürchten vor (+ *dat.***)** to fear, be afraid (of)

der Fuß, *pl.* **-¨e** foot

die Fußärztin, -nen female podiatrist

der Fußball, *pl.* **-¨e** soccer; soccer ball

der Fußballer, *pl.* **-** soccer player

die Fußballmanschaft, *pl.* **-en** soccer team

die Fußgängerzone, *pl.* **-n** pedestrian zone

G

gähnen to yawn

der Gang, *pl.* **-¨e** hallway; gait

ganz completely; whole

die Garage, *pl.* **-n** garage

das Gartenpalais, *pl.* **-** garden palace

der Gasbehälter, *pl.* **-** gas tank

die Gasse, *pl.* **-n** alley; small street

der Gast, *pl.* **-¨e** guest

das Gebäck, *pl.* **-e** pastry, baked goods

gebären, gebärt, gebor, hat geboren to give birth; to bear

das Gebäude, *pl.* **-** building

geben, gibt, gab, hat gegeben to give

die Geburtstadt, *pl.* **-¨e** city of birth

der Geburtstag, *pl.* **-e** birthday

das Geburtstagsgeschenk, *pl.* **-e** birthday gift

der Gedanke, *pl.* **-n** thought
gedeihen, gedeiht, gedieh, ist gediehen to thrive
das Gedicht, *pl.* **-e** poem
gefährlich dangerous
gefallen, gefällt, gefiel, ist gefallen to please
das Gefängnis, *pl.* **-se** jail; prison
gegen against
gegenüber across from, opposite
gehen um (+ *acc.***) geht, ging, ist gegangen** to be concerned about
gehen, geht, ging, ist gegangen, *v.i.* to go
gehorchen to obey
gehören zu (+ *dat.***)** to belong (to)
das Geld, *pl.* **-er** money
der Geldsack, *pl.* **-̈e** money bag
der Geldtransporter, *pl.* **-** armored vehicle used to transport money
gelingen, gelingt, gelang, ist gelungen to be sucessful
gelten, gilt, galt, hat gegolten to be valid
das Gemälde, *pl.* **-** painting
das Gemüse vegetable
die Gemütlichkeit coziness, intimacy
genug enough
die Geographie geography
das Gepäck luggage
gerade just
das Geräusch, *pl.* **-e** noise
gern gladly; with pleasure
geschafft completed
das Geschenk, *pl.* **-e** gift
die Geschichte, *pl.* **-n** story; history
der Geschichtslehrer, *pl.* **-** male history teacher
das Geschirr china; dishes
das Geschwister, *pl.* **-** sibling

gestern yesterday
gesund healthy
die Gesundheit health
das Getränk, *pl.* **-e** drink
das Gewicht, *pl.* **-er** weight
das Gewinn, *pl.* **-e** profit
gewinnen, gewinnt, gewann, hat gewonnen to win
der Gewinner, - winner
gewiss certain (of)
das Gewitter, - thunder and lightning storm
(sich) gewöhnen an (+ *acc.***)** get used (to)
giessen, gießt, goss, hat gegossen to pour
das Glas, *pl.* **-̈er** glass
glauben an (+ *acc.***)** believe (in)
gleich at once; same
gleichen to equate
gleiten, gleitet, glitt, ist geglitten to glide
der Globalismus, die Globalismen globalism
die Globalization globalization
der Glücksbringer, *pl.* **-** good luck charm
golden golden
der Gouverneur, *pl.* **-e** governor
der Gouverneurposten, - governorship
graben, gräbt, grub, hat gegraben to dig
der Grad, *pl.* **-e** degree
der Granit granite
gratulieren (zu + *dat.***)** to congratulate (on)
das Graubrot, *pl.* **-e** mixed rye and wheat bread
der Graupel sleet
greifen, greift, griff, hat gegriffen nach (+ *dat.***)** to reach or grasp (for)
das Griechenland Greece
groß big, tall

die Großmutter, *pl.* **-̈** grandmother
die Großstadt, *pl.* **-̈e** large city
der Großvater, *pl.* **-̈** grandfather
grün green
gründen to found; establish
die Gründung, *pl.* **-en** foundation
gucken to look (colloquial)
gut good; well
das Gymnasium, *pl.* **-** high school

H
das Haar, *pl.* **-e** hair
(sich) die Haare kämmen to comb one's hair
(sich) die Haare waschen, wäscht, wusch, hat gewaschen to wash one's hair
haben, hat, hatte, hat gehabt to have
die Haft custody
der Hagel, *pl.* **-** hail
halb half
halt just
halten, hält, hielt, hat gehalten für (+ *acc.***) / von (+** *dat.***)** to consider (as), take (for) / think about (opinion)
der Hamburger, *pl.* **-** hamburger
die Hand, *pl.* **-̈e** hand
der Handel trade
(sich) handeln um (+ *acc.***)** to deal (with), to be (about)
das Handtuch, *pl.* **-̈er** towel
hängen, hängt, hing, hat gehangen to hang
die Harmonie harmony
hauen to hit
der Hauptcharakter, *pl.* **-e** protagonist; main character

das Hauptkonzert, *pl.* **-e** main concert

die Hauptstadt, *pl.* **-¨e** capital city

das Haus, *pl.* **-¨er** house

die Hausaufgabe, *pl.* **-n** housework; chores

der Hausmeister, *pl.* **-** caretaker

der Hautarzt, *pl.* **-¨e** male dermatologist

heben, hebt, hob, hat gehaben to raise

heilig holy

die Heilmethode, *pl.* **-n** healing method

das Heilmittel remedy

die Heimfahrt, *pl.* **-en** trip home

heimlich secret

heiraten to marry

heißen, heißt, hieß, hat geheißen to be called

der Held, *pl.* **-en** hero

helfen, hilft, half, hat geholfen to help

das Hemd, *pl.* **-en** shirt

her here (motion towards speaker)

herausfordern zu (+ *dat.***)** *sep.* to challenge someone (to)

hereinkommen, kommt herein, kam herein, ist hereingekommen *sep.* to come in

hereintragen, trägt herein, trug herein, hat hereingetragen *sep.* carry in

herkommen, kommt her, kam her, ist hergekommen *sep.* to come here

herrlich marvelous

herunterfallen, fällt herunter, fiel herunter, ist heruntergefallen *sep.* to fall down

heute today

heutzutage nowadays

die Hexenmeisterin, *pl.* **-nen** witch

hier here

die Hilfe, *pl.* **-n** help

der Himmel, *pl.* **-** sky

hin there (motion away from speaker)

hinauswerfen, wirft hinaus, warf hinaus, hat hinausgeworfen *sep.* to throw out

hindern an (+ *dat.***)** to hinder, try to prevent something from happening

hingehen, geht hin, ging hin, ist hingegangen *sep.* to go away

(sich) hinsetzen *sep.* to sit down

hinter behind

hintrainieren *sep.* to train towards

hinweisen auf (+ *acc.***) weist hin, wies hin, hat hingewiesenv** to refer to, point to

hinwerfen, wirft hin, warf hin, hat hingeworfen *sep.* to throw down

das Hirschleder, *pl.* **-** deerskin

historisch historic

das Hobby, *pl.* **-s** or **die Hobbies** hobby

hoch high

der Hoch- *pl.* or **Tiefdruck,** **-** high or low pressure

die Hochzeit, *pl.* **-en** marriage

das Hockeyendspiel, *pl.* **-e** hockey final

hoffen auf (+ *acc.***)** to hope for

der Hoforganist, *pl.* **-en** chief organist for royalty

hohl hollow; cavernous

hören auf (+ *acc.***)** to listen to; obey

das Hörgerät, *pl.* **-e** hearing aid

die Hörschwierigkeit hearing impairment

die Hose, *pl.* **-n** pants

das Hotel, *pl.* **-s** hotel

der Hund, *pl.* **-e** dog

das Hündchen, *pl.* **-** puppy

der Hundertfüßer, *pl.* **-** centipede

das Hundertstel, *pl.* **-** hundredth

hungrig hungry

der Husten, *pl.* **-** cough

der Hut, *pl.* **-¨** hat

(sich) hüten vor (+ *dat.***)** to guard (oneself) (against)

I

der Idealismus idealism

identifizieren to identify

ignorieren to ignore

immer always

indem in that

der Indianer, *pl.* **-** male Native American

infolge because of

(sich) informieren über (+ *acc.***)** to find out or inform oneself (about)

inklusive including

innerhalb within; inside

das Instrument, *pl.* **-e** instrument

inszenieren to produce theatrically

intensiv intensive

interessant interesting

(sich) interessieren für (+ *acc.***)** to be interested (in)

das Internet Internet

das Interview, *pl.* **-s** interview

investieren to invest

der Ire, *pl.* **-n** Irishman

irgendwann some time; at any time

irgendwo anywhere
(sich) irren to err, make a mistake
das Irrtum, *pl.* **-ʺer** mistake, error

J
jagen to hunt
das Jahr, *pl.* **-e** year
jahrelang all year long
die Jahresendefilmvorführung, *pl.* **-** end of year film showing
das Jahrhundert, *pl.* **-e** century
der Januar, *pl.* **-e** January
je (mehr) . . . desto (besser) the (more) . . . the (better)
jeder each
jemand everyone
jenseits that side of
jobben to work
das Joggen jogging
das Jugendhotel, *pl.* **-** youth hotel
jung young
der Junge, *pl.* **-n** young man; boy
der Jüngling, *pl.* **-e** young man

K
der Kaffee, *pl.* **-s** coffee
der Kalender, *pl.* **-** calendar
kalt cold
(sich) kämmen to comb one's hair
kämpfen um (+ *acc.***)** to fight (for)
der Kandidat, *pl.* **-en** candidate
kandidieren für (+ *acc.***)** to run for office
der Kanton, *pl.* **-e** canton
das Karnevalerlebnis, *pl.* **-se** canival experience
die Karnevalfestivität, *pl.* **-en** carnival celebration

die Karriere, *pl.* **-n** career
die Karte, *pl.* **-n** card; ticket
der Käse cheese
der Käseburger, *pl.* **-** cheeseburger
die Kasse, *pl.* **-n** cashier
die Kategorie, *pl.* **-n** category
der Kater, *pl.* **-** male cat
das Kätzchen, *pl.* **-** kitten
die Katze, *pl.* **-n** female cat
kauen *v.t.* to chew
kaufen *v.t.* to buy
(sich etwas) kaufen to buy something for yourself
der Käufer, *pl.* **-** male shopper
kein none
der Keks, *pl.* **-e** cookie
der Keller, *pl.* **-** basement
kennen lernen to meet
kennen, kennt, kannte, hat gekannt to know (a person or place), be acquainted with
das Kind, *pl.* **-er** child
das Kindchen, *pl.* **-** little child
der Kinderarzt, *pl.* **-ʺe** male pediatrician
der Kindergarten, *pl.* **-ʺ** Kindergarten
das Kino, *pl.* **-s** movie theater
der Kinobesuch, *pl.* **-e** visit to the movies
klagen über (+ *acc.***)** to complain (about, usually an informal complaint)
die Klapperschlange, *pl.* **-n** rattlesnake
klar bright; clear
die Klarsichtfolie, *pl.* **-n** plastic wrap
die Klasse, *pl.* **-n** class
die Klassenarbeit, *pl.* **-en** classwork
der Klassenerfolg, *pl.* **-e** class success

der Klassenkamerad, *pl.* **-n** classmate
die Klassenparodie, *pl.* **-n** humorous class show
das Klassenprojekt, *pl.* **-e** class project
der Klassenschnappschuss, *pl.* **-ʺe** class snapshot
der Klassensprecher, *pl.* **-** male class president
die Klassensprecherin *pl.* **-nen** female class president
der Klassiker, *pl.* **-** classical author or composer
klassisch classic
klatschen to applaud, clap
das Klavier, *pl.* **-e** piano
der Klavierunterricht, *pl.* **-** piano lesson
das Kleid, *pl.* **-er** dress; clothing
das Kleinkind, *pl.* **-er** toddler; small child
der Kleinvogel, *pl.* **-ʺ** small bird
klingeln to ring
klug clever
kneifen to pinch
das Knie, *pl.* **-** knee
die Knieverletzung, *pl.* **-en** knee injury
die Koalition, *pl.* **-en** coalition
der Köcher, *pl.* **-er** quiver
der Koffer, *pl.* **-** suitcase
die Kombination, *pl.* **-en** combination
das Komikerteam, *pl.* **-s** comic team
komponieren to compose
der König, *pl.* **-e** king
die Königin, *pl.* **-nen** queen
konkurrieren um (+ *acc.***)** to be in competition (for)
können, kann, konnte, hat gekonnt can, to be allowed to
die Kontrolle, *pl.* **-en** control

kontrollieren to check; inspect; control

die Kontroverse, *pl.* **-en** controversy

(sich) konzentrieren auf (+ *acc.*) to concentrate on

das Konzert, *pl.* **-e** concert

der Konzertflötenspieler, *pl.* **-** flute player

der Konzertflügel, *pl.* **-** concert grand piano

die Konzerthalle, *pl.* **-n** concert hall

der Kopf, *pl.* **-ˮe** head

der Körper, *pl.* **-** body

kosten to cost

die Kosten, *pl.* expenses

krank sick

das Krankenhaus, *pl.* **-ˮer** hospital

die Krankenversicherung, *pl.* **-en** health insurance

der Krankenwagen, *pl.* **-** ambulance

die Krankheit, *pl.* **-en** illness

kreativ creative

der Krebsarzt, *pl.* **-ˮe** male oncologist, cancer doctor

kriechen, kriecht, kroch ist gekrochen crawl; creep

der Krieg, *pl.* **-e** war

kriegen to get

die Kriegsmarine, *pl.* **-en** navy

das Kriminalmuseum, die Kriminalmuseen museum of crime

das Kriterium, die Kriterien criterion

der Kritiker, *pl.* **-** critic

die Küche, *pl.* **-n** kitchen

der Kuchen, *pl.* **-** cake

das Kuchenrezept, *pl.* **-e** cake recipe

die Kultur, *pl.* **-en** culture

(sich) kümmern um (+ *acc.*) to look (after), take care (of)

die Kunst, *pl.* **-ˮe** art

die Kunstakademie, *pl.* **-n** art academy

die Kunstform, *pl.* **-en** artform

das Kunsthaus, *pl.* **-ˮer** art museum

der Kunsthistoriker, *pl.* **-** art historian

der Künstler, *pl.* **-** male artist

künstlerisch artistic

die Kurve, *pl.* **-n** curve

die Kusine, *pl.* **-n** female cousin

der Kuss, *pl.* **-ˮe** kiss

L

lachen über (+ *acc.*) to laugh (about)

lackieren to polish

laden, lädt, lud, hat geladen, *v.t.* to load

das Land, *pl.* **-ˮer** country

die Landschaft, *pl.* **-en** countryside, landscape

die Landung, **-en** landing

lang long

der Langlauf cross-country skiing

der Langläufer, *pl.* **-** male cross-country skier

lassen, lässt, ließ, hat gelassen to let; allow

das Laufen running

laufen, läuft, lief, ist gelaufen *pl.* to run

laut loud

leben von (+ *dat.*) to live (off), exist (from)

das Leben, *pl.* **-** life

das Leder, *pl.* **-** leather

das Lehrbuch, *pl.* **-ˮer** textbook

der Lehrer, *pl.* **-** male teacher

die Lehrerin, *pl.* **-nen** female teacher

das Lehrjahr, *pl.* **-e** learning year; apprenticeship

der Lehrling, *pl.* **-e** apprentice

die Leichenschauärztin, *pl.* **-nen** female coroner

leiden an (+ *dat.*) leidet, litt, hat gelitten to suffer from, be ill with

leider unfortunately

leihen, leiht, lieh, hat geliehen to borrow; to lend

leise quiet; soft

(ein Eid) leisten to take (swear) an oath

die Leistung, *pl.* **-en** achievement

lernen to learn

lesen, liest, las, hat gelesen, *v.t.* to read

letzt last

die Leute people

die Liebe, *pl.* **-n** love

lieben to love

die Liebesgeschichte, *pl.* **-n** love story; fairy tale

der Liebesgruß, *pl.* **-e** affectionate greeting

der Liebling, *pl.* **-e** darling, dear; favorite

der Lieblingsberg, *pl.* **-e** favorite mountain

der Lieblingsfilm, *pl.* **-e** favorite film

die Lieblingsmaskotte, *pl.* **-n** favorite mascot

die Lieblingssekretärin, *pl.* **-nen** favorite secretary

die Lieblingsszene, *pl.* **-n** favorite scene

der Lieblingswintersport favorite winter sport

das Liegen lying (position)

liegen, liegt, lag, hat gelegen to lie

die Limo, *pl.* **-s** soda

der Lipizzaner, **-** Lipizzaner horse

das Lokal, *pl.* **-e** (neighborhood) restaurant; pub

lösen to solve

der Löwe, *pl.* **-n** lion
die Lungentuberkulose, *pl.*
  -n tuberculosis
lustig cheerful; merry

M
machen to make; to do
das Mädchen, *pl.* **-** girl
mähen to mow
die Mahlzeit, *pl.* **-en**
  mealtime
der Mai, *pl.* **-e** May
das Mal, *pl.* **-e** time
malen to paint
die Malerei, *pl.* **-en** painting
manchmal sometimes
der Mann, *pl.* **-̈er** man
die Mannschaft, *pl.* **-en**
  team
das Manöver, *pl.* **-** maneuver
das Märchenschloss, *pl.* **-̈er**
  fairy tale castle
die Marienbrücke, *pl.*
  - Maria Bridge
der Marktplatz, *pl.* **-̈e**
  marketplace
der Marmor, *pl.* **-e** marble
marschieren to march
das Marzipanschweinchen,
  - candy pig made out of
  marzipan
massiv massive
die Mathaufgabe, *pl.* **-n**
  math homework
die Mathe math
der Matheathlet, *pl.* **-en**
  mathlete, competitor in
  math academic contests
die Mathestunde, *pl.* **-n**
  math lesson
die Matratze, *pl.* **-n** matress
die Medaille, *pl.* **-n** medal
die Medaillezeremonie, *pl.*
  -n awards ceremony
mehr more
die Mehrheit, *pl.* **-en**
  majority
meiden to avoid; to shun
die Meile, *pl.* **-n** mile

die Menge, *pl.* **-n** crowd
die Mensa school cafeteria
der Mensch, *pl.* **-en** human
  being
der Menschenaffe, *pl.* **-n** ape
messen, misst, maß, hat
  gemessen to measure
der Meter, *pl.* **-** meter
die Methode, *pl.* **-n** method
das Migrantenkind, *pl.* **-er**
  migrant children
das Militär, *pl.* **s** army
die Millionärin, *pl.* **-nen**
  female millionaire
die Minderheit, *pl.* **-en**
  minority
mindestens at least
die Minorität, *pl.* **-en**
  minority
die Mission, *pl.* **-en** mission
misslingen, misslingt,
  misslang, ist misslungen
  to be unsuccessful
mit with, by
mitarbeiten *sep.* to work
  with someone
mitbringen, bringt mit,
  brachte mit, hat
  mitgebracht *sep.* to bring
  with; to bring along
mitfahren, fährt mit, fuhr
  mit, ist mitgefahren *sep.*
  to drive with someone
mitfeiern *sep.* to celebrate
  with *s.o.*
mitkommen, kommt mit,
  kam mit, ist
  mitgekommen *sep.* to
  come along; to come with
mitmachen *sep.* to
  participate
mitnehmen, nimmt mit,
  nahm mit, hat
  mitgenommen *sep.* to
  take with; to take along
mitsingen, singt mit, sang
  mit, hat mitgesungen *sep.*
  to sing along
mitspielen *sep.* to play with

das Mittel, *pl.* **-** means
die Mitternacht midnight
der Mittwoch, *pl.* **-e**
  Wednesday
das Modell, *pl.* **-e** model
modern modern
mögen, mag, mochte, hat
  gemocht to like, like to
die Molkerei, *pl.* **-en** dairy
der Moment, *pl.* **e** moment
der Monat, *pl.* **-e** month
monatelang lasting for
  months
der Monsun, *pl.* **-e** monsoon
der Montag, *pl.* **-e** Monday
der Mord, *pl.* **-e** murder
der Mörder, *pl.* **-** male
  murderer
die Mörderin, *pl.* **-nen**
  female murderer
morgen tomorrow
der Morgen, *pl.* **-** morning
die Morgenroutine, *pl.* **-n**
  morning routine
müde tired
die Mühe, *pl.* **-n** effort
munter lively
das Museum, die Museen
  museum
die Musik, *pl.* **-en** music
das Musikstück, *pl.* **-e** piece
  of music
die Musikstunde, *pl.* **-n**
  music lesson
musizieren to play music
müssen, muss, musste, hat
  gemusst must, to have to
mysteriös mysterious

N
nach after, to, toward
nachahmen *sep.* to copy, to
  mimic
der Nachbar, *pl.* **-n** neighbor
das Nachbargymnasium, *pl.*
  - Nachbargymnasien
  nearby high school
die Nachbarstadt, *pl.* **-̈e**
  nearby town

nachdem after

nachdenken, denkt nach, dachte nach, hat nachgedacht *sep.* to contemplate, think deeply about, ponder

nachfahren, fährt nach, fuhr nach, ist nachgefahren *sep.* to follow someone in a moving vehicle

nachfolgen, folgt nach, folgte nach, ist nachgefolgen *sep.* to follow, succeed

nachfragen *sep.* to ask about; ask after

die Nachhilfestunde, *pl.* **-n** tutoring

das Nachkriegsleben, *pl.* **-** postwar life

die Nachkriegszeit, *pl.* **-en** postwar era

nachlassen, lässt nach, ließ nach, hat nachgelassen *sep.* to let up, slack off

nachmachen *sep.* to imitate

der Nachmittag, *pl.* **-e** afternoon

nachmittags in the afternoon

die Nachrichtenagentur, *pl.* **-en** news agency

nachschlagen, schlägt nach, schlug nach, hat nachgeschlagen *sep.* to look up; reference; check

nachsehen, sieht nach, sah nach, hat nachgesehen *sep.* to look after

nächst next

nah near

die Nähe, *pl.* **-n** vicinity

namens by the name of

der Narr, *pl.* **-en** fool

die Nation, *pl.* **-en** nation

natürlich naturally

der Nebel, *pl.* **-** fog

neben next to; near

nehmen, nimmt, nahm, hat genommen to take

neigen zu (+ *dat.*) to tend to (an opinion)

der Neinsager, *pl.* **-** naysayer

nennen, nennt, nannte, hat genannt to name

nett nice

der Netz, *pl.* **-e** net

neu new; young

der Neuankömmling, *pl.* **-e** newcomer

die Neurose, *pl.* **-n** neurosis

nicht not

nicht nur . . . sondern auch not only . . . but also

nie never

niederbrennen *sep.* to burn down

der Niederschlag, *pl.* **-̈e** precipitation

niedlich pretty

(sich) niegen zu (+*dat.*) to lean toward

niemals never

niemand no one

der Nikolaustag, *pl.* **-e** St. Nicholas Day (Dec. 6)

das Nilpferd, *pl.* **-e** hippopotamus

nirgendwo nowhere

der Nobelpreis, *pl.* **-e** Nobel prize

noch still; yet

der Nord(en) north

nordamerikanisch North American

nordisch northern

normalerweise normally

die Note, *pl.* **-n** grade; mark

der Notiz, *pl.* **-en** note

notwendig necessary

nur only

die Nuss, *pl.* **-̈e** nut

O

ob whether, if

das Oberteil, *pl.* **-e** top

obwohl although

oder or

die Öffentlichkeit public

offiziell official

öffnen, *v.t.* to open

oft often

ohne without

ohne . . . zu without . . . (verb)+ ing

das Ohr, *pl.* **-en** ear

der Oktober, - October

die Olympiastadt, *pl.* **-̈e** Olympic city

die Oma, *pl.* **-s** grandma

der Opal, *pl.* **-e** opal

die Oper, *pl.* **-n** opera

das Operwerk, *pl.* **-e** operatic work

der Orangutan, *pl.* **-s** orangutan

die Ordnung, *pl.* **-en** order

organiziert organized

der Orkan, *pl.* **-e** hurricane

österreichisch Austrian

der Ozean, *pl.* **-e** ocean

P

das Paar, *pl.* **-e** couple; pair

packen to pack

der Pandabär, *pl.* **-en** panda

der Papst, *pl.* **-̈e** pope

der Parallelriesenslalom, *pl.* **-s** parallel giant slalom

der Park, *pl.* **-s** park

die Parkanlage, *pl.* **-n** parking lot

die Partei, *pl.* **-en** political party

die Party, -s or **die Parties** party (social)

das Partygeflüster party gossip

der Partysnack, *pl.* **-s** party snacks

passen zu (+ *dat.*) to match, look good with

passieren, passiert, passierte, ist passiert to happen

der Patient, *pl.* **-en** patient (med.)

das Pauken cramming
pauken to cram
die Pause, *pl.* **-n** break
das Pausebrot, *pl.* **-e** snack
pazifisch Pacific
persönlich personal
die Perücke, *pl.* **-en** wig
der Pfau, *pl.* **-en** male peacock
die Pfauhenne, *pl.* **-n** female peacock, preacher
der Pfeil, *pl.* **-e** arrow
die Pferderasse, *pl.* **-n** breed of horse
der Pfifferling, *pl.* **-e** chanterelle (mushroom)
der Pfosten, *pl.* **-** pole
die Philosophie, *pl.* **-n** philosophy
die Physik physics
das Picknick, *pl.* **-s** picnic
der Pilot, *pl.* **-en** male pilot
die Pilotin, *pl.* **-nen** female pilot
der Pinguin, *pl.* **-e** penguin
die Pizza, die Pizzas or Pizzen pizza
planen to plan
der Platz, *pl.* **-¨e** plaza, square
plaudern to chat
die Politik politics
die Polizei police
der Polizeikommissar, *pl.* **-e** police commissioner
populär popular
die Portion, *pl.* **-en** portion
prächtig splendid
prachtvoll magnificent
praktizieren to practice
der Preis, *pl.* **-e** prize; price
preisgekrönt award-winning
der Preisgewinner, *pl.* **-** prizewinner
die Premiere, *pl.* **-n** premier
der Preuße, *pl.* **-n** Prussian
der Prinz, *pl.* **-en** prince
das Problem, *pl.* **-e** problem
der Professor, *pl.* **-en** male professor

die Propoganda propaganda
provozieren to provoke
der Psychiater, *pl.* **-** male psychiatrist
das Publikum public
putzen to clean
qualifizieren to qualify

Q

der Quarz, *pl.* **-e** quartz
die Quelle, *pl.* **-n** source

R

die Rakete, *pl.* **-n** rocket
der Rasen, *pl.* **-** lawn
(sich) rasieren to shave oneself
raten, rät, riet, hat geraten to guess, advise
der Rauch smoke
das Rauchen smoking
rauchen to smoke
der Raum, *pl.* **-¨e** room
die Raumfahrt, *pl.* **-en** space travel
das Raumfahrtprogramm, *pl.* **-** space travel program
rauschen to rush
reagieren auf (+ *acc.***)** to react to
die Reaktionszeit, *pl.* **-en** reaction time
der Realismus realism
der Realist, *pl.* **-en** realist
rechnen mit (+ *dat.***)** to count on something (to happen in the future), figure
die Rede, *pl.* **-en** speech
reden to speak
der Redner, *pl.* **-** male speaker
reduzieren to reduce
der Regen, *pl.* **-** rain
regieren to govern
die Regierung, *pl.* **-en** government
der Regisseur, *pl.* **-e** male movie director

die Regisseurin, *pl.* **-nen** female movie director
regnen to rain
reiben, reibt, rieb, hat gerieben to rub
reich rich
das Reichtum, *pl.* **-¨er** wealth
die Reise, *pl.* **-n** trip
der Reiseführer, *pl.* **-** trip leader
reisen to travel
reissen, reißt, riss, hat gerissen to rip
reiten, reitet, ritt, ist/hat geritten ride
die Reitkunst equitation; riding
der Rektor, *pl.* **-en** headmaster; male principal
die Rektorin, *pl.* **-nen** headmistress; female principal
die Relativitätstheorie, *pl.* **-n** theory of relativity
die Religion, *pl.* **-en** religion
rennen, rennt, rannte, ist gerannt to run
das Rennen racing
die Rennfahrerin, *pl.* **-nen** female racecar driver
das Rennpferd, *pl.* **-e** racehorse
der Rennrodel, *pl.* **-** luge
das Rennrodeln luge tobogganing
der Rennrodler, *pl.* **-** luge tobogganer
reparieren to repair
repräsentieren to represent
der Respekt respect
das Restaurant, *pl.* **-s** restaurant
das Resultat, *pl.* **-e** result
retten vor (+ *dat.***)** to save (from)
die Revolution, *pl.* **-en** revolution

richtig correct
riechen, riecht, roch, hat gerochen nach (+ *dat*.) to smell (of)
das Riesenrad, *pl.* **-¨er** ferris wheel
der Riesenslalom, *pl.* **-s** giant slalom
der Ring, *pl.* **-e** ring
ringen to wrestle, struggle
der Ringkämpfer, *pl.* **-** wrestler
der Riss, *pl.* **-e** rip, tear
die Rockband, *pl.* **-s** rock band
die Rockgruppe, *pl.* **-n** rock group
roh rough; raw
der Rollmops, *pl.* **-¨e** pickled herring
der Rosenmontag, *pl.* **-e** Monday before lent begins, big Carnival parade day
das Röslein, *pl.* **-** small, mini rose
rot red
die Routine, *pl.* **-n** routine
der Rückwind, *pl.* **-e** tailwind
rudern to row
der Ruderstock, *pl.* **-e** oar
ruhig quiet; still
rund round
runterhängend hanging down
der Russe, *pl.* **-n** Russian

S
die Sache, *pl.* **-n** thing
die Sachertorte, *pl.* **-n** Sacher tort, Austrian cake
die Sage, *pl.* **-n** saga; tale
sagen to say
sammeln to collect
die Sammlung, die Sammlungen collection
der Samstag, *pl.* **-e** Saturday
der Samstagabend, *pl.* **-e** Saturday night

samstags on Saturdays
der Sänger, *pl.* **-** singer
der Saphir, *pl.* **-e** sapphire
der Satz, *pl.* **-¨e** sentence
saubermachen *sep.* to make clean
saugen to suck
das Schach chess
der Schachspieler, *pl.* **-** chess player
schaden harm
schaffen to manage
(sich) schämen to be ashamed
schauen to look
der Schauer, *pl.* **-** rain shower
schaufeln, *v.t.* to shovel
die Schauspielerin, *pl.* **-nen** actress
scheiden, scheidet, schied, ist/hat geschieden to separate; part; divorce
die Scheidung, *pl.* **-en** separation
scheinen, scheint, schien, hat geschienen to appear; to seem; to shine
Schi laufen, läuft Schi, lief Schi, ist Schi gelaufen to go skiing
der Schi, die Schier (also der Ski, die Skier) ski
schicken to send
schieben, schiebt, schob, hat geschoben push
schießen, schießt, schoss, hat geschossen auf (+ *acc*.) to shoot (at)
die Schifahrerin, die Schifahrerinnen female skier
das Schild, *pl.* **-er** sign
der Schinken, *pl.* **-** ham
der Schispringer, *pl.* **-** ski jumper
der Schlaf sleep
schlafen, schläft, schlief, hat geschlafen to sleep

das Schlaftier, *pl.* **-e** stuffed animal; soft toy animal
schlagen, schlägt, schlug, hat geschlagen to hit; to beat
schlecht bad
schliessen, schließt, schloss, hat geschlossen close; lock
schließen, schließt, schloss, hat geschlossen aus (+ *dat*.) to end, lock, conclude (from), assume as a result of
schlimm bad
das Schloss, *pl.* **-¨er** castle
die Schlossrunde, *pl.* **-n** tour of castles
der Schlossturm, *pl.* **¨e** castle tower
die Schlussfeier, *pl.* **-n** final celebration
die Schlussprüfung, *pl.* **-en** final exam
schmecken nach (+ *dat*.) to taste (like)
schmeissen, schmeißt, schmiss, hat geschmissen to throw (colloquial)
schmelzen, schmilzt, schmolz, hat/ist geschmolzen to melt
schmieden to forge; to create
(sich) schminken to put on makeup
schmutzig dirty
der Schnee snow
die Schneepiste, *pl.* **-n** ski run
das Schneiden cutting
schneiden, schneidet, schnitt, hat geschnitten to cut
schnell fast; quick
die Schnelligkeit, *pl.* **-en** speed
der Schnellimbiss, *pl.* **-e** snack bar

der Schnitt, *pl.* **-e** cut, slice
das Schnitzel, *pl.* **-** veal
die Schokoladentorte, *pl.* **-n** chocolate cake
schon already
schön beautiful
schreiben, schreibt, schrieb, hat geschrieben to write
schreiben an (+ *acc.***)** to write to
schreiben in (+ *acc.***)** write in something
schreiben, schreibt, schrieb, hat geschrieben auf (+ *acc.***)** to write onto; write down
der Schreiber, *pl.* **-** writer
schreien, schreit, schrie, hat geschrien to scream; yell
der Schritt, *pl.* **-e** step
der Schuh, *pl.* **-e** shoe
der Schuhputzer, *pl.* **-** shoe shiner
der Schulabschluss, *pl.* **-¨e** end of school year
schuldig guilty (of)
die Schule, *pl.* **-n** school
der Schüler, *pl.* **-** pupil
der Schulfreund, *pl.* **-e** classmate
das Schulkind, *pl.* **er** school child; young student
das Schulpflicht, *pl.* **-en** compulsory education
der Schulrektor, *pl.* **-en** male principal of a school
das Schulzeugnis, *pl.* **-se** report card
schummeln to cheat
der Schuss, *pl.* **-¨e** shot
schwach weak
der Schwan, *pl.* **-¨e** swan
schweigen, schweigt, schwieg, hat geschwiegen to remain silent
schweizerisch Swiss
schwer difficult; heavy
die Schwester, *pl.* **-n** sister

die Schwesterschule, *pl.* **-n** sister school
schwimmen, schwimmt, schwamm, ist/hat geschwommen, *v.i.* to swim
schwingen, schwingt, schwang, hat geschwungen to swing
das SCUBA-Tauchen scuba diving
die See, *pl.* **-** sea
der See, *pl.* **-n** lake
der Seerobbe, *pl.* **-n** seal
sehen, sieht, sah, hat gesehen, *v.t.* to see
(sich) sehnen nach (+ *dat.***)** to have a longing for, long for
sehr very
sein, *v.i.* to be; his; its
seit since (temporal)
seit (dem) since (then)
die Sektbowle, *pl.* **-n** champagne punch
das Selbstbildnis, *pl.* **-se** self portrait
senden to send, broadcast
der Senior, *pl.* **-en** senior citizen
das Seniorenzentrum, die Seniorzentren senior citizen center
die Serviette, *pl.* **-n** table napkin
(sich) setzen to sit down
sicher certain (of)
das Siebtel seventh
der Sieg, *pl.* **-e** victory
siegen, *v.t.* to win
silber silver
das Silvesterfest, *pl.* **-e** New Year's Eve festivities
singen, singt, sang, hat gesungen to sing
der Sitzplatz, *pl.* **-¨e** seat
der Skandal, *pl.* **-e** scandal
der Ski, *pl.* **-er** ski
der Skiberg, *pl.* **-e** ski slope

die Skibrille, *pl.* **-n** skiing goggles
der Skifahrer, *pl.* **-** skier
der Skifan, *pl.* **-s** ski fan
der Skiläufer, *pl.* **-** skier
der Skislalom, *pl.* **-s** downhill ski racing
der Skispringer, *pl.* **-** ski jumper
der Smaragd, *pl.* **-e** emerald
der Smog, *pl.* **-s** smog
der Snowboarder, *pl.* **-** snowboarder
so so; thus
sobald as soon as
die Socke, *pl.* **-n** socks
sofort immediately
sofortig immediate
der Sohn, *pl.* **-¨e** son
solange as long as
sollen, soll, sollte, hat gesollt should; to have to
die Soloflugstunde, *pl.* **-n** solo flying lesson
der Sommer, *pl.* **-** summer
die Sonate, *pl.* **-n** sonata
sondern but rather, on the contrary
das Sonett, *pl.* **-e** sonnet
die Sonnenlampe, *pl.* **-n** sun lamp
der Sonntag, *pl.* **-e** Sunday
sooft as often as
(sich) sorgen um (+ *acc.***)** to worry about
(sich) Sorgen machen um (+ *acc.***)** to worry about
sorgfältig careful
sortieren to sort
sowohl . . . als auch both . . . and; both . . . as well as
spanisch Spanish
die Spanische Hofreitschule, *pl.* **-n** Viennese Spanish Riding School
spannend exciting
spät late
die Spende, *pl.* **-n** donation

die Spendenaktion, *pl.* **-en** fundraising

die Spezialität, *pl.* **-en** specialty

das Spiel, *pl.* **-e** game

das Spielen playing

spielen, *v.t.* to play

die Spielerei, *pl.* **-en** ridiculous games

spinnen, spinnt, spann, hat gesponnen to be crazy; spin tales

der Sporn, *pl.* **-s** spur (horse riding)

der Sport, *pl.* **-e** sport

die Sportart, *pl.* **-en** type of sport

die Sporthalle, *pl.* **-n** sports arena

der Sportler, *pl.* **-** sportsman; athlete

die Sportlerin, *pl.* **-nen** female sports figure

der Sportschuh, *pl.* **-e** athletic shoe

spotten über (+ *acc.***)** to make fun of; mock

sprechen, spricht, sprach, hat gesprochen über (+ *acc.***)** speak about (formally, about facts, research)

sprechen, spricht, sprach, hat gesprochen von (+ *dat.***)** speak about something (usually reminiscence)

springen, springen, sprang, ist gesprungen to jump

spülen to rinse; do dishes

der Staat, *pl.* **-e** state

der Staatsbürger, *pl.* **-** male citizen

die Staatsoper, *pl.* **-n** state opera

der Stachelschwein, *pl.* **-e** porcupine

die Stadt, *pl.* **-̈e** city

der Stadtbesuch, *pl.* **-e** city visit

die Stadtliga, die Stadtligen city league

der Stadtvater, *pl.* **-̈** city father; founder

das Stadtzentrum, die Stadtzentren city center

der Stahl steel

der Star, *pl.* **-s** star (person)

stark strong

stattfinden, findet statt, fand statt, hat stattgefunden *sep.* to take place

staubsaugen, staubsaugt, staubsaugte, hat staubgesaugt to vacuum

der Staubsauger, *pl.* **-** vacuum cleaner

stehen, steht, stand, hat/ist gestanden bei (+ *dat.***)** to stand (by someone), support someone

stehlen, stiehlt, stahl, hat gestohlen to steal

steigen, steigt, stieg, ist gestiegen to climb

das Steigen climbing

die Stelle, *pl.* **-n** place; position; job

stellen to place

sterben, stirbt, starb ist gestorben an (+ *dat.***)** to die of

der Stiefel, *pl.* **-** boot

stiften to endow; fund

der Stil, *pl.* **-e** style

stinken, stinkt, stank, hat gestunken, *v.i.* to smell badly

das Stinktier, *pl.* **-e** skunk

der Stock, *pl.* **-̈e** stick

der Stoff, *pl.* **-e** fabric

stoppen to stop

stören, *v.t.* to disturb

der Stoß, *pl.* **-̈e** pile, batch

die Strafe, *pl.* **-n** punishment

die Strasse, *pl.* **-n** street

das Straßenfest, *pl.* **-e** street festival

streben nach (+ *dat.***)** to strive for

der Streit, *pl.* **-e** quarrel

streiten, streitet, stritt, hat gestritten to quarrel

das Stück, *pl.* **-e** piece

der Studentenausweis, *pl.* **-e** student card

studieren, *v.t.* to study

das Studium, die Studien course of studies

der Stuhl, *pl.* **-̈e** chair

die Stunde, *pl., sep.* **-n** hour; lesson

stundenlang lasting for hours

der Sturm, *pl.* **-̈e** storm, gale-force winds

suchen nach (+ *dat.***)** to look (for), search (for)

der Supermarkt, *pl.* **-̈e** supermarket

surfen, *v.i.* to surf

sympatisch nice

die Symphonie, *pl.* **-n** symphony

synchronisieren to synchronize

die Szene, *pl.* **-n** scene

T

der Tag, *pl.* **-e** day

der Tagesablauf, *pl.* **-̈e** to-do list

das Tagesthema, die Tagesthemen theme of the day

täglich daily

die Tante; *pl.* **-n** aunt

der Tanz, *pl.* **-̈e** dance

tanzen, *v.i.* to dance

das Tanzen dancing

der Tänzer, *pl.* **-** male dancer

die Tänzerin, *pl.* **-nen** female dancer

die Tanzstunde, *pl.* **-n** dancing lesson

die Tasche, *pl.* **-n** pocket; pocketbook; purse

das Taschengeld, *pl.* **-er** small change; pocket money

die Tat, *pl.* **-en** act; deed

der Täter, *pl.* **-** perpetrator, person who performed the act

taub deaf

(sich) täuschen in (+ *dat.***)** be disappointed in someone

die Technik, *pl.* **-en** technique

das Teil, *pl.* **-e** part

teilnehmen, nimmt teil, nahm teil, hat teilgenommen an (+ *acc.***)** *sep.* to take part in

das Telefon, *pl.* **-e** telephone

telefonieren mit (+ *dat.***)** talk with someone on the phone

die Telefonnachricht, *pl.* **-en** telephone information

die Telefonnummer, *pl.* **-n** telephone number

die Temperaturskala, *pl.* **-s,** or **die Temperaturskalen** temperature scale

der Tennisspieler, *pl.* **-** tennis player

der Tenor, *pl.* **-ˮe** tenor

der Terrorist, *pl.* **-en** terrorist

der Test, *pl.* **-e** test

die Theaterkarte, *pl.* **-en** theater tickets

das Thema, die Themen theme

der Thron, *pl.* **-e** throne

tibetanisch Tibetan

tief deep

die Tierärztin, *pl.* **-nen** female veterinarian

das Tierchen, *pl.* **-** small animal

der Tiergarten, *pl.* **-ˮ** zoo

Tierumfrage, *pl.* **-n** animal survey

die Tierwärterin, *pl.* **-nen** female zookeeper

der Tiger, *pl.* **-** tiger

der Tintenfisch, *pl.* **-e** squid

der Tisch, *pl.* **-e** table

die Tochter, *pl.* **-ˮ** daughter

der Tod, *pl.* **-e** death

die Todeskrankheit, *pl.* **-en** terminal disease

tödlich fatal

toll great

der Topas, *pl.* **-e** topaz

der Tornado, *pl.* **-s** tornado

töten to kill

die Tour, *pl.* **-en** tour

der Tourist, *pl.* **-en** tourist

die Touristensehenswürdig-keit, *pl.* **en** tourist attraction

die Tradition, *pl.* **-en** tradition

tragen, trägt, trug, hat getragen, *v.t.* carry, wear

der Trainer, *pl.* **-** male coach

die Trainerin, *pl.* **-nen** female coach

der Trank, *pl.* **-ˮe** potion, drink

der Traum, *pl.* **-ˮe** dream

die Traumanalyse, *pl.* **-n** dream analysis

träumen von (+ *dat.***)** to dream (about)

traurig sad

treffen, trifft, traf, hat getroffen to meet

(sich) treffen, trifft, traf, hat getroffen mit (+ *dat.***)** to meet up with; hit

treiben, treibt, trieb, hat getrieben to drive; propel

das Trinken drinking

trinken, trinkt, trank, hat getrunken auf (+ *acc.***)** to drink to

der Triumpf, *pl.* **-e** triumph

der Trockner, *pl.* **-** drier

trotz in spite of, despite

tun, tut, tat, hat getan to do

die Tür, *pl.* **-en** door

U

das Üben practice

üben to practice

über over, across, about, above

übereinstimmen mit (+ *dat.***)** *sep.* to agree (with someone or something)

(sich etwas) überlegen to consider something

übermorgen the day after tomorrow

übernachten to stay overnight

überreden zu (+ *dat.***)** to convince someone to

überzeugen von (+ *dat.***)** to convince someone of

üblich usual

die Uhr, *pl.* **-en** clock

um around, for; at (time)

um . . . zu in order to

umbringen to kill

(sich) umdrehen to turn around

die Umfrage, *pl.* **-en** survey; poll

umgekehrt reversed

(sich) umziehen, zieht sich um, zog sich um, hat sich umgezogen *sep.* to change clothes

umziehen, zieht um, zog um, hat umgezogen *sep.* to move (from one location to another)

der Umzug, *pl.* **-ˮe** parade

unbedingt absolute(ly)

und and

der Unfall, *pl.* **-ˮe** accident

ungewöhnlich unusual

unglaublich unbelievable

unglücklich unlucky

unheimlich eerie; creepy
die Uni, *pl.* **-s** university (spoken)
die Uniform, *pl.* **-en** uniform
die Universität, *pl.* **-en** university
unmöglich impossible
unordentlich untidy
unser our
unter under, among
(sich) unterhalten, unterhält sich, unterhielt sich, hat sich unterhalten mit (+ *dat.***)** to entertain, converse with
der Unterricht, *pl.* **-e** lesson; teaching
die Unterwasserwelt, *pl.* **-en** undersea world
unterwegs on the way
unverschämt insolent
die Urgroßmutter, *pl.* **-¨** great grandmother
die Ursache, *pl.* **-en** cause
urteilen über (+ *acc.***)** to make a judgment about; judge
das US-Eishockeyteam, *pl.* **-s** U.S. ice hockey team

V
der Valentinstag, *pl.* **-e** St. Valentine's Day
der Vampir, *pl.* **-e** vampire
die Vase, *pl.* **-n** vase
der Vater, *pl.* **-¨** father
vegetarisch vegetarian
(sich) verabreden mit (+ *dat.***) / für (+** *acc.***)** to make a date with *s.o.* for *s.t.*
(sich) verabschieden von (+ *dat.***)** to say goodbye to
verachten to despise
veranstalten to organize; to hold an event
verbieten, verbietet, verbat, hat verboten to forbid

der Verbrennungsmotor, *pl.* **-en** internal combustion engine
verbringen, verbringt, verbrachte, hat verbracht to spend
verchromt chrome-plated
verdächtig suspicious; suspected (of)
verdienen to earn; to gain
vereinen to unite
verfügen über (+ *acc.***)** to have access to something
vergessen, vergisst, vergaß, hat vergessen to forget
vergleichen, vergleicht, verglich, hat verglichen to compare
das Verhältnis, *pl.* **-se** relationship
verkaufen to sell
(sich) verknallen in (+ *acc.***)** to develop a crush on
verlangen to ask for; to demand
verlangsamen to slow down
verlassen, verlässt, verließ, hat verlassen *sep.* to leave
(sich) verletzen to injure
(sich) verlieben in (+ *acc.***)** to fall in love with
verlieren to lose
(sich) verloben mit (+ *dat.***)** to become engaged to
vermissen to miss
veröffentlicht published (temporal)
verschenken to give away
verschieden different
verschwinden, verschwindet, verschwand, ist verschwunden to disappear
versprechen, verspricht, versprach, hat versprochen to promise
das Versteck, *pl.* **-e** hiding place

(etwas) verstehen, versteht, verstand, hat verstanden von *dat.* to understand, to know how to do something
der Versuch, *pl.* **-e** attempt
versuchen to try
verteilen to distribute
(sich) vertiefen in (+ *acc.***)** to lose oneself in something
vertreten, vertritt, vertrat, hat vertreten to represent
verzeihen, verzieht, verzieh, verziehen to pardon, forgive
verzichten auf (+ *acc.***)** to deny oneself something, do without
das Videospiel, *pl.* **-e** video game
viel much
viele many
das Viertel, *pl.* **-** fourth
das Vitamin, *pl.* **-e** vitamin
das Volk, *pl.* **-¨er** folks; common people; population
vollenden to complete
von *prep. dat.* of, from, by
vor in front of, before, ago
im voraus *sep.* ahead; in advance
voraussagen (*sep. prefix =* **voraus)** to predict
vorbeigehen, geht vorbei, ging vorbei, ist vorbeigegangen *sep.* to pass; to elapse
vorbereiten *sep.* to prepare
(sich) vorbereiten auf (+ *acc.***),** *sep.* to prepare oneself for
vorfahren, fährt vor, fuhr vor, ist vorgefahren *sep.* to drive in front of someone, precede, drive forward
vorführen *sep.* to perform

die Vorführung, *pl.* **-en** peformance

vorgehen, geht vor, ging vor, ist vorgegangen *sep.* to precede, go ahead of

vorhaben, hat vor, hatte vor, hat vorgehabt *sep.* to have planned

vorher beforehand

die Vorhersage, *pl.* **-en** prediction

vorig previous

vorlesen, liest vor, las vor, hat vorgelesen *sep.* to read aloud

(sich etwas) vornehmen, nimmt sich vor, nahm sich vor, hat sich vorgenommen to decide to do something

die Vorprobe, *pl.* **-n** reearsal

vorschlagen, schlägt vor, schlug vor, hat vorgeschlagen *sep.* to suggest

vorschreiben, schreibt vor, schrieb vor, hat vorgeschrieben *sep.* to prescribe

vorsingen, singt vor, sang vor, hat vorgesungen *sep.* to sing for *s.o.*

(sich) vorstellen *sep.* to introduce oneself

(sich etwas) vorstellen *sep.* to imagine something

W

wach awake

wachsen, wächst, wuchs, ist/hat gewachsen to grow

das Wachstum, *pl.* **-̈er** growth

der Wagen, *pl.* **-** car

wählen to choose; to elect

wahr true

während while, during

die Wahrheit, die Wahrheiten truth

die Waise, *pl.* **-n** orphan

der Wald, *pl.* **-̈er** forest

das Wanderjahr, *pl.* **-e** year of travel

wann when, whenever

das Warenzeichen, *pl.* **-** trademark

warm warm

warnen vor (+ *dat.***)** to warn (about)

warten auf (+ *acc.***)** to wait for

die Wartezeit, *pl.* **-en** waiting time

das Wartezimmer, *pl.* **-** waiting room

warum why

was what

die Wäsche, *pl.* **-n** laundry, wash

waschen, wäscht, wusch, hat gewaschen, *v.t.* to wash

die Waschmaschine, *pl.* **-n** washing machine

das Wasser, *pl.* **-̈ or -** water

der Wasserfall, *pl.* **-̈e** waterfall

wecken to wake *s.o.* up

der Wecker, *pl.* **-** alarm clock

weder . . . noch neither . . . nor

der Weg path; way

weg away

wegbleiben, bleibt weg, blieb weg, ist weggeblieben *sep.* to stay away

wegen on account of, because of

wegfahren, fährt weg, fuhr weg, ist weggefahren *sep.* to drive away, go away on vacation

weggehen, geht weg, ging weg, ist weggegangen *sep.* to go away

wegklauen *sep.* to steal away

weglaufen, läuft weg, lief weg, ist weggelaufen *sep.* to run away

wegnehmen, nimmt weg, nahm weg, hat weggenommen *sep.* to take away

wegreissen, reißt weg, riss weg, hat weggerissen *sep.* to tear away; snatch away

wegschmeißen, schmeißt weg, schmiss weg, hat weggeschmissen *sep.* to throw away (spoken)

wegsehen, sieht weg, sah weg, hat weggesehen *sep.* to look away

weh hurt; sore

(sich) wehtun, tut weh, tat weh, hat weh getan *sep.* to hurt (oneself)

weich soft

weichen to yield

die Weihnachten Christmas

weil because

die Weile while, during

weisen to point to

weiß white

weit far

weiter farther; further

die Welt, *pl.* **-en** world

weltbekannt world renowned

weltberühmt world famous

der Weltkrieg, die Weltkriege world war

weltweit worldwide

wem whom

wenig few

wenn if

wer who

werden, wird, wurde, ist geworden to become, (auxiliary verb) will

werfen, wirft, warf, hat geworfen to throw

wert worthy of

wertvoll valuable

das Wesen, *pl.* - being; creature; nature

der Wettbewerb, *pl.* **-e** competition

das Wetter, *pl.* - weather

widmen delicate

wieder again

die Wiedergeburt, *pl.* **-en** rebirth

wiegen, wiegt, wog, hat gewagen weigh

wild wild

der Wildvogel, *pl.* **-¨** wild bird

der Wille, *pl.* - will

der Wind, *pl.* **-e** wind

winden, windet, wand, hat gewunden to wind

der Winter winter

der Winterausverkauf, *pl.* **-¨e** winter sale

das Winterspiel, *pl.* **-e** winter sport

wir we

der Wirbelsturm, *pl.* **-¨e** tornado

wirklich really

(etwas) wissen, weiss, wusste, hat gewusst von (+ dat.) to know something factual

wo where

die Woche, *pl.* **-en** week

das Wochenende, *pl.* **-n** weekend

wohl probably

wohnen to live; reside

die Wohnung, *pl.* **-en** apartment

das Wohnzimmer, *pl.* - living room

der Wolkenkratzer, *pl.* - skyscraper

die Wolle, *pl.* **-n** wool

wollen, will, wollte, hat gewollt to want

das Wort, *pl.* **-¨er** or **-e** word (**Worte:** words in context. **Wörter:** individual words)

die Wortschatzherausforder-ung, *pl.* **-en** vocabulary challenge

worum for what; for which

wunderbar wonderful

das Wunderkind child prodigy

(sich) wundern über (+ acc.) to be amazed at

wunderschön magnificent

würdig worthy of

der Würfel, *pl.* - die (*pl.* dice); cube

X

der X-Strahl, *pl.* **-en** x-ray

Z

zahlen to pay

zählen auf (+ acc.) count on (someone or something happening)

der Zahn, *pl.* **-¨e** tooth

der Zahnartz, *pl.* **-¨e** male dentist

die Zahnarztin, *pl.* **-¨nen** female dentist

(sich) die Zähne putzen to brush one's teeth

zehn ten

zeichnen to draw; to sketch

das Zeichnen, *pl.* - drawing

zeigen auf (+ acc.) to point to

die Zeit, *pl.* **-en** time

die Zeitung, *pl.* **-en** newspaper

der Zeitungsartikel, *pl.* - newspaper article

zerbrechen, zerbricht, zerbrach, hat zerbrochen to break

zerstören to destroy

die Ziege, *pl.* **-n** goat

ziehen, zieht, zog, hat gezogen pull

das Zimmer, - room

zittern vor (+ dat.) to shake (from, because of)

zu to; too

zudecken *sep.* to cover up

zuerst first; at first

zuhören, *v.t., sep.* to listen to

die Zukunft, *pl.* **-¨e** future

zulassen, lässt zu, ließ zu, hat zugelassen *sep.* to admit, agree to

zuletzt finally

zumachen *sep.* to turn off, close

zunehmen, nimmt zu, nahm zu, hat zugenommen *sep.* to increase, gain weight

zuordnen *sep.* to assign to

zurückbringen, bringt zurück, brachte zurück, hat zurückgebracht *sep.* to bring back

zurückfahren, fährt zurück, fuhr zurück, ist zurückgefahren *sep.* to drive back

zurückgeben, gibt zurück, gab zurück, hat zurückgegeben *sep.* to give back

zurückgehen, geht zurück, ging zurück, ist zurückgegangen *sep.* to go back

zurückkommen, kommt zurück, kam zurück, ist zurückgekommen *sep.* to come back

zurückrufen, ruft zurück, rief zurück, hat zurückgerufen *sep.* to call back

zurückschreiben, schreibt zurück, schrieb zurück, hat zurückgeschrieben *sep.* to write back, reply

zurücksetzen *sep.* to set back, reset

zurückzahlen *sep.* to pay back, repay

zusammen together

zusammenbinden, bindet zusammen, ban zusammen, hat zusammengebunden *sep.* to tie together

der Zusammenbruch, *pl.* **-¨e** collapse

zusammenfahren, fährt zusammen, fuhr zusammen, ist zusammengefahren *sep.* to crash into another car, drive together with someone

zusammenfallen, fällt zusammen, fiel zusammen, ist zusammengefallen *sep.* to coincide

zusammenhalten, hält zusammen, hielt zusammen, hat zusammengehalten *sep.* to stick together (people)

zusammenhängen, hängt zusammen, hing zusammen, hat zusammengehangen *sep.* to associate, hang around together

zusammenkleben *sep.* to glue together

zusammenschlagen, schlägt zusammen, schlug zusammen, hat zusammengeschlagen *sep.* to break apart by force

zusammenstehen, steht zusammen, stand zusammen, hat zusammengestanden *sep.* to stand together

zuschauen *sep.* to watch

der Zuschauer, *pl.* **-** spectator

zwanzig twenty

das Zwanzigstel, *pl.* **-** twentieth (fraction)

der Zwanzigste, *pl.* **-n** twentieth (ordinal)

zwei two

die Zwei, *pl.* **-en** two

zweifeln an (+ *dat.***)** to doubt

die Zwiebel, *pl.* **-n** onion

der Zwilling, *pl.* **-e** twin

zwingen, zwingt, zwang, hat gezwungen zu (+ *dat.***)** to force (to)

zwischen between

zwitschern to chirp